A Borders Schoolmaster

The Written Effects of
William Lorrain, A.M.
1772 - 1841

with additions by
Audrey Mitchell

KELSO

CAMEOS

© Copyright Audrey Mitchell, March 2000.

Printed in the Scottish Borders by Kelso Graphics.

Dedicated to Schoolteachers,
past and present, everywhere

CONTENTS

INTRODUCTION

During the Second World War, householders were advised to clear their premises of any spare combustible materials. From the attic of a house in Jedburgh there appeared a collection of papers which was spotted by Mr. John Fotheringhame, schoolmaster in Denholm. He took them to his colleague Mr. Alex. Cameron who sorted them into chronological order. They turned out to be an assortment of letters, bills, accounts etc. belonging to William Lorrain, a Borders Schoolmaster.

When, in 1978, a group of people living in Melrose produced a small book about the history of their town in 1826, Mr. Fotheringhame recalled a letter in the Lorrain collection from a Melrose gingham manufacturer:

Melrose June 30th 1814

Dear Sir,

I have just now received yours of the 28th currt. I have no Ginghams on hand at present that would answer your purpose of my manufacturey. - Trade has been so bad for a long time I had almost given up the making of fine Ginghams. I could however make you a piece like this swatch in the course of six weeks but I believe it will cost as high as they ever did the price of cotton yarn is so much advanced I have inclosed a few swatches of such Ginghams as I have on hand, but they are not of my manufacturing. - If I hear no word in by return of Fly I will set forward a check agreeable to this pattern. I am
> *Dear Sir*
> *your most obedt servt*
> *Geo. Laurie*

Two months later Laurie writes apologetically to Mrs. Lorrain:

Melrose, 25th Augt 1814

Madam,
I am extremely sorry it will not by in my power to execute your order which I promised to do. The white & Lilac yarn which I have in

hand are so different in their qualities they cannot match in one web. - I have tryed both Glasgow & Edinburgh but cannot get less than £6.16 worth in one parcel which I am very unwilling to purchase now that of little or nothing in the manufacturing line. I could make you a piece of Red or Pink Check same quality and pattern if it will answer you can let me know when convenient. -

> *I am*
> *Madam*
> *Your humble Serv.*
> *Geo. Laurie*

The sample fragments of material enclosed with the former letter were of great interest to Anne and Macdonald Scott, artists who then lived at the Pendstead in Melrose. The letters were handed over to their custody and travelled with them when they moved to Walton Hall in Kelso. The collection lay dormant for many years during which time a warm friendship grew between the Scotts and the Mitchells. Mr. Scott eventually trusted me with a sight of the letters and when I expressed great interest in preparing them for publication he handed them to me for this purpose. The destination of the originals is the Archive at St. Mary's Mill in Selkirk where they will be safely guarded and available for public perusal.

The period covered begins in 1800 when William Lorrain moved from Callander to Selkirk and continues during his ten years at Jedburgh Grammar School. A small number of items date after Lorrain's removal to Glasgow and these include some family correspondence after his death. The record of Lorrain's lifestyle, experiences, contacts, and community involvement gives a fascinating insight into the social history of the period. The status of the schoolmaster, the expectation of parents, the ravages of illness and the timelessness of humour are all highlighted. I was given invaluable assistance in deciphering a variety of spidery handwritings by my friend Moira McGregor and she too developed a keen interest in the personalities of the correspondents. We were careful not to alter spelling or punctuation, however idiocyncratic!

The political effects of the Napoleonic Wars are experienced at a personal level when French prisoners arrive in the Borders. Many of the letters from Lorrain's assistants Espinasse and Doubzere were written in French and I am indebted to my friend Marie-Hélène Mallen for her expert translation. For the two letters written in 1818 by Lorrain to James Veitch, and for the picture on p.68, I am grateful to the present Mr. Veitch of Inchbonny. I also thankfully acknowledge the help of Mary McLeish, Jim Carroll and Dorothy Mobed in carrying out research.

William Lorrain was obviously an able and ambitious man. Despite the poor rates of pay for schoolmasters, he appears to have been astute in handling money and was often asked for loans by family, friends and strangers alike, as this letter shows:

Deare Sir,

I am enformed By Mr. Harkeness that You have a Hundred pownd to Give owte at this time. John Buckham Esqr Bush & Me will take the Money if you will acksept of owr Bill if you will let us have the Money Be So Good as write as we want the Money at the Beginning of next Month

Yow perhaps do not Know Mutch abowte Me the Reson I want the Money for is that I canot lift what is My owne till My dawgr arive at adge Which it is Secowred Upon land in Scottland

Sir I am Your Most
Obdt humle Servt
William Crozier

June 26th 1809 Broombwlks

Several correspondents express disappointment that Lorrain has failed to visit them as promised - whether he was genuinely too busy or was more interested in pursuing his career it is difficult to tell. He himself complains of not hearing from old friends in Jedburgh after the move to Glasgow, but his obituary in the "Glasgow Herald" states that he was so popular in Jedburgh that the people never forgave him for leaving. Readers will form their own opinion from their interpretation of this cameo of life in the early 19th century. There is something to interest everyone and no doubt many of the names and places will be familiar to all who take an interest in Border history.

Audrey Mitchell
Kelso
March 2000

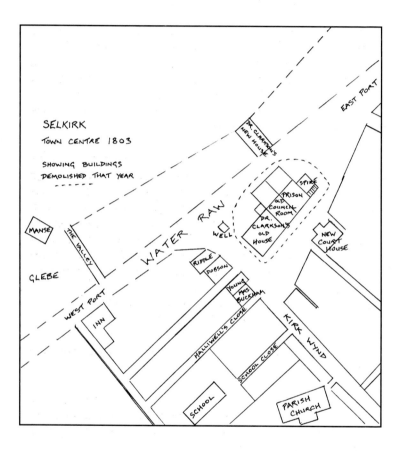

SELKIRK

TOWN CENTRE 1803

SHOWING BUILDINGS
DEMOLISHED THAT YEAR
- - - - - - -

EAST PORT

DR. CLARKSON'S NEW HOUSE

SPIRE

PRISON
OLD COUNCIL ROOM
DR. CLARKSON'S OLD HOUSE

WELL

NEW COURT HOUSE

WATER RAW

MANSE

THE VALLEY

GLEBE

WEST PORT

RIDDLE
DOBSON

YOUNG MRS BUCKHAM

INN

HALLIWELL'S CLOSE

SCHOOL CLOSE

KIRK WYND

SCHOOL

PARISH CHURCH

Chapter 1

SELKIRK

*Great care has been taken in accurately transcibing all letters -
errors in spelling and punctuation are as per original*

William Lorrain was born in 1772 near Canonbie, Dumfriesshire, in
the parish of Half Morton, to farmer Walter Lorrain and his wife Mary
Currie. William attended school in Kirkpatrick-Fleming and walked
from home to Aberdeen at the age of 21 to study for an Arts degree at
Marischal College. In 1796 he was awarded the Gray Mathematics
Bursary and after his graduation the following year he became master
at the Grammar School in Callander.

*"These certify that the bearer William Lorrain A.M. came to this place
to teach our school, about three years and a half ago, well recommended
by Doctor Hamilton of the Marischal College, Aberdeen, in respect of his
abilities and Conduct: that he has taught the higher branches of education
during that period, with diligence and success; which hath been annually
attested in the most public manner by the gentlemen who examined his
Scholars previous to the Vacation: and that he has thereby earned the
best wishes of his Employers, & merits encouragement, wherever a more
extensive sphere of usefulness may occurr.
Given at Callander upon the 12th of April 1800 and attested by
James Robertson".*

Callander 19th April 1800

Dear Sir,

*In consequence of my being a candidate for the vacancy of the Grammar
School of Stirling, am desired by my Friends there to forward letters
from the different Gentlemen who examined my School, certifying their
opinion of my Scholars and me -*

*Yours by the bearer agreeable to the above specifying the number of
years you examined my School will singularly oblige -*

> *Dear Sir*
> *Yours respectfully -*
>
> *William Lorrain.*

These are to certify that I was present at the public examination of the Grammar School of Callander in Autumn 1799 and can freely say that the appearance made by the scholars upon that occasion gave a very strong proof of the abilities and attention of their teacher Mr. Lorrain. I can also add that as far as I know Mr. Lorrain is a most unexceptionable person in every respect -

William Stirling Minister

Sir,

I received yours and if my subscription can in the least add to the ample Testimonies of merit you have already received as Teacher of the Grammar School at Callander for several years past I chearfully give it. and I am Sir

Your most obedient Servant
Dun. Stewart
Balq.(uhidde)r Manse 22d April 1800

"*The Parish School of Selkirk having become vacant by the death of Mr. Porter, a Schoolmaster qualified to teach Latin Greek French and Mathematics, is immediately wanted to supply the vacancy-*

Candidates are requested to lodge, in the hands of Andrew Henderson writer in Selkirk Certificates of their moral Character and abilities to teach the above languages, betwixt and the 21st May next".

William Lorrain was duly appointed schoolmaster and moved to Selkirk. The town in 1800 was described as having "a dolorous appearance". Not only was there high unemployment, but poor weather during successive seasons and the effects of foreign wars had an adverse effect. There were internal bickerings among the bailies and such was the animosity between the Langs and the Hendersons that to support one faction was to make an enemy of the other. This unpleasantness permeated civic life, affecting not only bailies and councillors but also craftsmen, whose business often relied on their patronage. When Andrew Henderson resigned as Town Clerk in 1803, he became Senior Bailie in place of George Rodger, who became Town Clerk.

In that same year, the dilapidated buildings in the town centre - the old Council Room, the prison and spire, and Mr. Clarkson the surgeon's old house - were all demolished to leave an open square. A new Court House was built and the poet Southey, visiting in 1805, thought it seemed out of place in such a town. He remarked on the dark rough-cast houses and the local custom of painting the window-frames exactly to the shape of the wood, which was anything but square!

The Parish School at this time was situated in the churchyard, and both the church (which had an earthen floor) and burial ground suffered at the hands of the scholars. An annual cock-fight was held at the school each Fastern's E'en (Lent), with the Chief Magistrate sitting at the headmaster's desk as judge. The birds which were defeated had their necks wrung and became the property of the Dominie. The boy bringing the winning cock became "king" and entitled to lead a "hand ba'" chase around the town. When the town centre buildings were demolished in 1803 leaving plenty of room, the cloth market was ordered to transfer there from the schoolyard.

William Lorrain, like all his contemporaries, had to appear before the Presbytery to be examined on civil and religious principles and sign the Confession of Faith. He was then bound to attend the Established Kirk. The parish minister at this time was Rev. Thomas Robertson, who had been ordained at Selkirk in 1772 and married Robina Lang, daughter of the farmer at Broomhill. Three years later Rev. Robertson was fined for carrying marl from the mosses belonging to the town of Selkirk and although he appealed to the Court of Session, the Council met and resolved to defend their position.

Rev. Robertson wrote the first Statistical Account for Selkirk in 1791 and his unsympathetic attitude towards the poor was such that it comes as no surprise to find the Council prepared to prosecute him for non-payment of the poor-rates. Thomas Robertson died on 5th September 1805, aged 69, and it would appear that his widow not only inherited everything, to the exclusion of his friends, but cleared the garden down to the last leek and box hedge, leaving nothing for the incoming minister, Rev. John Campbell.

William Lorrain writes to Rev. Robertson:

Selkirk Saturday 9 Oclock p.m. 1802

Sir

I have just now got yours and beg leave to say that Mr. Beattie agreeable to the request of his Clergyman came to Selkirk for the sole purpose to sign the Conf of Faith but as there was no presbytery that day he was desired to attend he was disappointed   This I believe was attested by his Clergyman in the last Presbytery - Mr. Beattie from this moment holds himself in readyness to obey the Presbyterys orders in Signing the Con. of F. and give evidence of his abilities to teach such branches of education as he professes -

Selkirk 15th May 1802

Dear Sir

As Mr. Beattie purposes to meet my Scholars every Sunday afternoon to hear them repeat their Psalms and Questions and read the Scriptures it is hoped that you will as is usual on Such occasions countenance him on Sunday first between 5 and 6 oclock to sanction the meeting of the children with prayers or what other admonitions you may think proper or useful- and oblige
> *D. Sir*
>> *Your Most obt huble servt.*
>> *Wm Lorrain*

One of Lorrain's close friends at this time was William Berry Shaw, whose first of many letters is dated February 1803. *(p.189)* Shaw was courting Eliza Scott of Deloraine while Lorrain's choice, Dorothea ("Dolly") Scott, aged 24, lived with her father Thomas Scott at Bowhill, the property of the Duke of Buccleuch near Selkirk.

A colleague of William Lorrain's, teaching at George Watson's Hospital, Edinburgh writes:

Geo. W. Hospital Janry 17th 1802

My Dear Sir

Yours I received by Mr. Bell and was happy to hear of Your Welfare. I have made the desired purchase Which I hope Will Satisfy you and answer the fair finger for Which it is intended. If it does not fit you may return it to be exchanged. My taste & opinion corresponding with

Your Dulcinea's, I have sent a plain one.   I sincerely Wish You Great happiness in Your married State & think you wise in taking to Yourself a Wife.   I am happy to hear Your School is So very *throng & hope your Assistant to whom remember me gives Satisfaction.   Mr. Robertson & Miss Beatson join in Wishing You much health & happiness.   I am in haste

My Dear Sir,

Yours Sincerely

D. Smith

(with a parcel)

[* throng = very busy - ed]

Mr. William Lorrain
   Bought of Wm. Turnbull

1802

June 15	1 yard New Stript Quilting		£ -	9 -
	2 yards Cotton Lining	1/6	3.	4¹/₂
	1 yards Milled Cassimere	10/6	17.	
	2¹/₂ yards White fustian	1/6	3.	9
	yard Lining 1/8 5d ¹/₂ yard Cold.fustian 2/-	1/-	1.	5
	Booking		.	1
18	2 yards Superfine Royal Blue Cloth 21/-		£2. 2.	-
	yard Black Velvet	18/-	4.	6
	1¹/₂ yards White fustian	1/6	2.	3
	¹/₂ yard Sheeting	2/-	1.	0

£4. 4. 5

Dr. Sir

   *Above you have a Copy of your Accompt which I hope you find Right.
I have sent your Patterns Superfines, also Breeches and Vests.   I doubt not but some of them will Please.   Your commands will oblige.*

Dear Sir,

Your most Obedient Servt

Will. Turnbull

Edinb. 9 March 1803.
(with a parcel)

Savanna la Mar, Jamaica, 15th March 1803

Honoured Sir,

I am truly Happy in acknowledging the Receipt of your very acceptable and agreeable Letter by the January Packet, by which I was extremely happy to learn you were well, and I sincerely hope you will long continue so. I am very sorry to hear of the death of poor Robert Robertson, I understand he died very suddenly at Edinburgh, he was a promising youth, and no doubt his loss will be severely felt, by his Parents, and other Relations. Have you heard from Callender lately, I hope my schoolfellows and other old acquaintance in that quarter are well, I have wrote Dr. Robertson and my Schoolfellows repeatedly, but they have never had the good manners to honour me with a single one, therefore do not think it worth my while to write them any more. I fancy you remember John Graham of Drunkey, poor young Man, he died about three months ago, and I believe his Relations know nothing of it as yet. Nothing can equal the Pleasure I feel in sitting down to write you a Letter and nothing adds more to it, than when I receive a Letter from yourself.

Trade is very dull in this Country at present, nothing at all doing and faillieurs Happening amongst us every day, God knows what is to become of those in Business, the times actually look worse than they did in the year 1793, you may then easily conceive in what a distressed situation the Country is in, at this present moment. When did you see or hear from Archibald McNab, I hope he is well and doing well, when you see or write him, please deliver my kind Compliments to him and tell him I shall be extremely happy to hear from him, when he finds it convenient, and I shall be very punctual in answering his Letters, likewise to Robert Buchanan of the Trean, is he still at Glasgow, or has he removed to Edinburgh. Sandy Robertson came out here the other day in the John Captain Duncan from Glasgow. I think it would have been better, if his Father had kept him to the weaving Business, than in sending him out to this Country, for he is such a thick Headed fellow, he will be fit for nothing else but a Penn keeper. How many Boarders have you got now, the Gentlemen whom I mentioned in my last were going to send of their Children, has declined it for a year longer but you may rely that no endeavours on my side shall be wanting, in endeavouring to get you these Gentlemens Children, for there is no man Breathing, I would go a greater length to serve than you, and I shall never forget the attention you paid me whilst I was at Callender, and if it is ever in my power to serve you in any degree whatever, I shall make it my Study to do it with pleasure. How does my old friend Gilbert McEwen come on, has he and your successor made up the quarrell they had, when you write him deliver an old Scholar's Compliment to him and his good Lady. I enjoy good Health at present thank God, and I am extremely Happy with my Situation.

I expect to have a Long Letter from you by the first opportunity after the receipt of this Letter. Have nothing more at present to add, But wishing you Success Health and Happiness. I remain

Dear Sir
Yours very Affectionately
Daniel George Colquhoun

By the Packet
Q D C

Sir

Having heard a very favorable account of your School at Selkirk from my friend the Rev Dr. Douglas Galashiells, I wish to know if you could take a young man about 13 or 14 years of age as Boarder and Scholar. He is under the charge of a particular friend of mine, who tells me he has been three years at Latin, is a good Scholar, and of an agreeable temper.

Be so good as to let me know your terms of Board Education etc. as soon as convenient as my friend proposes to remove him from the School he is now at about the beginning of next month.

I am sir
Your most Obedt
Humble Servt

Edinr 15 March 1803   Mattw Sandilands

Writer to the Signet

[Alexander Pringle, a son of Pringle of Whytbank, had repurchased the family estate of Yair which had been sold to the Duke of Buccleuch at a time of financial difficulty - Ed.].

Yair 31st Augt 1803

Mr. Pringle is sorry at being prevented from accepting of Mr. Lorrains Invitation to attend the Examination of his School, which it was fully his Intention to have done, by unavoidable circumstances; but he has done himself the pleasure to send two of his sons with Mr. MacArthur to be present.

In April 1803 a Bill was passed "for the betterment of schoolmasters in Scotland". The terms were revealing as they stated that from Martinmas the amount of salary paid to a parochial schoolmaster "shall not be less than average annual wages of a day-labourer, nor above that of two day-labourers in that part of the country where the parish is situated". A schoolhouse must be provided, together with a proper dwelling-house and garden of at least ³/₄ acre for the master.

William Lorrain and Dorothea Scott were married on 14th April 1803 and their first child, William Buckham, was born in January 1804. By now William Lorrain had decided that it was time to move from Selkirk. He had been summoned to appear before the Town Council to answer charges that the manner in which he was conducting the school did not meet with parental approval, but he failed to attend. A vacancy had occured for a headmaster at Jedburgh Grammar School, from which James Brewster, father of famous scientist David, had retired due to ill-health. Until this time there had been two separate schools, the Grammar and the English, in Jedburgh but a vacancy in both at the same time gave the Heritors an opportunity to amalgamate the two and to pay a double salary which might attract a high calibre of teacher. Lorrain was obviously interested in the Jedburgh post from an early date, for the birth of his son William was first registered there on 15th January 1804 and the christening at Selkirk on 5th February.

Lorrain confided his intentions to Gilbert MacEwen in Callander, who had been mentioned in Daniel Colquhoun's letter, and received a reply:

Callander 16 January 1804

My Dear Sir

I am this moment favoured by yours of the 7 Current etc. as formerly - Our Carrier puts up in Clerks Grassmarket who says he'll not be there till Thursday the 26 Jny is the proper person to take over the Cheese - he is so forgetful that I am afraid he'll not call at the Quarters of the Selkirk Carrier altho' not far from Clerks - I saw the advertisement of Jedburgh. Dowie is a candidate and showed me a Letter he had from Dr. Sommerville giving an acct of the usual number of Scholars fees and Salary The letter seemed very candid and not filled with imaginary or expected advantages - no word of stent poor rates or Sess Clerks. I could understand this School for sometime back was but indifferently attended. I am afraid it is too near Kelso* but you can best judge being nearer *hand - It surely ought to be a better situation than Selkirk -*

Whether or not the Clergyman here will give certificates to Dowie that may be of service to him may probably depend upon Robt. Buchanan, Trean being thought more plyable to go on here etc.

Salarys and settlement between Messrs Dowie and Buchanan

Dowie	£16. 13. 4	Parochial Salary
	1. 6. 8	Garden
	4. 0. 0	for a House till one is given him.
	£22. 0. 0	

Buchanan	£5. 11. 1	Parochial salary
	12. 0. 0	Sunday do
	£17. 11. 1	

The School fees and Hansel to be equally divided between them - Dowie to teach the Sunday School for the Winter half year. The other the Summer half year - The Sess Clerkship given to the one who the minister and Elders think most worthy during pleasure. Dowie is installed in the meantime but must provide a precentor off the Emoluments which are now almost equally divided between the Clerk and Bellman (Mint servt Man) which makes no object - School fees per Quarter for Latin 7/6 Arithc 5/- English and Writing 3/- English 2/- French 7/6 Geogy 7/6 etc. Dowie does not seem pleased enough with the arrangements - Yet upon the whole I think both the Situations are considerably bettered If they agree themselves and keep up the respectability of the School they will be tolerably well provided -

Since I returned from Edinr in October was throng and a good deal of the time from home at Keir Kippendavie, Doune and Monteath south side of the hill - and for the ensuing year I have more surveying than I'll be able to finish so that I am by no means sorry yet at quitting the School what may happen before I die - God knows -

We are all well and Mrs. MacEwen joins in wishing long and happy life to you and Mrs. Lorrain -

I am   My dear Sir
Yours sincerely
Gilbert MacEwen.

After writing the above in a great hurry on receipt of yours on Monday, it lay bye in the P. O. drawer till now - I spoke to Dowie upon the Jedburgh affair - he says that he'll drop canvassing if you intend to come forward, but that he would start for Selkirk if you thought there would be any prospect of success or that the situation is preferable to Callen - this you can easily tell from the foregoing statement - that he may see I have represented his case - I would like you would write your opinion in a Letter I may show him: or write himself -

G. MacE.

[* The reference to Jedburgh being "too near Kelso" was due to the excellent reputation of John Dymock, master of Kelso Grammar School, who was an outstanding teacher of languages. - Ed]

At the end of January 1804 the countryside erupted in what became known as the "False Alarm". A series of beacons had been positioned within sight of one another to be torched in the event of invasion by Napoleon's forces and one of these was set alight in error. In no time there was general uproar as men responded to the call to arms all over the Borders, Selkirk included. Trumpet and drum were sounded; gallants gathered at the Cross and were given tearful farewells by wives and sweethearts as they marched off to Dalkeith, to be sent home again to a hero's welcome. An actor named Flintoff had a theatre in Mr. Lang's barn at the end of Bogie's Close and he gave free entrance to the Volunteers and their ladies.

Aberdeen 19th March 1804

My Dear Friend,

I have yours of the 17 Ulto presently before me - It comes attended as usual with apologies and excuses which you wish to cram down my throat whether right or wrong - For one part of your apology namely your having become a Father I give you Credit and certainly would have excused your delay of writing for a short time that you might be able to furnish me with this intelligence but the other, to wit your intention of leaving Selkirk is not admissable as an excuse for one days delay - However as the case stands I have no alternative but condemn or acquit and as I would always wish to lean to the merciful side I shall yet forgive you; this I am the more readily induced to do when I consider that I have sometimes been an offender myself - I hasten now to congratulate you and Mrs. Lorrain on the late addition to your Family, on her happy recovery and on the health & promising appearance of your Heir, permit me to add my sincere wishes that he may live to be a comfort to his Parents & a blessing to Society -

I cannot help, my Friend, admiring your Correctness I assure you I shall not undertake to calculate so exactly to a day, nor shall I blush to yield the palm of victory to you in the way of Calculation when I consider the distinguished rank you hold as a Mathematician - How far this applies I leave you to judge -

Now with respect to your official Situation I observe your intention to make a Change - and highly approve of your motive - I am sorry that your Constitution has suffered any thing; but such being the case you ought to embrace the first opportunity that occurs of obviating that Evil and I am inclined to think the situation that now offers is a favourable one, more especially as you say the Endowment is good & the labour much less than at Selkirk - Were the Emoluments even less than those of your present Situation you certainly ought to prefer that in view if it appears more advantageous for health, for it is a Blessing of the greatest value and much must be sacrificed to it - I hope you will have your expectations fully gratified in the place you have in view -

You have happily anticipated my Query respecting Matrimony and your answer is exactly what I should have expected, For Whoever meets with a good partner as I have the strongest reason to suppose you have done must continue to relish the Married State more and more especially after they have been more strongly united together by a Pledge of their mutual affection - Reasoning with me on the subjects of Celibacy or Batchelorism is in vain for my ideas of its absurdity are the same as your own, indeed not so much from experimental Knowledge as from Theory and from a Regard to Consistency, my views being directed to a change of state in a very short time - Before many Moons shall revolve I expect to be united to the object of my affection, to her whose affections are centerd in me - If this state of mutual attachment affords the brightest prospect of happiness, as I think it does we have a very fair chance for it - My Notion of Matrimonial Felicity however is rather moderate than otherwise, for after some experience I have learned that no Situation in life is likely to produce that degree of happiness which in prospect we are apt to apportion it therefore a moderate expectation runs the lest hazard of a disappointment - When matters are somewhat further advanced I shall inform you more particularly meantime I am happy to say that at present

I am in good health and spirits and thriving as well as may be supposed in these times I beg to hear from you again as soon as convenient and with best wishes to Mrs. Lorrain & your health & happiness with that of your young man

> *I am My Dear Friend yours sincerely*
> *John Smith younger*

The appointment of William Lorrain to Jedburgh Grammar School, incorporating the English school, was made by the joint committee of Heritors and Town Council on 4th April, 1804 and his employment would start at Martinmas (11th November). The salary was to be £42.3.0 and a schoolhouse in Canongate which was purchased from trustees of the late Andrew Preston, cooper and church-officer. Preston's trustees were two well-known ministers; Rev. Dr. Thomas Somerville of Jedburgh and Rev. Dr. Robert Douglas of Galashiels.

In May William Lorrain's father wrote with bad news from home; his brother James was very ill and thought to be near death. *(p.97)*

In August Walter Lorrain junior, William's 20-year-old brother, decided to follow William's career as a schoolmaster. He appears to have stayed with William and Dolly at Selkirk before setting out to walk to Edinburgh. *(p.98)*

In September Lorrain received a letter from Rev. Dr. Douglas who was looking for a teacher for his parish :

Galashiels 1st Sept. 1804

D Sir

Last night I found time to draw up hastily the scroll of an advertisement about the examination of the school, which I enclosed to Mr. Clarkson. I have this evening as hastily drawn up and signed the attestation in favour of Mr. A. on the other page which I think may serve, tho' a little leisure might have produced a better one.

By a line from Mr. Dalzell I am told Mr. Lockerby is engaged. If you can hear of any other, or recollect any body that would answer us, as I wd. reckon it a favour to inform me & assist me in engaging him. He will have £23 of salary, at least 20 scholars at 5Sh. pr qr. & 30 if he acquits himself well - but he must provide lodging, board and a teaching room for himself. His entry is Mart. or sooner if he pleases. I should think one in your line could scent one out for us. Perhaps some of the rejected Candidates for your succession might be glad of our berth. Let us see you soon and have all your eyes about you.

Yours sincerely -

Rob. Douglas

Dr. Douglas had been minister at Galashiels since 1770 and had purchased a property known as Cartley Hole from Walter Turnbull, Melrose schoolmaster. In 1811 he sold it to Walter Scott, Sheriff and author, and it was renamed Abbotsford.

William Lorrain wrote to Bailie Rodger at Bridgelands:

Selkirk 3d Septem 1804

Dear Sir,

I thank you most kindly for your goodness in favouring me with a sight of the Advertisement relative to the Business of the 29th last. I have only used the freedom to make one slight alteration and that is respecting the Method exhibited in my School which I claim as my own exclusive right - The arrangements which you that day saw were all made by myself, in every respect even to the sound of a letter or the spelling of a word nor can Mr. Armstrong have any more right to the method which I have in Teaching Writing etc. or order than your apprentice has to any of your Law Processes because he wrote the words which you put in his mouth or put it in a copy before him - I am convinced that by this time from what I have stated you see the propriety of the right which I claim - If I cannot obtain that claim I'll consider it as the best of favours if you will expunge my name entirely from the advertisement -

Method alone is what establishes one teacher over another and to be deprived of this or even a part of it without reason is hard indeed -

With best wishes to Mrs. Rodger,

I ever am

Dear Sir,

Yours most truly,

Wm. Lorrain

Jedb. 20th Sept. 1804

Sir, I ould tak hit as a particular favour if you Could Get for me 6 or 8 ston of plaster hair our Job is lik to stop for want of that article I have aplad to Hawick Kellso Berwick and this place and Cannot get hit - I am sory to Truble you but som of your acqaintences will Get hit & send hit to Hawick & our peopl will Call for hit at Wallter Aitkens Carrier what hit Coms in shall be returned by our Carrier I am Sir yours

Richd Telfer

Mr. Lorane
Gramer & Engles Schol Mr
Selkirk

care Mr. Walter Aitkin Carrier Hawick

Dalkeith 17 Octr 1804

Dear Sir,

I regretted very much I did not see you when you were in Town, but I had the pleasure of hearing you were in good spirits

I wish you would make Sandy go through a Course of Book-keeping immediately, as on account of Mr. Simpson's ailing state he is really very much wanted at home - I do not know whose System you teach whether Mair's or Hamilton's, but I know from experience, that it is of much importance that Sandy should fully understand & comprehend the principles, and not be satisfied with merely writing a sett of Books. I was obliged to keep Books in a regular business soon after my leaving School and I am confident I should not have been competent for the business had I not completely understood what I had learnt, and even then many things will occur that never can be seen or taught in any Theory or System at School - The greatest difficulty, I recollect well, I had in learning this branch of education was in not seeing clearly how any other than a Person could be made Dr. or Cr. The fictitious Drs or Crs puzzled me exceedingly merely because I think the principle was not properly explained which however is very simple - That Cash, Cloth, Wine, Adventure & Susannah Bell's receivable etc. etc. should be debited or charged with what was paid for them, and credited when they are sold or parted with for another commodity requires but a common degree of attention to see that these may as well be made Drs as a Person to whom you give value - This extensive knowledge may not be required in keeping the Books here, but it will give him a much more enlarged view of business, if he is first *properly qualified by being a good Arithmetician - How the Devil does he yet spell so ill - it is a Shame*

Hector Munro has been put into the Jedburgh Fly by Mistake and has spent several days at the Bush much to his liking I dare say, and if you do not endeavour to get him back, he will give himself little trouble about you

I beg you will set Sandy about Book-keeping instantly which he may finish easily, at least a plain simple course, in six weeks and send him home qualified to carry on the business - I confess I cannot understand how the fellow is so d—nd clever as to spell so miserably

I shall expect to hear from you soon and I beg my best Complt to Mrs. Lorraine and my friend Mr. Clarkson

I always am,

Dear Sir,

Yours most faithfully,

John Russel

I have returned a Letter & marked
the bad spelling, blunders & bad Grammar,
but I should not even be well pleased to see his Letters well done either in Grammar or Spelling, unless it was done by himself easily and without any effort   If he has not time to write which is always his excuse, he ought not to write at all, but how has he not time in a week: he knows the Carrier's day and a Letter can be no worse of being kept a day or two.

Towards the end of 1804 William and Dolly Lorrain, with baby William, settled in the schoolhouse in Jedburgh and prepared to face the New Year.

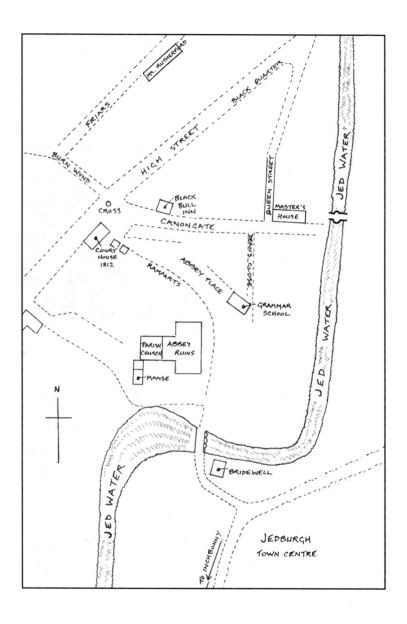

MR. RUTHERFURD

FRIARS

BLACK QUARTER

HIGH STREET

BURN WYND

JED WATER

CROSS

BLACK
BULL
INN

QUEEN STREET

MASTER'S
HOUSE

CANONGATE

COURT
HOUSE
1812

RAMPARTS

ABBEY PLACE

CASTLE STREET

GRAMMAR
SCHOOL

PARISH
CHURCH

ABBEY
RUINS

MANSE

N

JED WATER

JED WATER

BRIDEWELL

TO INCHBONNY

JEDBURGH
TOWN CENTRE

Chapter 3

JEDBURGH 1805-08

*Great care has been taken in accurately transcibing all letters -
errors in spelling and punctuation are as per original*

Jedburgh 1800 from a painting by Thomas Girtin

Girtin's picture of Jedburgh painted around 1800, taken from the ruinous remains of the Castle, shows mainly thatched houses, some with outside stairs to the upper storey. Originally, there had been a "tongue" of houses down the middle of the Canongate, but these and the old prison were demolished, to leave an open Market Place. In 1755, Newgate gaol was built at the entrance to Abbey churchyard, not far from the Tolbooth, and a spire was added in 1761. Across Abbey Bridge the first Bridewell in Scotland, influenced by prison reform doctrines, was built in 1789 and this was also used as an Asylum for Lunatics.

The County Hall and Town House, completed in 1812, were used for magistrates holding Courts, and for public meetings of burgesses, their Clerk having an office and record-room upstairs. Two apartments on the ground floor were for Public Weights. When the Circuit Court visited Jedburgh, there were ceremonial trumpets, processions and costumes, the Burgh officers bearing halberds.

The rough state of the roads in Girtin's painting gives an indication of the discomfort experienced by coach passengers. Coaches left the Black Bull Inn in Canongate and went to Edinburgh via Drygrange and Lauder on Wednesday and Saturday. The fare was 14s.

The Rector's House to which William Lorrain moved in 1804 was situated at 38 Canongate, with a large open space behind, half garden, half orchard, reaching back to Queen Mary's house. The premises boasted a "Necessary House" and coal-house. It was the birthplace, in 1781, of David Brewster, scientist, son of Lorrain's predecessor, James Brewster. The Grammar School occupied the building now known as the "Carter's Rest", opposite the Abbey which provided much of the stone. There had been an English School, kept by the Burgh, but this was amalgamated with the Grammar School on Lorrain's appointment.

"The Carter's Rest" - formerly Jedburgh Grammar School

Lorrain received a letter from the minister at Yetholm.

Yetholm   7th Janry 1805

Dear Sir,

I take the opportunity of an acquaintance being at Jedburgh to write you a few lines. William told me that you intended to give the Scholars the play the whole Saturday and the friday afternoon, at the end of every month. As bringing him home seems rather to encourage him I promised to send for him the first time he gets the play if the weather be tolerably good; & therefore request of you to let me know by a few lines the friday eight days before & whether the play be given on the friday. He seems both to like his situation in your house, and to continue at his learning, and therefore I am satisfied that in this respect such an indulgence will do him no harm. If you have as yet formed any judgement of the progress in his learning that may be expected; I will be obliged to you to let me know. My wife joins me in offering the best Compts of the Season to you and Mrs. Lorrain & wish to hear if William's Cold be any better.

> *I am Dear Sir*
> *Your most Obedient humle Servt*
> *William Blackie*

Despite having boys boarding with them, the Lorrains seem to have been suffering considerable inconvenience due to the unfinished state of the house, as this extract from the meeting of the Heritors shows:

[*Archibald Douglas of Adderston (or Edderstone) who had been chosen to preside over the committee was a brother of George Douglas of Cavers. - Ed]

*At Jedburgh the twenty fifth day of March eighteen hundred and five years. The Heritors of the Parish of Jedburgh having met in consequence of appointment of a former meeting and edictal citation and letters wrote to the Absent Heritors made choice of *Archibald Douglas of Adderston Esq. for their Preses and it having been inter alia represented to the meeting that Mr. Lorrains Kitchen loft was not floored they requested the Committee formerly named & appointed for conducting the Repairs and improvements of Mr. Lorrains House viz Provost Billerwell Mr. Potts and Mr. Wilson would purchase some of the deals of the old Manse from Mr. Winterup for that purpose and employ Tradesmen to get it properly* *floored so soon as the deals could be procured from Mr. Winterup. As the same contained in the Minutes of Sederunt of said Heritors & subscribed by their said Preses bears. - Extracted upon this and the preceding page by*

Rob Rutherfurd clk.

[Robert Rutherfurd (or Rutherford) of Friars was Inspector of Taxes in Jedburgh and was related to Dolly Lorrain, his mother Janet having been daughter to Walter Scott of Nether Bonchester. *(see family tree p.108)* His brother Archibald was a bookseller in Kelso - Ed].

My Dear Sir & Mrs. Lorrain   *(undated)*

Mrs. Rutherfurd wonders you have not come over - If not engaged we will be glad to see one or both as convenient.

Yours truly

Friars   Tuesday afternoon   *R. Rutherfurd*

Now that Dolly Lorrain was living at a distance, her father Thomas Scott began writing from Bowhill to keep her in touch with the family news. *(p.109)*

The country was recruiting soldiers to fight Bonaparte and one of William Lorrain's duties as schoolmaster was to draw up lists for Militia and fix them on to the door of the kirk. *(p.125)*

Four months before the Battle of Trafalgar, Thomas Gibbs, a naval man stationed at Queenborough in Kent, wrote to his son:

My Dear Boy
    Yours of the 20d came to hand and that we are very well as this leaves us and Much Wish you had said Weather Mr. Lorrain had Received My letter as the one I sent to your Mother the day before never came to hand Your Cousin Jane wished to know if you delivered her Letters: and that we are happy to hear you like the Country and have No Doubt of Mr. and Mrs. Ls kindness and have No Doubt but you will behave according to them and all your Friend for good behaviour will Make Friends and hope that you will give your Mind to your Edducation and that will make the time pass Easy Miss Barron and Broadbank are dead your Cousin Henry is left the Squrrell and gone into the Success(?) Frigate

your Uncle H and all very sorry that Thos has let him go: Mr. Morriss had a letter from Capt. M. last Week and that the youngsters were all well and that they have taken a Prize a Ship a long shore near the Bay of Hondoras: and I keep doing a little   James Gibbs is at Chatham

Mine your Mothers and Girls Most Respectfull Compliments to Mr. and Mrs. Lorrain and that W was happy about their having my Letter Trust and hope they will let you have yours Want for Mr. L. to Draw on Me at Mr. R Saxbys Butchers no. 57 Tower Street as Most Convenient to Himself Your Uncles Aunts all round are Well your old Play Mates often enquire after you: and I think you improve in you letter and hope it will continue and Remain

Queenborough	*Yours Most Affectionate*
30th June 1805	*Father Thos Gibbs*

P.S. Little John desires Me to tell you he is very well: Uncle Aunt H. with Janes best Compliments to Mr. and Mrs. L, Mother Self and the Girls Most Gratefull Compliments to Mr Smith and Friends When Opportunity; T.G.

Thos Gibbs at Mr. Lorrains Academy Jedburg Scotland   Post paid At Mr. R. Saxby Butcher No. 57 Tower Street London

On 30th June, 1805, the Lorrains' second son, Thomas, was born.

Dear Sir,
Inclosed you have a Draft for Wm. Homes Account he will be removed about the first of next September and return to this House - if he does not understand English Grammar I think it will be necessary he should learn it before Harvest
*   I am Dear Sir*

Harcarse House	*Yours with regard*
21 Apr. 1806	*P. Smith*
Compt to William	

Mrs. Blounts compliments to Mr. Loraine and is extremely sorry to trouble him, but is under the necessity of requesting he will desire the boys to play before the school as their being constantly so immediately before the door of Mr. Blounts house keeps it quite dirty and several times of late the windows have narrowly escaped being broken by throwing stones.

Wednesday morning

Dear Sir

The bad weather, and chilblained toes of our boys, together with a belief that there would not be much going forward in the School the two days in the end of this week, has induced Mrs. Usher and me to keep them here till Monday morning; and therefore I must beg that you will impute their non attendance on the first day of the meeting of the School, to the folly of their parents, and not to the boys themselves. Having occasion to send two carts to Jedburgh I write this by the men merely to prevent you from being surprised at the boys not making their appearance. I intend that they shall set out on Monday in proper time to be present at the afternoon school.

Mrs. Usher joins me in wishing you Mrs. Lorrain and family many happy returns of the season.

Yours most sincerely

Courthill 1st Janry 1807   Thomas Usher.

A third son, Walter Scott, was born to the Lorrains on 5th April 1807.

? Tom Hau April 7th 1807

Sir/

I hope you'll be so good as take the Trouble alongst with my son Robert to enclose me a Bank Check which you'll get from Mr. W. Riddell Writer of £1000 sterg. also the full interest of both these Bonds that is Dew upon them/ This you'll send in notes etc./ I have Discharged them and hopes you'll Seal up the Check and Notes in a letter and send James of on Thursday Morning as airly as possible with them as I could not come to Jedr. myself at this time. Hopes you'll Excuse this, let me know what Robr. is to do after the 4th of June as I think that must be his time of leaving you - Can he be of no use to you after that time or any of your Neighbours as he is fond of staying in Jedburgh but before then I shall see you and him when we shall settle every thing in hopes you'll Get this business finished in the Evening and my son of on Thursday Morning. I am

Dear Sir

Your Most obe Servt

John Elliot.

William Lorrain's career as a writer began at this time, with the publication of "Book-keeping by Double Entry". Sales seem to have been slow, according to James Smith writing from St. Andrew's *(p.225)*

Dear Sir,

  I should be very glad to have your opinion and advice as to the branches of education to which it would be most proper for George Pott to apply during the ensuing winter at Edinburgh. As he will probably take another winter, if not other two, at Edinburgh, I have been thinking that he would reap more advantage with private teachers than by attending the public classes of the College during the first winter; and that he might attend Mr. Dufrain for French, Mr. Scott for reading English, Mr. Laidlaw for Mathematics, Professor Coventry for Agriculture, and that, if it was not taking too much in hand at once, he might also take a course of Geography with some reputable teacher of that branch; but as you are better acquainted than I am with the progress that he has already made, and a better judge of what it would be most advantageous for him to apply to next, I hope you will have the goodness to favour me with your opinion, both as to the branches of education, and the teachers, which you think it would be most proper for him to attend.

 I understand by a letter from James to his Mother that he is in want of a hat, and therefore, if he has not already got a new one, I beg you will be so good as order one for him. *I am, with great regard*

           Dear Sir,

Courthill 15th October 1807   *Yours most sincerely,*
              Thomas Usher

Dear Sir,

  Your favour of the 6th inclosing Mr. Fair's receipt for the money I have received, and am much obliged to you for your attention to that matter. I was happy to learn that the letter which we concerted, when I had last the pleasure of seeing you here, had so good an effect.

 I understand there is at present a Dancing School in Jedburgh. If you approve of it, and if you think the teacher a proper one, I think it would not be amiss that both the Penchrise boys and our's should go to it, because they will soon get past the proper age & size for learning dancing; but if our boys toes are not better I am afraid they could do nothing at the dancing, and probably to attempt it would make their toes worse. Of this you and Dr. Wilson will judge; and I leave it entirely to you to let any or all of the four boys go to the Dancing School as you think best. I always am

    Dear Sir

     Yours most sincerely,
Courthill 10th Feby 1808   *Thomas Usher*

Addressed to Master Gibson - Undated

My dear Thomas,

    I send you by the Fly a plum-cake, and Papa another sixpence, concluding you are now Dux - Tell Mr. Lorrain I am obliged to him for writing and believe me yours

Affectionately

I Wootton

It was at the end of 1807 that the first of Mark Aitken's letters *(p.159)* appeared and he proved a very entertaining correspondent. Like many other aspiring ministers, he bided his time by becoming a tutor to children of the gentry. Another budding schoolmaster was Thomas Robson *(p.173)* who had just started his career at Newcastleton.

Schoolmasters in Scotland were uniting in their efforts to improve the lot of their profession as a whole. *(p.225)* One of the chief instigators of action was John Dymock, Rector at Kelso Grammar School who wrote to Lorrain inviting him to a meeting:

Sir,

    For a day or two past, I have been considering the Draughts of Our Bill with a view to make out a Report for the Schoolmasters of this Presbytery - But previous to the transmitting of our opinion, I would wish to know something of the sentiments of our Brethern in the neighbouring Parishes. With that intention, I wrote Mr. White of Dunse today requesting he would meet with you or a Delegate from the Presbytery of Jedburgh at my house tomorrow sennight at one oClock - should you find that inconvenient, we will forward to you a Copy of our Report and you can transmit us yours in return - The first is the preferable plan could you make it convenient - We Grammar Schoolmasters are too little acquainted at present which in future I hope will not be the case -

I am

Sir

Your Most Obdnt

John Dymock

2 oclock 12 Dec. 1806

P.S. Will be happy to hear from you in the course of a post or two J.D.

John Dymock had been Rector at Kelso since 1791 and had acquired a reputation for excellence. His wife, Jean Lockhart, assisted him in looking after the boarders, as Dolly Lorrain did in Jedburgh. Despite their good standing, the Dymocks were considered to have been negligent in their care of two boys. Tom Mein and Will Ogilvie were pupils in 1803; they were punished for not attending to their letters by being confined to the school on a Saturday. The school floor had been washed and the boys' shoes taken to be cleaned, so they developed bad colds. Their relatives found them huddled, wrapped in blankets, on uncomfortable chairs and crying in their misery. They were removed from the school and took six weeks to recover from their ordeal.

There were nine Dymock children to share the accommodation in the schoolhouse, and Mrs. Dymock's mother and sister lived with them. When Mrs. Dymock died in September 1805, her eldest son was only 11 years old and the youngest an infant. Mrs. Lockhart, Dymock's mother-in-law, died the following January and his sister-in-law in January 1808.

An advertisement appeared in the Kelso Mail:

March 3   "Latin Rudiment Class" J. Dymock will open a Latin Rudiment
1808   Class on Monday 4th April next. It is his intention to take in
            a class of that kind, in future, only once a year.

However, events moved quickly for the following month an announcement appeared in the same paper:

April 4   Kelso Grammar School In consequence of the appointment
            of Mr. Dymock, rector of the Grammar School of Kelso, to
            supply a vacancy in the public school of Glasgow, a
            successor to his office is immediately wanted. He must be
            qualified to teach the Latin, Greek and French languages;
            also Roman Antiquities and Ancient and Modern
            Geography. As the salary is large, and the other
            emoluments, from the flourishing state of the school, and
            the advantageous situation of the place, may be expected
            to be very considerable, it is hoped that none but able and
            experienced teachers will apply.

William Lorrain decided to investigate his chances of a transfer from Jedburgh and contacted his friend Ebenezer Clarkson, the Selkirk surgeon whose son was boarding with the Lorrains at Jedburgh. Clarkson wrote to report on progress:

Dear Sir,

      I am just arrived from Traquair from attending Mrs. Nicol in Labour - As Mr. Rodger is to be with you tomorrow - I take the opportunity to send you the enclosed as a proof that all the Pringles are not alike - Mr. Nicol wishes you all the success you wish Tell My Dear little Fellow I fully intended, but had not time to write him - By a Servant from Eilliestown yesterday I wrote very strongly for more recommendations than one - Was as the enclosed   Yours

³/₄ past 9   *E. C.*

Enclosed   *No. 55 George Square, Edinburgh 11 April 1808*

Dear Sir,

      I have been favoured with yours of the 8th Instant, and in compliance with your request, now enclose a letter to Sir George Douglas soliciting his patronage and good offices in behalf of Mr. Lorrains application to succeed to the vacancy in the Grammar School of Kelso occasioned by the removal of the present Incumbent to Glasgow - on your account I most cordially wish it may be of the service to him you seem to expect.

        I remain, Dear Sir,
          Yours very truly,
            Alexr. Pringle.

Alexander has just come in very happy at a prize being adjudged to him, for one of the best decertations in Latin delivered in at Mr. Cristisons Second Class at College.

                  Selkirk 30th April -08
Dear Sir,

      I was duly favoured with yours and am glad to think you have such good prospect of success in Kelso - Mr. Pringle of Whit. had lately written to Mr. Ogilvie of Chesters for his aid and assistance in your behalf - In his answer (which I saw) he says, "keep yourself quite easy about Mr. Lorrain, for the Kelso folks have determined to give him the School" - What nonsense to conclude that Ma—t-y had anything to do with my enquiry about your ploy at the term - you have even been saying something about it this day week to some of our folks. J. A. this was terrible as the story is spreading like Muirburn — & Jedburgh is quoted - I only meant to say that if it was the same thing to you I should like Eben to be over after or at the term for the Vacation but 'tis not improbable but I may take a trip over to Jedburgh before that - Best Compts to Mrs. Lorrain   I am Ever Sincerely yours,

E. Clarkson

Kelso Manse
6 May 1808

Dear Sir,

As you expressed much anxiety respecting the resolutions to which the Heritors might come about limiting the number of Boarders &c. I lose no time in informing you of the result of a Meeting of Heritors & Stentmasters which was yesterday held in this house for the purpose of fixing certain doubtful points previous to the election.

The Heritors and Stentmasters had some discussion about the part of the salary which has been for a long time paid by the latter to the Rector viz. £11. 2 .2 . This sum was after the passing of the School Act 1803 increased by the town, "during pleasure" , to £20 but even had Mr. Dymock remained the addition would have been taken away. The town you know now say that the original eleven pounds is also voluntarily & especially in their option to give or withhold as the late Act gives them no voice in the election, and no power over the school. The Heritors present seemed of a different opinion, but were not inclined to engage in a contest about the matter. It was therefore resolved to promise no more than the £22. 4. 4   i.e. the maximum under the late Act paid by the Heritors. They at the same time were encouraged by what the Stentmasters said to hope that if they shall be pleased with the new appointment the sum so long paid, at least, will be continued.

I was asked if the Rector might expect to be nominated Session Clerk, and answered, tho' with some reservation, which could not apply to such candidates as you, that he might.

Latin and Greek were fixed as the only languages to be taught in future at the public School - Latin fee is to be advanced from 7/6 to 10/ pr. qr. Latin & Greek to be advanced from 10/6 to 15/- As Greek is seldom or never taught at our school without Latin to any pupil, no price was fixed for Greek alone.

The Rector was allowed to teach French or any other branches except those taught by the English Master, at his private hours, & to fix his own fees. The public hours were fixed to be from April till Vacation Morning 7-9 Forenoon 10-12 Afternoon 2-4. In winter Mg. None - Forenoon 9-12 Afternoon 2-4. After considerable discussion, and some difference of opinion as to the number to be fixed as the maximum of Boarders (tho' the meeting agreed that a limit should somewhere be fixed) it was settled that the future number of Boarders kept by the Rector should not exceed Twelve. It was added, tho' not without some hesitation, that tho' the Rector might do all for those pupils who were boarders that he inclined, in general, he yet must either not drill them in private for their public school exercises, or if he does, must arrange them in a class by themselves. I am inclined to hope the Rector will be allowed still to exercise his own discretion on this last point.

The last measure adopted by the Meeting, was a declaration that the English School should henceforth be quite independent of the Rector, tho' it is not meant to be considered as a separate parochial school.

Though I have little leisure at present, I have thought it my duty to give you this particular statement, that you might not remain ignorant in points which might materially tend to affect your future views in relation to this business.

Messrs Gillies and Muirhead arrived in Kelso last night in the same coach, tho' apparently ignorant of each others persons & intentions, till they met at the Manse. They talk of being in Kelso for two or three days.

The Heritors are to meet at the Manse on Tuesday to, arrange & talk about the recommendations. The day of election is Thursday, if time &c. permit.

With every good wish for your family, I am Dr. Sir
Your Most Obedt. Serv.
R. Lundie.

Galashiels 11 May 1808
Dr. Sir,

I was favoured with yours of the 7th and think you have acted properly. When at Kelso on the 26 of April, I regretted that I could not see Mr. Haldane & Mr. Walker of Wooden, the only Electors of my acquaintance. I found Mr. Lundie rather inclined to limit the boarders & increase the board. He spoke of 20 boarders at 40 gns. each being nearly equal to 30 at £30 each - attended with less trouble to the Master, - more for the advantage of the boys - & gratifying to the prejudices of the inhabitants. The last mentioned circumstance is the Crigo mali and began to operate against Dymock. The Heritors allow the maximum of the late Act. The town has been in use for 50 years or more to give 200 merks more. Sometime ago they added about £9 st. to make the salary £42 - but, upon finding that the late act gave them no vote, & conceiving their children neglected by Mr. D. for the sake of his boarders, they actually withdrew the last addition of near £9 some years ago, & threatened to withdraw the other 200 mks which I find they have now done. This, too, laid the foundation of the opposition school, of which you speak. All this I was told, or inferred from what I learned while conversing with several of the Town's people - & cannot help thinking the Electors were mighty silly to yield to their prejudices about limiting the boarders to 12, when they withdrew the whole salary they contributed.

You may see I write hurriedly being thrang preparing for my Sacr. on Sunday. Had you got Kelso, Mr. Brown's friend would have continued your Boarder. I am not without hopes of procuring him for you at Jedb. Accept my best wishes for your own & family's welfare.

I am, Dr. Sir,

Yours sincerely,

favoured by Mr. Balmer   Rob. Douglas

Kelso at this time had an English School in addition to the Grammar School and the teacher was John Weir. He and William Lorrain had apparently had a discussion in private at the time of the Grammar School vacancy. Weir used the information given by his colleague to make a case for his own betterment, published in the Kelso Mail, 1808 May 26:

Letter to the editor:

" Sir, I have learned, not without considerable surprise, that several persons in Kelso and the neighbourhood are complaining much of a small advance which is to take place, from the first of July next, in the English School fees, by authority of the heritors.... Since the time of the separation of the Latin from the English School of Kelso, about 28 years ago, a very trifling advance of fees has once only taken place; and there is no doubt that in consequence of the diminished value of money, even the intended school fees will be lower, in fact, than those which were at first established. The following is a correct account of the present and the intended fees:

	Present fees	Advanced fees
English per quarter	£0 .3 .0	£0 .3 .6
English & Writing	£0 .3 .6	£0 .4 .6
Writing & Arithmetic	£0 .4 .0	£0 .5 .6

When English happens to be taught along with writing and arithmetic an additional shilling is to be exacted. It thus appears that 6d is the whole advance for learning to read English per quarter, 1/- for writing, and 1/6 for arithmetic; an advance so extremely moderate that it is not easy to conceive that any objection should be made to it in a town like this, unless that it is too small. Let these most reasonable fees be compared with the increased wages of labour and the advanced price of commodities of every kind, and then let any candid man say whether the new school fees be either extravagant or unjust. In Jedburgh, a town neither more populous nor more flourishing than Kelso, the fees for writing and arithmetic have been considerably higher for several years past than the new Kelso fees, and have also been paid per advance. Yet the school of Jedburgh has never been better attended, nor have the wages been ever more willingly and regularly paid than since the rise took place. There is this peculiarity in the situation of the English teacher of Kelso, that he has no dwelling house, and that his salary amounts only to £5 .11 .1d, though he is obliged to employ an assistant at his own expense. This unquestionably renders the small advance of wages an act rather of narrow justice than of liberality. What other equal quantity of human labour can be purchased proportionately cheap? Education, Sir, including the principles of religious knowledge, has justly been deemed one great cause of the prosperity of Scotland, and the respectability of its inhabitants; and those who are so poor as to be unable to bestow this advantage upon their children, have seldom had reason to complain that public or private assistance has been withheld. But it is not to be endured that the respectable character of a teacher of youth is to be degraded by unprofitable labour into a public drudge. Nor is it consistent with the usual good sense and liberality of the inhabitants of Kelso to desire it."

AMICUS

John Weir received a letter from William Lorrain:

Jedburgh 2nd June 1808

Dear Sir,

On my return home last night from the neighbourhood of Carlisle where I had been spending a few days of Vacation, I was surprised at a Section of a letter dated 26th May to the Editor of the Kelso Mail of same date, by one who subscribes himself AMICUS.

The information which I forwarded you a month ago respecting the Fees of Jedburgh School, was in confidence and friendship, and not intended for the Subject of the Kelso Mail; and sorry am I to suppose that you should betray either, or have any hand in, such a (rash, thoughtless, and unfair) piece of public correspondence - If there exist any differences between the Heritors Schoolmrs. or Town of Kelso, what has Jedburgh to do with such differences? Is it not unfair and officious, publickly to mark out and point at the situation of any individual? By this does Mr. AMICUS wish to intone the same miseries upon that individual, that now brood over the public mind of Kelso? Is this like or does it deserve the name AMICUS? So well acquainted with the public mind of Kelso is Mr. AMICUS not aware of the evil consequences of rousing the designing in other Quarters? To such the bare mention of ills is their commission - why does he not call forward more examples for the inspection of the Public than Jedburgh and why does he not give a full detail of all the Rates of Fees in Jedburgh School since he pleases to mention it? By this he only serves you to the injury of another for the Section has occasioned speculation anent your cause, as in points of controversy, it is always looked upon as a bad precedent where only one example can be adduced - Once I intended to take public notice of the Section aluded to as it most certainly deserved without writing you, had I not been actuated from the principle of doing as I would be done to - As Mr. AMICUS must be known to you, I hope you will point out to him the absolute necessity of curing the wound which he has made, or I must, from the duty which I owe myself and the respect I bear the support of my situation, take public notice of it., and in such a manner as clearly to show, upon a candid, fair and impartial comparison of the Schools of Kelso and Jedburgh, that the former is much higher rated than the latter. This I am sorry to do as it must operate against your interest - I shall expect to hear from you in a day or two.

I am

Dear Sir

Yours sincerely

Wm. Lorrain

[*William Gillies, mentioned by Rev. Lundie, was appointed new Rector of Kelso Grammar School and took his place soon after. - Ed]

June 13
1808

Kelso Grammar School The public are respectfully informed that the Grammar School of Kelso was opened on the 6th inst by Mr. Gillies, who has a good accommodation for a few more young gentlemen as boarders. It shall be his study to promote, by every means in his power, the improvement and comfort of his pupils, and he indulges the hope that, from his experience in the education of youth, he may be enabled to give satisfaction to those parents and guardians who may honour him with their confidence. It is scarcely necessary to add that the situation of Kelso is healthy and uncommonly pleasant. Mr. Gillies avails himself of the present opportunity of stating that he proposes to open a Rudiment class once only in the course of the year, immediately after the autumn vacation. It has often been found that in consequence of the admission of beginners at several different periods of the year the classes become so numerous, and the time and labour of a master so much divided, as to render it extremely difficult, perhaps impossible, for him to pay due attention to all; he therefore hopes that the public will acquiesce in an arrangement which he considers as alike conducive to the comfort of the teacher and the benefit of the school.

August 22

The Annual Examination of the Grammar School of Kelso took place on Thursday last. In consequence of the interval between the removal of Mr. Dymock and the present appointment of Mr. Gillies to succeed him as rector, the examination was of a more general nature than it would otherwise have been. The more advanced pupils, however, read and explained the Latin classics with much accuracy, and a few of them showed a very considerable knowledge of the Greek language. From the high professional character of Mr. Gillies, we entertain the hope that the reputation of Kelso school will be fully maintained, and from his personal respectability we are warranted to add that his pupils will acquire virtuous habits as well as classical knowledge.

Chapter 3

JEDBURGH 1808-15

*Great care has been taken in accurately transcibing all letters -
errors in spelling and punctuation are as per original*

The beginning of the 19th century was a time of invention, exploration and progress in many fields. The citizens of Jedburgh were as enterprising as any, and James Veitch of Inchbonny (1771-1838) was amongst the foremost. Under the tuition of James Small, Veitch learned the art of plough-making and was awarded a prize of £100 by the Highland Society for his own design. It wasn't long before his fame spread to other parts, thanks to people like William Lorrain, who received the following letter:

Dear Sir,

I had the pleasure of travelling with you in the Stage-Coach between Hawick & Langholm rather more than twelve months ago; when you showed me the model of a plough made by one Vetch in the neighbourhood of Jedburgh. I am in want of a plough at present & I will take it as an obligation, if you would have the goodness to desire him to send me one immediately with an account of the charge. It may be directed to me at Westerkirk to be left at Ancrum Bridge to the care of Mr. Thomson Carrier Hawick.   *I am, with much regard,*

Dear Sir,

Your most obedn. &

Westerkirk 8 July   *very humble Sevt.*
        1808   *William Little*

Meanwhile, the Lorrain children - William, Thomas and Walter - were suffering the miseries of measles. They were not alone, as this letter from James Pott, (whose father Gideon rented the farm of Penchrise from Elliot of Stobs) shows:

Pencrise 3d July 1808

Dear Sir,

Alexr. and I last week were seized with the Measles, and have to our great joy got them over, which have indeed very much enfeebled us; and frustrated our expectations of coming down to you soon but as soon as our strength will permit us, be assured of us being with you. I

hope your family has now got them over likewise in a favourable manner.
- Be so good as write next week, and send up my Nankin small clothes. I
am

> *Dear Sir,*
>> *Yours &c.*
>>> *James Pott*

P.S. All join me in best Compts to you, Mrs. Lorrain and family. J.P.

Described by his peers as a pedant, James Pott went on to become a Writer to the Signet in 1818. There seems to have been a connection between the Pott family and the Ushers at Courthill.

Dear Sir,

> *The reason of our boys not being sent to Jedburgh yesterday was because all my people were so much engaged in getting the corn into the stackyard that I could not spare a man to go along with them.*

> *Subjoined you will find an order on Mr. Fair for £60, of which you will be so good as place £30 to my credit for John & James. The other £30 you may apply in the first place for paying what is due for the Board and Education etc. of James Pott since 1st July when last account ended, and place the balance to my credit for the board and education etc. of Alexander Pott.*

> *Mrs. Usher has sent a Cheese for Mrs. Lorrain, and joins me in best Compts to her and you. I ever am*

> > *Dear Sir,*

Courthill 20th Septemr   *Yours most sincerely*
     1808   *Thomas Usher*

> > > > *Orchd Cottage 20 Sept. 1808*

Dear Sir,

> *I hope it will not make much difference in your arrangement of my son's class He not having come over last night. He certainly intended it and things were ordered accordingly - & his Box sent to the Carrier which will come to your house this day - The day being so wett we thought it of no importance as I imagine you seldom make a full muster the first day after the vacation.*

> *Having some friends with me at present I could not conveniently come over with him but will have the pleasure of calling on you some day soon*

I am satisfied he is in good hands and the more readily commit him to the care of you and Mrs. Lorrain convinced that every attention will be paid to him that is proper -   I remain with best compliments to Mrs. Lorrain

        Dear Sir,
              Your obdt. servant
              John Wilson.

Sir,

    We regret the very bad state of the Roads has prevented Thomas from returning at the time you mentioned the School met after the Holidays - We have been very well pleased with his improvement under your care and he has been a very good Boy - he is to ride into Jedburgh tomorrow if the weather will permit - I fear the ride may be rather fatiguing for him, as he has never rode so far - but Mr, Tulloch thinks the Carriage would not pass easily yet, from the blowing of the snow - and trust he will not suffer beyond being tired - I observe his every day Clothes are much worn, and shall be obliged by your procuring him a new Jacket & Pair of Pantaloons - his best pair are short for him now, so they had better be turned into every day wear & a new Jacket of such Cloth as they are got to wear with them, a pair of Pantaloons of the same Cloth will answer well with his Sunday Jacket - He also requires a pair of Braces (gallowses) which I will thank you much to order for him immediately - these he has at present Cut his Shirts sadly, & besides are very uneasy they make him stoop from tightness in short you will be so good as get any thing necessary for him when you see occasion

    with good wishes to you & family in which Mr Tulloch joins I am Sir
             Your most Obedt Servt
               J. Tulloch

Ellistown House
8th Janry 1809

We always wish his Clothes to be Blue - and before you order his new ones, if you will have the goodness to look at his pantaloons - you will see they are good second Cloth - his dress Jacket is superfine but that would not do for common wear - I will send him another blue waistcoat - he has a note for Mrs Erskine which if Wednesday is a good day he can go with.

It was at this time that William Lorrain's brother Joseph died *(p.100)* and he was apparently too preoccupied to visit his parents, to the grief of his ageing father. From a later communication *(p.102)*, it seems that William was contemplating a financial involvement in a farm being rented by his brother John. He retained an interest in land and agriculture and his skill in costing and financial matters was useful to several of his circle.

A fourth son, James Montesquieu Beattie Lorrain, was born in September, 1809.

Leith 22nd Decr 1809

Dear Sir,

 Your esteemed favour of the 20th I recd this morning. I actually anticipated that Tomas would not be a bit better than I find he has been from your information as well as Mrs Reids partial account of him. He is a Monster of iniquity, & a disgrace to human nature. Something must be done & that without delay. I would come without waiting a day if I knew how to put an end to his unprecedented infamous conduct. I shall tomorrow see how far it is possible to have him removed to a place of confinement; for he is Worse than any Maniac I ever heard of. Interim if he is again outrageous, I beg as a particular favour you will get an Order from the Majistrates or Sheriff to put on a Strait Jacket & lodge him at the Bridge end till we fix on another place of safety. - If this cannot be done tell him when I hear of any further disturbance he may expect to be taken without notice to the nearest Seaport & put on board a Man of War. - Indeed I offend him too much, but I will keep my promise, if he will retire 10 miles from Jedburgh & not Molest my Mother & Sister. I will pay a board & lodging for him to the extent of £30 per Ann. - This you may either tell him or not as you may see necessary - indeed you are Wellcome to show him all or any part of what I write you. - My Mother & Sister shall be protected; if it were possible to remove them as well as Mrs. Reid from Jedbh for a time. He would then be under the necessity of putting up with any Lodging that may be provided for him. Robt is studying very closs so that it would be a pity to take him of even for a week, but be assured I will be ..(illegible)....any in 10 days. I will see Mr. C. Baxter & take his opinion on all these irksome matters.

 I now most sincerely thank you for your attention in writing me so particularly, & I beg in future you do not wait for Mrs. Reids bearer, but let me hear every part when he is not in Order. Mrs. Scott & Robt. join me in good wishes to Mrs. L. self & family - a happy Xmas etc. etc.

 I am Mo Truly Dr. Sir

  Yrs J. Scott

[The suggestion of lodging Thomas "at the Bridge" refers to the Bridewell at the old Jedburgh bridge end where Lunatics were held. The threat of putting him on a "Man o' War" gives some idea of prevailing conditions at sea - Ed].

Courthill 31st January 1810

Dear Sir,

I was favoured with your letter of 30th of last month mentioning that you had got from the Schoolmaster of Hobkirk a receipt for the proportion of salary due to him by Mr. Elliot of Harwood, and I would have sent the money before now but am not certain of the amount. If you will have the goodness to send either the receipt itself, or a line mentioning the sum contained in it, by the boys when they come home on Friday first, I shall not fail to send the money by them when they return to School next week. I always am

Dear Sir,

Yours most sincerely,

Thomas Usher

The boys would mention to you that when they last returned to school I had not received your letter intimating Dr. Wilson's opinion that it might be proper (on account of Thomas Stephenson's fever) that they should remain at home till he could say that they might return with safety. Had your letter come to hand before they went away we certainly would have detained them at home till we had heard from you again; and upon receiving your letter we wished that you had just sent them back with the man who accompanied them; but, no bad consequences having followed, it is better that they remained. I do not know how you may now be pleased with the progress they are making. It is probable parental partiality may have deceived me; but last time they were here I was remarkably well pleased with both of them, and with the progress they seemed to me to have made.

Excuse this palaver

Dear Sir,

Having an opportunity of conveyance today I use the freedom of sending up my two boys to your School, tho' I cannot accompany them myself to introduce them - but will wait on you as soon as I possibly can. In the meantime, as I told you, I wish to fit them for bussiness by giving them a good English Education. The oldest will need brushing up in reading & writing - & in the Arithmetick he has got, before he goes further I suppose. He knows little, or nothing of English grammar yet. He has learned a little Latin, which, if it be of no further use to him, will perhaps make French easier by & by. My youngest boy is far back, poor fellow. He is sensible of this, & is easily damped by anything like an affront. He is capable of considerable application but seems not very quick - especially in committing anything to memory. He has been going on with reading & begun writing. I beg pardon for troubling you with all this, but thought it proper to give you a hint of what they have been doing, as I wish them to be carried on as fast as prudence & their capacity will permit - but submit entirely to your discretion

I am,

Sir,

Roxb: 27 Feby   *Your most humble servant*

1810   *Andrew Bell*

P.S. The boys have taken with them some books they were using here - & Mr. Thomson the Stationer I suppose will can provide them with what more you prescribe for them.

Many of your Scholars, besides your Boarders, attend you to Church, I will esteem it a favour if you allow my children to do so.   *A.B.*

In February 1810 a committee met to discuss Lorrain's proposal to enlarge the school but agreed to delay action for a year, apart from allowing the ceiling to be raised to admit more air. They were concerned that no more pupils "than he can with ease and safety accommodate" should be taken as boarders. The wisdom of this advice is evident:

Orchd. Cottage 8th March 1810

Dear Sir,

  I am extremely sorry to hear that the fever still continues in your House and also in the Town of Jedh. I have kept my son at home since *Candlemas in hopes that the decease might be extirpated and that he might return with safety to his studies -

  He being idle and loosing his time here I am advised to send him to Edinr. which I am not a little puzzled about - but I think for his sake I shall probably Comply as there no person who knows the Nature of the fever can say when it will be safe for you to take back your boarders in the meantime you may please send me your Acct and have the goodness to order over by Geo. Adamson the Books & other Box with the Keys of both - which is proper at all events to get properly aired - I beg to present Compts to Mrs. Lorain in which I am joined by Miss Watson & your pupil & we sincerely sympathise with you in this unfortunate business - I am

Dear Sir,

Your very obed servt

John Wilson

[* Candlemas - 2nd February - Ed.]

Dear Sir,

I took it into my head to examine William upon some very trifling Latin words, and I really must say he is much more deficient than I could have thought it possible. - I do not conceive it necessary to break the boys heart by forcing him to attend: but I am afraid that unless he is in some degree checked, that habit of listlessness which he has acquired, will increase upon him, & ruin his future prospects. - But the degree, I leave entirely to yourself. -

I have informed him how very much displeased I am with him. - I have given him no handsel; - but if you will be good enough to bring him up to my room, next Tuesday & say that he has promised amendment, I shall relent.

I wish you & your family many happy returns of the Season: & what I do assure you will prove upon trial much stronger & sweeter than all these good wishes - I send you a bottle of real Noyau which be so kind as to accept of -

I remain Dear Sir,

Yours very truly,

Charles Kerr

Abbotrule, Jany 1 -1811

[Charles Kerr, related to the Kerrs of Lothian, was an ill-tempered man who upset many of his contemporaries. He became a Writer to the Signet in 1789 and purchased the post of Paymaster in an infantry regiment in 1800, returning to Abbotrule on half pay. His son William seems to have been a delicate lad, for he died in 1822 - Ed].

Dear Sir   *Abbotrule 23rd Sept 1811*

    I am really very much difficulted what to do about William. You are sensible that he has made no progress at school and I am perfectly convinced that to whatever school I should just now send him, it would be the same thing. For the present therefore I shall keep him at home and make the most of him, until something better occurrs.

    In mean time I request that Mrs. Lorrain & you will accept of Mrs. Kerr's & my very grateful thanks for your kind attention to him.

    Be so good as to send me your acct.

      Your very obt Sert

        Charles Kerr

Dear Sir   *Abbotrule   Saturday*

    I certainly ought to have seen you before now, to have thanked both Mrs. Lorrain & you for your kind attention to Willy, and so far as a boy of his age may be supposed to feel circumstances of that nature, he was loud in his acknowledgements to both, nor will he soon forget your kindness. I have been too much engaged of late to offer you my thanks in person; be kind enough now to receive them, - I shall ever acknowledge your conduct as a debt of gratitude.

    William has accompanied my family to Dublin: I have no longer therefore the prospect of his being with you. Make out his account which I shall immediately pay. Do not stint his charges.

    I remain Dear Sir

      Your very obdt Servt

        Charles Kerr

          Lanton Place   17th Febr 1811

My Dear Sir,

    I am extremely sorry Thomas has behaved so ill and I am much alarmed for his safety as the night is so very inclement. I sincerely hope however that his temerity will not carry him to such a length as to venture himself out to the open fields, which if he has done I am much afraid he will never reach home, but as the bearer tells me you have despatched a person to the Swinie Toll to intercept him if he goes that way (and that way he must go if he thinks of reaching Langburnshiels). I do not see what more can be done, because it is absolutely impossible to find him in the fields tonight. - I would however gladly hope that the foolish creature may still be in the town, and that before the bearer returns with this he will have returned to you, but should that not be the case, you will cause every search to be made in the Town and should that prove fruitless and if before the morning he is not come back to you, then I will thank you to despatch a person very early in the morning to Langburnshiels and desire him on his way to call at Mr. Smiths Hartsheughmill for I know no other place he has the smallest likelihood to couch at. - I shall see you in the morning when I shall be glad to hear good news.   I always am

My Dear Sir,

Yours very sincerely,

George Bell

My Dear Sir,

  You gratified me much with your account of your attempts to improve James: it shewed an honesty & an interest that are not always to be met with. I saw & regretted what you mention: but being obliged to be often from home my regrets were fruitless. I shall never however consider that time as ill spent which is employed in fixing the attention ; well knowing how difficult it is to acquire, & how important it is, after it is acquired. Indeed the more I think of James, the more pleased I am at my present choice - he will see his defects & I hope endeavour to profit by his advantages.

  I have written him a long letter - where the heart is engaged, words come of course: but I do it with the double view of attaching him to home & improving his mind. These little buds & blossoms of humanity are naturally dear to a parents heart: & we wish that they shall respect & love us wherever they are. I envy you the advantage you possess as to a French teacher: altho' I often spoke with natives while in Edinr I feel rusted: & besides a living language is always changing. As I have the opportunity of one Anderson a Plant man from Hawick I send you my Copy of Moores Grammar with the Fragments & addenda of Dalzel. You can easily copy it over & return the Book with James in harvest - As a bon bouche I have also sent a Copy of Fraser of the High Schools English version & a number of Latin words I got from Mr. French - He allowed me to copy them from a Manuscript Book before he retired from office. - But the servant tells me that unless he goes immediately the good family at Craighaugh will be to bed so I can only add that with best Compliments to Mrs. Lorrain

I am My dear Sir

Eskdm Manse	*Yours truly*
13 May 1811	*Wm. Brown*

To enlarge the Packet I shall also add Hills Phrases - but request they may be taken care of.

The French teacher mentioned by Rev. Brown had arrived in Jedburgh at the end of March 1811, part of a contingent of prisoners-of-war who were billeted in the town. Life in Jedburgh, as in other Border towns in a like position, was transformed by the influx of foreigners. They brought excitement, (not least to the female section of the populace!), new ideas, skills and interest. The prisoners were paroled and had boundaries beyond which they were not allowed to venture; townsfolk kept a watchful eye to ensure these rules were not broken. A small group was quartered under the Clock Tower, but the rest stayed in private dwellings which gave them an identity - "Nanie Thomson's Frenchman" or "Widow Ross's Frenchman". Although they were generally polite and well-mannered, the prisoners had to endure a good deal of ill-mannered jeering, taunting and even stonethrowing at the hands of local schoolboys. A local man, known as "Jock the Kecken" took delight in undoing attempts by the Frenchmen to make beautiful flower-beds and sundials.

Assisting Mr. Lorrain was Francois Espinasse, a young naval Lieutenant *(p.137)* who was obviously exasperated by the behaviour of some of his pupils.

Dear Sir, I send you Mr. William Veitch's letter in answer to mine, which I inclose in here -

Mr. Veitch,
        Sir,
                As it is necessary to maintain the young gentlemen placed under my tuition, in good order and in the respect we ought to have for each other, when assembled together at School, I desire you, Sir, as it is by no means your intention to Stand to this rule, not to attend any longer a class where the example you set might prove prejudicial to us all.

                Your - - - -

Sir,
        It is with heartfelt grief (I can assure you) that I have offended you in such a degree - I am well aware how easily children copy and imitate bad examples, and it is undoubtidly your duty to maintain your dignity as a Teacher - and it is my duty as a Scholar to obey you my Superiour in that respect - I am willing to obey - nay even bound to obey as long as I am your Scholar - I surely have done something I am not sensible of for

I did not expect this

The only way by which I can prove what I have here said is to come back, at your pleasure, and do my duty as an obedient Scholar - The reason why I offer myself is this - I cannot bear the thought of having a difference with anybody - and it would deprive me of receiving any further improvement from you - I am extremely much obliged to you for the benefit I have already got from you -

I will come to morrow - and when the class is dismissed you can tell me your resolution -

I am your most obedient and wellwishing pupil

W. Veitch

[By November M. Espinasse had been transferred to Valleyfield. *(p.137)* - Ed]

Fairlaw 17th May 1811

Dear Sir,

I received yours of the first hoping you were all in good health. I am surprised that you have not heard from William since he left you. We had a letter from him of the eight of April when he was in good health, he arrived at Woodbridge on the eight of March where he found all his friends in good health and spirits excepting Major Moncrieff who was at that time in a very poor state, and whose death you will have since seen in your newspaper, and who succeeds him I have not yet heard, but I expect to hear from William as soon as his place is supplied and any other alteration that may take place in the Regiment which certainly will not be long as they were expecting to march to some other quarters when he wrote to us, but on account of the Volunteering into the Line which was to take place in the Militia Regiments no removal was likely to be for the space of a few weeks untill the volunteering was over, but he not knowing how soon they would be removed might very probably be the cause of being so long in writing you, in order to give you the particulars of his situation etc.   My Father joins me with best respects to Mrs. Lorrain. -

I am Dear Sir
Yours with respect
Wm. Home

EXTRACTS from a PROSPECTUS
for JEDBURGH GRAMMAR SCHOOL 1811
by kind permission of the `National Library of Scotland

Messrs. Lorrain, Aitken and Rutherford teach the following branches of Education, viz. the Latin, Greek and French languages; the Elements of Euclid, Plane and Spherical Trigonometries, Conic Sections, Algebra, Geography Ancient and Modern, Navigation, Land Surveying, Mensuration of Solids, Superfices, Heights and Distances, Book-Keeping, by Single and Double Entries, Practical Arithmetic, as contained in Hutton, Bonnycastle and Wiseman; and the English Language Grammatically, according to Lindley Murray, and Walker's Critical Pronouncing Dictionary.

REGULATIONS

I. Every Gentleman, upon entering the house, is to produce a list of his wearing apparel, books etc. which list shall be fixed to the inside of his trunk containing such articles.

II. Every Gentleman has his seat at table pointed out to him, which he keeps while he remains in the house; and upon entering the Public School, at the foot of whatever class he joins, he takes his seat, which he changes weekly according to his merit.

III No Gentleman in the Public School, is allowed to show his neighbours penknife, ball or top etc. without forfeiting such articles; or to talk, or walk from seat to seat, or to call aloud to his schoolfellows, or to the masters, without losing a place in his class or being otherwise punished, according to the nature of the offence.

IV No Gentleman is to whistle in the house, or call names or seek redress at his own pleasure upon such of his schoolfellows as have given him cause of offence or to use vulgar phrases, but to attend to his language and conduct in every respect.

V. No Gentleman is permitted to go a-walking along the banks of the Jed, or a-trouting or a-bathing during summer, or a-skating etc, in the winter, without having the place of amusement pointed out to him, or being accompanied by one of the Masters.

VI. No Gentleman is allowed to pay *visits*, without a direct application in writing from his parents, tutors or friends, or to stroll about the public streets during the hours of amusement.

VII. None will be allowed to have fire-arms of any description, or any offensive weapons, or gun-powder, squibs, rockets etc. or to make a practice of going into the kitchen, or any apartment belonging to the servants of the house, or of entering his bedroom before noon, lest servants may be interrupted in making beds and cleaning apartments.

VIII. Every Gentleman is to pay the strictest obedience and attention to the Masters, whether in or out of the hours of teaching; as nothing will be required but what is for the advantage of the pupil: - Reproof is the first expedient made use of to the offender, punishment the second, and expulsion the last.

IX. No Gentleman is allowed to play at games for money, to contract debts, to have the odious habit of swearing, of using indecent expressions, or of committing a fault and screening it by anything that has semblance of a false-hood, or of behaving with ill manners at table, or to any of his companions, or to any gentleman whatever.

X. Any thing broken or destroyed is to be added to the account, and a separate and particular statement made of it to parents or tutors, when it does not appear that the thing has happened by accident. Inattention, or negligence of any kind, will be punished by with-holding the allowance made by friends for pocket-money, which is recommended not to exceed threepence per week.

XI. Every Gentleman in going to or getting out of bed, is to retire without the least noise or disorder; is not to go from room to room, or from bed to bed, or in the night to frighten, or otherwise disturb his neighbours while they are sleeping, or behave in any other way contrary to good order.

XII. All transgressions whatever, which are contrary to good order, though not mentioned in the above Regulations, are to be censured according to the nature of the offence.

TERMS OF BOARD

Are £34 per annum, exclusive of medical attendance washing and education, and payment in advance by the half-year. Medical attendance, washing and education are charged as follows, viz. Medical Attendance at £1. 1. 0 per annum; washing amounts to 40s. per annum and Education is charged at the *rate* of fees fixed upon by the Minister and Heritors of the Parish.

No charge will be made for less time than one quarter of a year.

There are two Vacations in the year. The one of fourteen days at Whitsunday; and the other of four weeks in September. For such Gentlemen as remain with Mr. Lorrain during these vacations, an extra charge of £1. 8. 6 will be made for that of Whitsunday and of £2. 16. 6 for that of September.

Gattonside House 10th June 1811

Dear Sir,

    I was favoured with your letter of the 23d of last month enclosing your Accounts amounting to £55.0.11½ for Henry Wiles during last year - for which I hope very shortly to send you a draft upon Edinburgh

    I fully agree with you that by Autumn next Henry should either go to an University or be put to the profession for which he is intended: and I request you will accordingly consider it as fixed that he is to leave Jedburgh at the end of the quarter new commenced

    I exceeding regret, that the situation of West India affairs is such as to prevent his Father from returning to Great Britain this year as was confidently expected: amongst other circumstances this disappointment has laid a responsibility upon me which I would willingly have avoided - A Seafaring Life however seems fully determined upon for the Boy, which I am glad to see he seems much inclined to. I have had a letter from Capt. Flinders of the Royal Navy respecting Henry, and I thought that Gentleman would likewise have wrote to you but which I understand he has not.

    I have to request that during the time our young friend remains with you, he may be principally occupied in Writing Arithmitic and Geometry, particularly the latter which is so essential to Naval men in every Service.

    I remain Dr. Sir,
        Your Obedient Servt
        J. W. Brown

Newtown June 19th 1811

Dear Sir,

    I take the opportunity of acknowledging your Letter of the 17th April by John Robson - I was very happy to find by it that you had brought Mr. Thomas into proper subordination, & that the cause of Complaints which you mentioned in your former Note had in a great measure subsided - As you very justly observed a due submission and respect to authority is absolutely necessary - Mr. Thomas' disposition is such as requires a good deal of breaking in - John is all mildness and requires to be encouraged - He seems to have regained his health perfectly since he left School - Be pleased to present my respects to Mrs. Lorrain   Send in your account to Oxnam Nook at the expiration of six Months

    I am Dear Sir
        Yours truly
        Wm. Jobson

Addressed to Oxnam Nook:

Dear Mother   Jedburgh School
        As my quarter is now at an end, I hope you will let me ride out in all this summer, for I ashure you it is a great confinement for to stay here all this summer, I am now going on with book keeping and two more of which one is a border, who is going from Mr. Lorain to go out and in. and as it will not do for me If I do not do it tow. For I will not can keep with them. my quarter is now down, and I hope you will not refuse. I am Dear Mother
                        Your Affectionate son   Thomas Robson   1811

Dear Sir,
        I received yours & have to thank you for the care you have taken to form the mind of my son. I perfectly approve of your plan, and would gladly hope that it will enable him to enter the mercantile line with some chance of success. You know as well as I do, what are necessary for a boy in his situation. A good hand & an accurate accountant are the foundation: & whatever mor he can acquire so much the better. I believe that French & German are of excellent use - but the latter he can get when he goes to Leith. I was in company with a London merchant lately who recommended Mathematics, altho' I could not see for what reason. Perhaps the Gentleman himself had a turn that way. I should rather have thought that Geography would have been of more advantage. - My intention is to continue him with you till next harvest at least, so that I hope he will be able to profit a good deal. I am sure it will not be your fault if he does not. - Poor fellow, he goes off tomorrow to Branxholm braes to go down in the Chaise with Mr. & Mrs. Grieve & Robert to your house. I am happy that your boarders are increasing & if I can do anything to promote it, it shall be done with the greatest pleasure.
        May I take the liberty to say, that by adopting a single very simple regulation, you will have it very much in your own power. I mean the making the boys repeat the Shorter Catechism every Sabbath evening: & the whole school every Saturday. I understand from James that the lower classes learn their Questions regularly. But it is the complaint of parents that Boys who are further advanced become rusted. I cannot say so myself, for James is not much deficient: but we had Miss Pott of Penchrise with us some time ago who told us that her mother regretted it in her sons: & several others I understand have mentioned the same thing. Have some respect then My dear Sir for their prejudices, & for

your own interest: & adopt of your own accord what may be of infinite advantage to young minds in future life. To an immortal being it appears absurd to polish the Casket & neglect the jewel. You may say that it is not done in many Grammar Schools that you could mention. It is the more pity: but a well principled mind will be guided by a sense of accountability & not of fashion. The favourite doctrine of the Devils & indeed of all who differ from our Standards is to decry the good old practice of teaching the Catechism: because they well know that if it is not acquired when young, it will never be learned when old. I say nothing of our Acts of Assembly which require it of parochial teachers - You are actuated I hope by higher motives: & would be happy to meet with mercy in the next world who have been trained to piety by your means. - Let me request you my dear Sir to excuse my freedom. I never could be by halves a friend, & a regard for your interest was what induced me. It was but lately that I recommended you to two families who had children & who objected to my request on the ground that they feared the religious education of their children would be neglected. They had indeed made enquiries before - for your character is rising - & they thought it a pity that so essential a department was overlooked. I told them you prayed every evening in School - & read the Bible in your School. I wish I had then known that you insisted as I find you do, on your boarders saying their prayers, every morning & evening, & getting a portion of a psalm every sabbath. Do my Dr. Sir adopt this single regulation & you will find it both for your interest & happiness: for what can be more pleasant than to teach them a sensible & manly system of religious truth. - The whole of this is under the rose.

Remember me kindly to Mrs. Lorrain & believe me to be Dr. Sir
Yours truly
Wm. Brown

Eskdalemuir
26 Sept. 1811

Leith 18th Oct 1811

Dear Sir,

I enclose you the account for Sugar paid 27th ult which you will please pay Mr. Robt Rutherford as I have placed it to his debit.

My Mother & Mrs. Reid are now with us, who Mrs. Scott join in giving you & Mrs. Lorrain Joy in the *addition to your small family. We are glad to hear both Mother & Child doing well. -

When I can do any thing for you here I shall be very happy to receive your instructions. I am

        With Good Wishes ever

           Dear Sir,

               Yours Truly

                  John Scott

John Scott Esq.,   *Leith 27 Sept 1811*
for Mr. Wm. Loraine

Bot of Alexr & Jno. Douglas

12 Single Loaves	*1. 0. 0*	*@ 107/-*	*£ 5.*	*7.*	*0*
Raw Sugar	*2. 1. 14*	*@ 70/-*	*£ 8.*	*6.*	*3*
		Cask		*2.*	*6*
			£13.	*15.*	*9*

Settled & Stamp
Alexr & Jno Douglas

*The "addition to the family" refers to the birth of Dorothea, the Lorrains' only daughter, who was christened on 17th November 1811

M. Doubzere, the French teacher who had replaced M. Espinasse, formally invited Mr. Lorrain to attend the funeral of one of his compatriots:

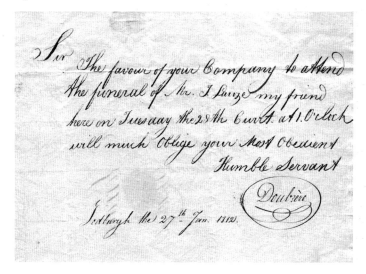

Doubzere was faring no better than his predecessor with the conduct of his pupils:

Sir,   *(In English)*
I am under the necessity of writing you of the behaviour of my scholars which is very troublesome, and in particular of Mr. J. & Gabriel Murray* who never learns their lessons nor yet brings their versions, making an excuse that they forgot them, Jas. Brown's version is never right, and Mr. Thomas Stavert he is very noisy.

Please inform the scholars to behave better, and your boarders, to bring the Key regularly at four o'clock, as it was half past four before it came tonight.

I am Sir,
Your humble Servt.
Doubzere

Jedburgh 14th Feby. 1812

[*The Murray boys came from the farm of Corsbie near Gordon, which their father rented from the Marquis of Tweeddale. The family were influential in the area and Mr. Murray wrote the first Statistical Account for Legerwood in 1791. Thomas Stavert lived at Hoscote, parish of Roberton. - Ed]

Sir,   *(In English)*
I have no doubt that after my last letter you reprimanded those of your Scholars to whom I teach the french language, therefore I am very sorry that my Duty obliges me to inform you that your reprimands have made but little impression on Mr. John Murray who for three days past, has neither wrote his versions, nor learned his lessons, and always continues to make a noise in the School, and quarrel with his School fellows. I wish to pass over in Silence the misconduct of a few, in condition that they behave themselves better for the future; for if the noise continues, after the 9th Currt. which is the first day of a new quarter, I will return you the Key of the School, for I should be very much grieved that the parents should reproach me with the little progress their children make under my tuition.

I am your humble and obedient
Servant   Doubzere

Jedburgh the 2d March 1812

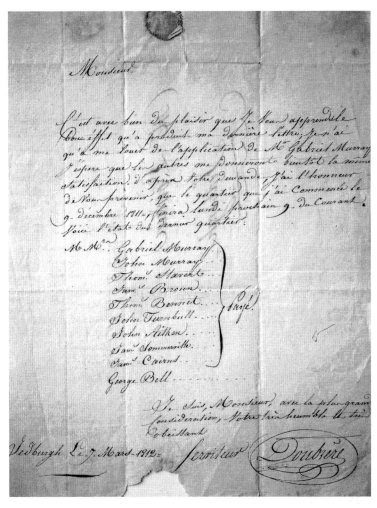

Sir,   *(In French)*

    It is with great pleasure that I inform you of the good effect that my last letter has had; I can only praise the application of Mr. Gabriel Murray. I hope that the others will soon give me the same satisfaction. At your request, I beg to inform you that the quarter which I began on 9th December 1811 will finish next Monday the 9th of this month. Here is the state of the last quarter:

Messrs. Gabriel Murray...
  John Murray...
  Thomas Stavert...
  James Brown...
  Thomas Bennet...
  John Turnbull...
  John Aitken...
  James Sommerville..
  James Cairns...
  George Bell...

} Paid

I remain, Sir, with the greatest esteem,
Your very humble and very obedient

Jedburgh 7th March 1812   Servant
         Doubzere

        Eskdalemuir 19 Jany 1812

My Dear Sir,
  After the whole family are gone to bed I do not think I violate the sanctity of the evening by writing you to thank you for your long & very satisfactory letter. I can by no means however comply with one part of it - that viz which refers to concealment: for I count it but justice done you to shew it prudently to those it may concern. A man's character is his fortune - & a teacher's especially comes under this description. Go on, my dear Sir, to merit a well earned fame; & do not be surprised if this world should hate you. You need not say Odi profanum vulgus et arceo: but you may put up a better prayer, that God would bring them to a better mind. After all, misrepresentation is commonly the effect of ignorance & deserves our pity. - I do not indeed know a finer field of usefulness than you are favoured with. You have a great influence over a great variety of character - & at a time of life too when the mind can be easily moulded as wax by the seal. To you it is entrusted to communicate instruction of various kinds: & I make no doubt that whilst you impress on minds of the more advanced the admirable beauties of the Classics you will direct all to a serious acquaintance with revealed truth. I was horrified - but not astonished - at the conduct of the parents to which you refer - for it is but too common among those who aim at thinkg above the

Vulgar. They feel not the influence of divine things on their own minds: & therefore they deny them to their children. It is happy however when these children fall into such good hands as yours, who will interest yourself in them as a second parent. - I am gratified with the accounts you give me of James. His situation here was exceedingly unfavourable to habits of study. He had no rival in the Class; an abundantly indolent master; & I was often from home: altho when at home I endeavoured to do my duty - for I have always been fond of instructing the young - am an enthusiast about Greek & Latin - & happily possess an active mind which impells me to the acquisition of useful knowledge.

Tell James that amidst the hurry of my Examinations & other avocations I neglected to write him last week - & think it scarce needful now that the month is half elapsed: but that he may get the box he speaks of, & any other thing that is commonly got by the other boarders. Only it must always be with your permission.

Mentioning my Examinations, would you believe that in this retired place, a large barn will often be well filled with those who are to be examined, or who come as hearers? None are exempted but those who exempt themselves: & all is done with the utmost cordiality. The heads of families always set the example from the firm persuasion that their conduct will be put in the most favourable light: & the others are entirely at their ease. I always examine from a Skeleton of the Question - & recapitulate the whole in the form of an address when we have done. I flatter myself you would be pleased if you sat in a corner & saw the cordiality that subsists among us. - Poor Sir John Johnston you would see is gone the way of all the earth. His Corpse is lying in great state at Westerhall & is to be consigned to the dust on Tuesday 21st. Ly J. in consideration of his former regard for me has numbered me among the few, besides the Tenantry, whom she wishes to attend. I am happy to hear that his last moments were as they ought to be. He was sensible that it was death for some time - begged his servants to keep from swearing & passion, - his own predominant vices, - lamented his former conduct - & died with folded hands, entreating mercy from the Saviour.

But 12 oclock strikes - nature requires refreshment. - How delightful the time when sleep shall be for ever discarded, & our active faculties shall be unceasingly employed in the Service of God!

   Yours truly,

    Wm. Brown

Tuesday Evening - 11 oclock. I am just returned from Westerhall where I have been dining after the interment of my late friend. We had a vast number of spectators & I count it an honour done me to be one of those who handed him down to the narrow house.

A note at the foot of the next letter advises that it is sent by a blind man who was taught to write and spell by William Lorrain.

Selkirk 10 July 1812

My Dear Friend,

Since I saw you here silence black as egyptian darkness has reigned betwixt us without one glim of hope, your eastern sun seems to be set and enveloped in clouds whose beams are hid from mortal eye, and for what reason I cannot conceive. I expected to hear from you before this particularly from Mr. Bell but nothing has yet arrived which surprises me to think that I always thought among the best of friends and yet will not write nor give me a reason why, but I will say no more on this subject till I hear from you which I hope will not be long as I expected you would have called again before you went away when you stayed so long in the town but I suppose you love the gentry so well that you forget your poor humble servant I am sure I would have entertained you ....as well as any of them had you done so; Mr. Hendersons young ladies have given up the singing but Dr. Clarksons two sons are attending the Publick School. Your friend at the post offis is not come home yet but she is no worse is the account given to me ...write me when you receive this and give me all your news. In the hope of hearing from you very very soon

   I remain Dear Sir
    With the greatest respect
     Your most obedient humbel servant
      James ....(illegible)
Remember me kindly to Mrs. Lorrain

Eskdalemuir 26th Sept. 1812

Dr. Sir,

You will receive by James £21.4/- which settles the account for last half year. - As he is intended for a mercht the person who has promised to do for him is anxious that he should be a good writer & accomptant; understand English Grammar, Bookkeeping & French: with whatever other branches will fit him for a Counting House. He also mentions Mathematics, I suppose to fix his mind: & if you can give him any part of them that will be useful to him afterwards you can do it. Make him above all things however an expert Accomptant & Bookkeeper as a sine qua non - and if you could give him a taste for history, which by the by he seems to like better than he did; it would inform his mind. Dr. Robertsons works & Hume might be put into his hands at a leisure hour. Give my kind Compts. to Mrs. Lorrain & believe me to be Dear Sir

Yours etc.

Wm. Brown

The Scotts of Raeburn, St. Boswells (Lessudden), were related to Sir Walter Scott. William, eldest son of Walter and Jean Scott, became a merchant with business in Penang. His brothers Robert and Hugh joined the naval service of the East India Co., while their unmarried sister Barbara lived at home. Robert was listed as a single man in the family tree, but in fact he had three sons, Harry, Charles and George. In 1810 they were christened at Maxpoffle, William's home, by the Rev. William Balfour and the entry of their baptism says they were born in the East Indies.

Lessudden House

28th Sepr. 12

Sir,

As the boys return to you today I send these few lines merely to say that it is my intention to take Harry to London with me some time in the latter end of Octr. You will oblige me by making him pay particular attention to Reading & Spelling for the remainder of the time that he is to be at your School

I am Sir

Your most Ob. Ser

Rot. Scott

Dear Madam,

Be so kind as send by the Bearer all Harry Scotts clothes Boots Shoes etc. as his Father takes him to London in a few days. I hope your family are all getting well again as it is a sad loss to the Boys so much idle time, my Brother wishes to know whether they are likely soon to get back as if not, he will be obliged to make other arrangements for them.
Dear Madam

Yours

B. Scott

Lessudden House 11th 1812

Harry says James Brown will know all his Books. Be so kind as send a small bit of blue cloth to mend a coat

Dear Sir   *Branxholm Braes 28th Sept. 1812*

    As it may be some time before I be in Jedburgh, I send you the Amount of Roberts acct. £51-6-5d - Inclosed are £51 and my Servant will pay you the odd 6/5d - I wish you may not find that Robert has been very idle during the Vacation - With compts. to Mrs Lorrain

                I am Sir
                   Your obed. Sert.
                   James Grieve

                   B. Braes 18th Octr. 1812

Dear Sir,

    I am much obliged to you for your attention in sending Robert to Mr. Renwicks - but I think it safest to bring him home for a short time - I hope the precautions taken to prevent Infection will prove effective and I sincerely wish your own Family may escape it - I will expect to hear from you in a short time -

                I am Dear Sir
                Yours sincerely
                James Grieve

William Lorrain notified Rev. Brown at Eskdalemuir, but missed him. Mr. Moffat who replied was the brother of Mrs. Brown, née Margaret Moffat.

Dear Sir,

    Mr. Brown went off this morning on a visit to his Friends at Peebles, before your letter came here, Mrs. Brown seeing the Postmark, took the liberty to open it and sent it up to Mr. Laidlaw immediately; as he intends sending for his son tomorrow, and his servant can also bleed a horse for James, I have advised my Sister also to send for James home, till such time as you can receive him with safety again.

    Mrs, Brown begs to be kindly remembered to you and Mrs. Lorain, and hopes the infection will nor reach any of your Family

    I am
        Dr. Sir
            Yours Truly
Manse
20th Oct. 1812   *John Moffat*

6 April

My dear Sir

  I am at present in arrear both to you & my son: but I prefer writing to you on several accounts. In the first place I have to thank you for your sensible & well composed Essay which I think will do you credit, & may be the means of stirring up your brethren to a unity of plan as to teaching. I also write this to warn you as the Irishman said that James's four shirts are on the road addressed to you, but cannot say as to the Conveyance till tomorrow that I get to Langm - and thirdly, like a good Parson, I send this to inform you of my intended plan as to my son. I intend therefore to take him home for a few months before sending him to Edinr. that I may Urge him lightly as Burns did Young Davoc, on what he has been doing, inspire him with a love for home, before he is set afloat on the Sea of life, & rivet these religious & moral principles which you have been at pains to implant. For these objects I intend devoting several hours every day: & fixing his stated hours to five or six. - When he goes to Edinr besides any branches of Education which may be thought necessary I have it in view to ask my friend Mr. Scott of the Excise to take him into his office to accustom him to keep accounts & sum up columns with expedition. This will both keep him off the street, and further his future views.

 I am happy that trade is beginning to brighten: & shall be glad indeed if the Russians can effect their purpose of emancipating the Continent.

 As for the plan you propose with James till Whitsunday, my long silence is a proof that I approved of it. Tell him that we are all well & send him our best wishes.

 I request to be kindly remembered to Mrs. L. & with respect to Yourself am most gratefully yours

  Wm. Brown

 You will oblige me by sending about the beginning of May the Amount of Expenses - at least nearly: that I may know what to send. There are certain kindnesses & cares however which can never be paid for with money, & for which I must stand forever your debtor.

D/Sir I am at Hawick for stipend & in place of taking the money home I have drawn a Bill in your name on the Bank which I have left with Mrs. William Curll Walters Wynd Hawick & also the shirts which she says she can get to you tomorrow. You may bid any call for the Bill when you please & place it to my Credit. I have to be home tonight to get the sowing & planting over

Write me to say that the shirts have come safe.

(With two parcels carriage paid)

VUE DE L'ABBAYE DE JEDBURGH

Dedié à Mesdames *Vendu à Jmeh-Penny*

View of the Abbey of Jedburgh - 1812 - M. Jean-Marie Bazin

from the corner of Abbey Place where Bazin, of St. Malo, lodged

Dedicated to James Veitch of Inchbonny

Reproduced by kind permission of Mr William Veitch of Inchbonny

Extreme left by building
"Nanny Tamson's Frenchman"

Flock of sheep

Carriage from Stewartfield
(later Hartrigge)

Miss Jenny Somerville daughter
of Dr. Thomas Somerville

French prisoner
and soldier

"Jumping Joseph"
(Rev. Thomson of
Morebattle)

Johnnie Wark
(with letters)

French prisoners
reading papers

"Will the maltman"
(man with barrel)

Bazin & M. Jehenne
(French prisoner)

Mr Shortreed
(Sheriff Substitute)

James Veitch (maker of
ploughs and telescopes)

Funeral procession
behind Bell-man

Kelso   14th May 1813

Dear Sir

    *I herewith enclose you a bill on the Bank of Scotland for £54.4.0
which will be payment in full of Gabriel & John's board and education etc.
to the 22nd April last, and for which I will thank you to send me a receipt*
      I am Dr Sir
            Your most obdt. Servt
            John Murray
            Corsbie

...and from Branxholm Braes, where Robert Grieve later succeeded his
father as farmer:

B. Braes 20 May 1813

Dear Sir

    *I enclose you £37.4 in payment of the Account due you for
Robert & John - have the goodness to acknowledge the Receipt of it -*
      I am Sir
            Your obdt Serv
            James Grieve

Dear Sir,

    *If I am so fortunate as to find you disengaged, I shall be happy if
you will eat an egg here tonight about ¹/₂ past 8.   If this is out of your
power, I would take it very kind if you could take the trouble to look up
should you be passing; if not I shall make bold to look into the school
sometime tomorrow or saturday.*
        Yours faithfully,
          William Bell
            Jedb. Thursday
              *Christie's Inn
[*Black Bull Inn, Canongate - Ed]

Berwick 29th Sept. 1813

My Dear James

    *I got home a little before four and found your Grandfather
much better than when we left him, but he is still confined to the House,
with a large shoe on - What I write you about tonight, mainly is this -
after my arrival I began to examine my money, and immediately found*

*that three pound notes were amissing - They were of Mowbray & Co's
bank here (the Berwick & Kelso Bank it used to be) and I remember
perfectly having them in my hand at Jedburgh when I paid the bill. There
was four at that time and I took one off for the bill and think I must have
left the three upon the Inn table or upon the floor - however I beg you will
enquire at the Inn if such a thing was found thereabouts for, as far as I
recollect, I think they were left upon the table - Should they know nothing
about them I must just submit patiently and take more care in future - it
is curious enough after the lecture I gave you this morning about
carelessness - and telling you you would lose your head if it was loose -*

> *Write about it and Believe me always*
> *Yours affectionately*
> *Wm Bell*

Shew Mr. Lorrain this letter I can only get half a sheet of paper.

> *Bairnkine friday (undated)*

Dear Sir,
> *Will you be so good as mark the lessons Robert is to get and I
will make him learn them at Home for a few days. as the weather has
become so bad he is not able to go your length; already he has caught a
Severe cold. And I would wish him better or he set out again.*
> *with best wishes*
> *I remain, Dear Sir,*
> *Yours most faithfully,*
> *John Pringle*

Winter covered the river Jed with ice and, as ever, boys were tempted
to venture on to its surface, with disastrous results. William Lorrain
notified the parents of his pupils that their sons were safe.

> *1st Decr 1813*

Dear Sir
> *While we feel for the Parents of the Children who were drowned
on the breaking of the ice on the Jed - we are grateful to you for the timely
intimation of it, so as to preclude the chance of the accident reaching us
in such a way as to give alarm for our little Fellows - As you are so near
the water the precautions you take for the safety of your Boarders are
judicious, and will be effectual.*

Mrs. McMurdo enjoys Edwards letter, I had not prepared her for it, and she did not think him capable of writing so well - it is the commencement of a Correspondence she hopes may be happy and last long -

I congratulate him & Robert on keeping so well up in their Classes - which is to be attributed to your kind attention to them.

Many thanks for the Sermon you sent which I will pay for when I have the pleasure of seeing you - some years ago I met with Mr. Shaw at Col. Lockhart's, Borthwick Brae, where he was much respected. If the sale of Mr. Hardie's Sermons are still sold for the benefit of his widow, I shall wish to purchase them - are they to be had at Jedburgh?

I send Gil Blas &c with regard and good wishes to Mrs. Lorrain and your young Family

> *I remain Dr. Sir,*
> > *Your faithful*
> > > *humble Servant*
> > > > *Chas. McMurdo*

Mrs. Lorrain's father, Thomas Scott of Bonchester, *(p.108)* had a younger brother, Rev. William Scott of Southdean. William had a son, Adam, who married Margaret Elliot, daughter of a Jedburgh doctor, and she inherited Arkleton on the death of her brother Robert. Adam and Margaret adopted the name Elliot in addition to Scott. There seems to have been some confusion in the recording of birth dates and Adam appealed to Lorrain:

> *39 York Place*
> *21 Decr 1813*

Dear Sir

> *Accept of my thanks for the trouble you have taken in procuring and sending me the Certificate of my birth. from examing an old family bible of my Mother's I think there can be no doubt but there is an error in that Certificate, for there I find my Brother Tom's birth recorded on the same day of the month and year in which the Presbytery Clerk inserts mine, and that I was born on the 13th June 1776 which of course makes me two years younger - Mrs. Elliot has been tuging me about the boll of flour which you was good enough to order for us.*

I remain Dear Sir
> *Yours truly*
> > *A. Scott Elliot*

Noted by Mr. Lorrain:
[Thomas born 29th May 1773
Adam born 9th June 1775
Wm born 27th Sept. 1779]

Dear Sir,
May I now request you will be kind enough to hand me the Presbytery Clerks Certificate of my age Viz the 29 June 1775 as quoted in your obliging favour of the 2d Inst which without a doubt must be perfectly correct - Expecting soon to have the pleasure of seeing you in Jedburgh & without making any apology at present for all the trouble I have given you I remain Dear Sir
Yours very truly,
A. Scott Elliot
Edin   15 Feby 1814

8 Oclock
Ancrum Tuesday Morning
Dear Sir,
You will please deliver the inclosed certificate to Mr. Wm. Gibson or Mr. Wm. Telfer which will oblige.
Sir,
Your Most Obdt
John Scott

P.S. I am sorry I cannot have the pleasure of an hours conversation with you. My wife is so poorly that I cannot be from home.
J.S.

Enclosed Certificate:
That the Bearer William Telfer late of the parish of Jedburgh, and Agnes Gibson, late servant at Chesters in the parish of Ancrum, were three times proclaimed in order to marriage within the Parish Church here, and no objections offered. Given at Ancrum this 20th Decr 1813

John Scott, Sess. Clk.

Dear Sir,

Will you be so obliging as inform Mrs. Waugh that her Aqua would have been sent long before now, had it no been that our Distiller has most cruelly disappointed us, we however expect a large quantity to be delivered us either today or tomorrow, when she may rely on her order being executed by next weeks carrier -

> *We are Dear Sir,*
> *Your very obliged ser*
> *Anderson & Oliphant*
> *Edinr   31 Decr 1813*

Another pupil from the Kelso area attending Jedburgh Grammar School was Alexander Robertson of Ednam. The Robertsons were an old Quaker family and Samuel had inherited the mill at Ednam from his father, Peter. When Samuel died in 1807, his eldest son Peter became responsible for the rest of the family and this included the education of brother Alexander.

Ednam 3d January 1814

Dear Sir,

I am very much obliged by your attention in letting me know how Alexander had behaved himself both in & out of School - I was happy to hear such a favourable Acct, sincerely hope he will continue to deserve your good opinion - I agree with you with respect to his writing, he must have a time before he gets quit of his bad scrawl - With respects to Mrs. Lorrain

> *I am,   Dear Sir,*
> *Your Obd. Servt.*

> *Peter Robertson*

The Lorrain family was extended at this time by the birth of Francis Currie Lorrain, born in January 1814.

Berwick 7th May 1814

Dear Sir,

As Mr. Clunie is engaged today he has deputed me to answer your favor by Mr Thompson - It gives us very great pleasure to hear of our Dear Boy's Health & improvement - I have no fault to find with him but his breach of promise in not writing often - he could easily have written me a few lines - instead of a Copy - I hope he will adopt this method and let me hear from him - we understand there is a Carrier leaves Jedburgh every friday morning to Kelso - In that case if you will have the goodness to send David with his trunk under his care - Mr. Clunie will be at Kelso on friday the 20th and convey him safe home - he will inquire for his father at the Cross Keys. All this family join in affectionate love to David & best respects to Mrs. Lorrain with

dear Sir yours truly

W. Clunie

Berwick 12 Augt 1814

Dear Sir,

I write this expecting to have it forwarded from Kelso Mkt to you - it will not, I am sorry to say it, be in my power to attend your Examination on the 25th since I have to be at Duns Fair the next day, but I shall be up at your Fair on 23rd - & with your permission, will take David home with me, that night.

Your accounts of him are very agreeable & I hope he will continue to merit your approbation. Mrs. Clunie joins me in respects to Mrs. Lorrain & you - our love to David.

Yrs very truly

John Clunie

undated

Mrs. Young, Mr. Selby and Miss Selby's present their compts to Mr. Lorrain & Mr. Scott & would be extremely happy of their company tomorrow to dinner at 3 Oclock.

Hunthill

Thursday morning

Boon May 27th 1814

Dear Madam,

I take the opportunity of sending the key of my Trunk and will take it very kind if you will collect my clothes together as I am not to return. My Brother will come in my place. My Father & Mother unite with me in best respects to Mr. Lorrain and you.

I am

Dear Madam,

Yours ever

A. Brodie

The French prisoners-of-war were repatriated in June 1814 and the school lost their native French speaker, M. Doubzere. At least one parent decided that the loss of this expertise made a difference.

Dear Sir,

I suppose the French Teacher will have left Jedburgh when Edward returns to you - I have therefore to desire that he may cease, for the present, to study the French language - which will give more time for his attendance to the Latin etc.

I leave this tomorrow for some weeks - which occasions my writing now. I am Dr Sir,

> *Yours sincerely,*
> > *Chas. McMurdo*

Melrose 3d June 1814

Mrs. McMurdo begs leave to thank Mr. Lorrain for the very kind treatment he has shown her Boys since they have been under his care -

Mrs. M. requests of Mr. Lorrain to purchase a good Hat for each of them at Jedburgh. There is none fine to be got in Melrose. Pray let your Doctor see Roberts shoulder now, it is getting much better.

Melrose 13 June

Dear Sir,

I have resolved that David shall now give up the Latin at School that he may have no excuse for neglecting the Figures. I think, however, that he may still join the Class in the Greek which should not take up much of his time, as he may prepare his lesson at home. I hope he will not be allowed to sit idle. He has no time to lose.

> *I am*
> > *Dear Sir,*
> > > *yours sincerely,*
> > > > *David Brown*

Crailing 27th June 1814

Gattonside House   4 August 1814

Sir,

In consequence of your letter of the 1st inst. I send over James Wiles to you by the Fly of this day.

You will consider him as a Boarder who is to remain with you during the ensuing Vacation and make your arrangements accordingly - I shall probably wish to have him over to this place to spend a few days in the course of Vacation, but do not mean any deduction from your charge on the Account.

I wish you to pay great attention to James' Writing Arithmetic and English.   He is intended for a Counting house and I do not think his Father intends that he should learn Latin - English Grammar, however will be of immediate advantage. Book keeping will be useful to him and if his time is not fully occupied by these studies I shall consider of the mode of filling it up

When you have seen what the Boy can do, I will thank you for a Report of his talents and Acquirements - of the manner in which you divide his time and Studies, and any Plan which may occur to you as best suited to the Views of his Father in the Education of his Son

In the Trunk of Clothes etc. which accompanies James there is a Catalogue of them - He seemed in want of Shirts and half a doz. are making at this place for him, which will be forwarded to you

He seems to me a well disposed promising Boy, and I hope will do Credit to your Seminary. His brother Henry was well when we heard from him about two months ago. The great diminution which is expected to take place in the R. Navy however, and the death of his good friend Captn Flinders are against him at this time

I am Sir,

>Your Obedient Servant,
>>Jas. Brown

Corsbie October 10th 1814

Dear Sir,

Having occasion to send to Jedburgh, I take the opportunity of enquiring after you and your family and hope to hear by the Bearer that you are all in good health - I also take the opportunity of saying that whenever you think proper to send my Sons's Account the money will be remitted first opportunity - With Compts to Mrs. Lorraine

I am Dear Sir

>Yours very sincerely,
>>John Murray

Harry Scott, son of Robert Scott of Lessudden, is now established in the family business in Malaya, but his younger brother is still with the Lorrains. Harry writes an interesting account of his new life...

Penang, 25th Nov. 1814

My Dear Sir,

I daresay you think I have forgot you alltogether for not writing you sooner, but it is not likely I shall have such another opportunity for a long time, I now take the liberty of writing you a few lines Mr. Thomas Hutton who is returning home in the freighter Ship called the Lady Neugent from Penang - We had a very pleasant passage all the way out and were upwards of 6 months in getting here - I have now to relate to you the unhappy Circumstances which has happened since my arrival at this place - On the 27th Sept. Last a Dreadfull fire having taken place in the native part of the town and the wind blowing very heard at the time it soon communicated the fire from house to house untill it got down to the Beach. - The loss to individuals is great indeed but I have not assertained the exact amount, but reports say about 5 Lackes of Dollar, that is £60,000 Sterling - The Doris frigate arrived here about the latter end of the month of Oct. from China and brings us intelligence of a very unpleasant nature from China an acct. of a China war having taken place within the last two or three months they have not only prohibited all communication with the Indiamen but even with all the country ships and it is feared there will be much difficulty in obviating it. - It is I understand to be in consequence of the interference of our English Ships of War having blockaded the American Privateers. Jacobjones the Ranger and several other american ships in the port of China but no letters have been recd and we are not exactly informed of the circumstances.

The Arabella Bengal ship had been taken by the Ranger but retaken by the Doris and subsequently lost on the Coast of China. - I shall enclose in my Brothers letter a few lines from the Penang Newspaper of two other Dreadful fires which took place in Novr which he will let you see.-

I beg to be kindly remembered to Mrs. Lorrain the Children and all good folkes about Jedburgh. -

I remain

> *Dear sir,*
>> *Yours ever truly*
>>> *H. Scott*

P.S. I shall expect a long letter from you & George by the first opportunity, if you will be so good as to inclose your letter in my Brothers it will be forwarded to me. - I am quite well at present.

H.S.

Dunse April 25 1815

Sir,

    Mr. Rutherford desired me to send Alexds School Books along with him, They were accordingly sent in the gig, but were unluckily forgot to be taken out of it & have been returned to me, I have therefore sent them by the Kelso Carrier & hope they will reach Jedburgh this Week, There is also two Shirts a Vest and pair of Stockings in the Box and a pair of Shoes, these were put up in case Mr. Rutherford could not have taken Alexd Geddes's Trunk with him. I did not mention these articles in my letter to Mrs. Lorrain as I thought it impossible they could be forgot -

    I also beged the favor of Mr. Rutherford to mention to you Sir that I wished you to give Alexr what Pocket Money you allow to your other Boys but I wish it to be a very moderate allowance as I think in most Situations of Life Economy is a lesson all Boys ought to learn. -

    Alexr Geddes was also very desirous to have a Bed to himself if convenient for you, Sir to Permit this I will be much obliged to you to allow it, but of this you are the best judge. I sincerely hope Alexr will not prove a very troublsome inmate & that he will improve under your care. - I am sorry to trouble you with this letter but Mr. Rutherford told me that my request to him to mention these things to you had escaped his Memory. - Be so obliging as inform me sometime hence how Alexr goes on, you will I trust Pardon the trouble I give you, we are much interested in his doing well. - My sister unites with me in best compts to you & Mrs Lorrain

    I remain Sir

        Your Hble Servant

        H. Loraine

Be so obliging as enquire
for the Box on Friday

Berwick May 18 1815

Dear Sir,

    In reply to your favor - I think Andrew may leave Jedburgh next wednesday morning with the Carrier - Our Fair is on the friday - I mentioned to Robt Douglass some time ago - that if his Clothes were not

*in good order he might get a dress from Mr. Turnbull, this he forgot, -
will you be so good as send Andrew to get one a good servicable Grey -
made in the same way he usually has them - They can have them ready
for his coming down - any of his old ones will do for the Cart - Mr.
Turnbull may send his Bill with him - or deliver it to yourself - to transmit
- and the payment shall be returned with him - and any other Bill that
may be due - these matters I leave for you to do in your customary way
- Please to give him a few pence for the road - 6d or 1/- as you think right
-*

With respects to Mrs. Lorrain
    I am Dr Sir
        Your very obdt Servt
            John Reid

                      Berwick June 15 1815
Dear Sir,
    *Your charge leaves us today, he has been kept for Bathing a
little, and still has an inflamed eye - should the inflamation not go away
in a few days I will be obliged by your desiring Dr. Young to examine it
and to apply such cooling remedies as he may think best for its removal-
some cooling medicine I think would be necessary for him at any rate*
    *His mother was for keeping him a week longer - but as that was doing
him little good - being so much engaged with some of his former playfellows
- and not over fond of his Book - I thought it best to send him off - The
two shillings you gave him are entire - he will deliver them again   he
thinks a penny very little as some of his neighbours get more - you may
therefore advance to twopence occasionally*
    Mrs. R. joins in respects to Mrs. Lorrain & self - with Dear Sir
        Your most Ob Serv
            John Reid

Events were now taking place in Glasgow which were to change the
course of William Lorrain's career. The High School was about to
appoint a Rector for the first time since 1782. Four masters had enjoyed
equal status since that time, but it was decided to institute a fifth class
and to appoint a Rector who would take the senior class for Latin, Greek
and Geography. William Chrystal, one of the existing masters, was
promoted but advised that he would not have control over the other
masters. His former post was then advertised and William Lorrain was
urged to apply. Ebenezer Clarkson was approached for a reference:

My dear Sir,   I left Jedburgh on Thursday last to meet Mr. Chrystal in Edinburgh who has been lately elected Rector of the Grammar School of Glasgow, to consult with him and my other friends here about the propriety of offering myself a Candidate for the Situation in that School which has become vacant by Mr. Chrystals appointment -

After maturely weighing the matter, I have yielded to the advice of my friends to put in my claim for this Situation - And I have good reason to believe that, notwithstanding the number of respectable Candidates who have appeared, and very powerful interest by which some of them are supported, my chance of success is very considerable. From what I have said you have, I presume, anticipated my object in writing to you at present -

It must promote my views very effectively to procure letters of recommendation from Gentlemen of Respectability to whom I am personally known, & who have had the means of appreciating my Character as a Teacher.

Now I am most fully satisfied of the very deep interest which you take in my welfare, - and that it will give you sincere pleasure to exert yourself in my behalf on the present occasion. - I therefore apply to you with the greatest confidence - which the sincerity of your well-tried friendship authorizes me to cherish. - And I trust that your power to serve me will be equal to your wishes. -

Both your professional Character & situation as Chief Majistrate of Selkirk will give weight to any statements which you may think proper to make in your Letter. And I think it will be of consequence to me if you can procure the signatures of any of the respectable heritors of Selkirk, or separate letters from themselves. - But I have still a heavier demand to make upon your friendship, which I hope you will be able to grant me without doing any violence to your own feelings. For I believe you know me too well to think for a moment that I would press you to exert yourself for me in any way inconsistent with your own feelings of delicacy & propriety - The favour then which I have to ask is that you would try to procure for me the interest of the Duke of Buccleuch - which would be of mighty service to me. - This favour you may able to procure either in your individual capacity or as Chief Majistrate of the burgh of Selkirk for my services among you. In either capacities I fondly hope that your request will be granted. And I believe the Duke, in consideration of the great length of time that my Father in Law was in the service of the late Duke at Bowhill will be inclined to do a kind office to his Daughter & to me as her Husband. - I know that His Grace always requires the most respectable references for Character & abilities - before he will act. Now in additon to the weight of your own recommendation, you can refer him to Dr. Douglas Dr. Charters & Dr. Somerville - of whose good opinion I have had the happiness to have received many proofs. - I again repeat, that I have the greatest confidence in your friendship & I have equal confidence that you will manage the whole matter in a way far better than I can dictate to you - Perhaps to one of your discernment & warmth of friendship I have said more than enough - but this you will ascribe to that anxiety which we naturally feel to gain the object of our wishes. - I trust that you will forward any letters in my favour as soon as possible to Jedburgh - as they must be sent off to Glasgow with all possible despatch. I shall have the pleasure of seeing you in a few days when I shall explain matters more fully to you. -

Selkirk 10th July 1815

The Magistrates of Selkirk hereby Certify that Mr. William Lorrain Presently Rector of the Grammar School of Jedburgh, was for several years Rector of the Schools here, during which period he gave the most universal satisfaction as a Teacher, and it was with the deepest regret he left Selkirk - they can therefore with great confidence recommend him as a fit person to succeed to the present Vacancy at Glasgow.

> Eben Clarkson
> Wm. Lamb
> Geo. Young
> Geo. Robertson

Selkirk 10th July 1815

The Magistrates of Selkirk hereby certify that Mr
William Lorrain Presently Rector of the Grammar
School of Sedburgh, was for several years Rector of
the Schools here, during which period he gave the
most universal satisfaction as a teacher, and it was
with the deepest regret he left Selkirk — they can
therefore with great confidence recommend him as
a fit person to succeed to the present vacancy at Glasgow.

Robt Sanderson
Wm Lamb
Geo. Young
Geo: Robertson

83

and from John Riddell of Riddell, who became collector of taxes in Jedburgh.....

Riddell July 6 1815

My Dear Sir,

> *I beg leave to recommend to your kind protection Mr Loraine, who is at present a candidate for the Rectorship of the Grammar School at Glasgow - He has for many years taught with success at Jedburgh, & at Selkirk & I have no doubt is worthy of your favor -*
> *Believe me*
> > *My Dear Sir*
> > > *With great truth*
> > > > *Your Faithful*
> > > > > *John Buchanan Riddell*

Robert Findlay, Esq.

Already the wheels were in motion to find a successor for Lorrain at Jedburgh, and Mr. Robertson, who is recommended by Mr. Chrystal, did become Rector of Jedburgh Grammar School until he moved to Musselburgh in 1820.

21 Augt 1815

My Dear Colleague,

> *I beg to introduce to your acquaintance & friendly services my friend Mr. Robertson from St. Ninian's whom I have mentioned to you in my letters once & again -*
> *As he has a vacation at present I have advised him while at Edinr to visit your good town & learn how the land lies - There is none to whom I can introduce him with so much confidence of friendship as yourself - You cannot forget the anxious state of suspense in which you must have been lately in which he also was not unconcerned. The result however was very different to you & him, tho' his claims & pretensions to my certain knowledge were very well founded - Let me request you to do any thing for him that is fair & consistent with other claims - You are not to be blamed for Mr. R's coming to look after your vacancy & tho' he make some advances before others come forward and have things set in a favouable train for ultimate success the dilatory will have themselves / and me if you please / to blame. Let his visit be known or kept secret as you know to be best - I know he will do credit to those who may recommend*

him, & you may act for him on this presumption in the meantime. He will shew such letters as he has & more may be procured if needful -

The Patrons of the School may want a Teacher long & give themselves & others much trouble by delay yet after all their trouble, if they let him go, they will very probably get none who are his equal - I leave the matter wholly to your good sense & on the faith of our future intimacy request you to do what you can -

  I am My Dear Sir,
   Yours most truly,
    William Chrystal

Per favour
Mr. Robertson
St. Ninians

       Jedburgh 31st Augt 1815

Gentlemen

  I hereby beg leave to intimate to you that from & after the Term of Martinmas first I resign my situation as Schoolmaster of the Burgh and Parish of Jedburgh. With every wish for the best Interests and happiness of the Rising Generation; & with grateful Remembrance for the liberal conduct of the heritors of Jedburgh.

   I am
    Gentlemen
     Your obt huble servt
     Wm Lorrain

Chapter 4

THE HIGH SCHOOL OF GLASGOW

*Great care has been taken in accurately transcibing all letters -
errors in spelling and punctuation are as per original*

The High School in Glasgow was first mentioned in the 15th century as a Grammar School connected to the Cathedral. By the time William Lorrain joined the staff of the school, it was situated in George Street, to which it had moved in 1787. The school building was used by others in the community and the fees for letting, e.g. of the main hall for public worship, were a useful addition to the school revenue.

The building was far from ideal and the low classroom which William Lorrain first occupied at the west end was inconvenient and noisy because of the number of classes entering by the same stair. He was soon moved to an upper apartment at the other end of the building.

Lorrain initially kept in contact with Jedburgh, returning for the meeting of the Society of Schoolmasters in June 1816. He corresponded with his friend James Veitch at Inchbonny; Sir Walter Scott was also friendly with Veitch, whom he described as "a very remarkable man, a self-taught philosopher, astronomer, mathematician ... certainly one of the most extraordinary persons I ever knew". Scott had a clock made by Veitch, who also made telescopes of a high calibre. On 27th August 1811, Veitch was first to spot a comet which remained visible in the area for 510 days.

Lorrain writes:

Glasgow 27th July 1818

Dear Sir,

Your much esteemed and instructive letter I duly received and frequently perused - showed it to Mr. Buchanan who showed it to the Messrs. Harts; with whom I have not yet formed an acquaintance, which is entirely my own fault, as Mr. Buchanan has repeatedly offered to introduce me. The circumstance that you mention respecting the protuberances on the edge of the full Moon, has been frequently noticed by the Harts, by the instrument of the Observatory here - Mr. Buchanan is a married man about forty years of age, and a respectable Teacher of English in this City. He is I think a native of Peebles, was bred a cotton

*weaver, then served under Nelson in Egypt returned to Glasgow, and
became a Knight of the Taws in which he succeeds remarkably well and
at his leisure hours amuses himself in grinding and making telescopes
which he seems really to understand. The distress of his wife prevented
him from paying you a visit this season, but he hopes to see you next.
You no doubt will be thinking that I am neglectful, this was not the case.
I only put off for the purpose of writing you by Mr. B. and then when this
failed I thought that when in Dumfries-shire I might probably spare as
much time as to enable me to return home by Jedburgh; and in this also
I was disappointed - I very lately was introduced to a Mr. Crichton a
Mathematical Instrument maker, who appears a remarkably acute man,
perhaps you have heard of him. He is acquainted with Dr. Brewster and
though old and feeble still works with his son who, seems to possess a
considerable portion of his father's spirit. The season has been and still
is excellent; though this be the case, yet our Markets have been on the
advance of late. Trade here this season is good, yet both the merchant
and weavers are complaining of low prices and bad times, but all this you
observe is neither in the times nor prices, but in the extravagant views of
individuals concerned.*

*My family at present thank God enjoys good health, and every individual
of it pursuing the daily task. My children are all at school except the
youngest, which is not quite five years old - How is my old shop now
filled? Say in your next, in which favour me with all the news of the place.
My wife and I are often speaking of you and yours; she request to join
me to your wife, you and Children.*

> *I ever am
> Dear Sir,
> Yours truly,
> Wm. Lorrain*

*P.S. Do not neglect to write me by every opportunity, whether you hear
from me or not; which practice I shall endeavour to observe towards you.*
> *W.L.*

> *Glasgow, 17th Nov. 1818*
My Dear Sir,
> *Your favour met with a most hearty welcome, as I have much
pleasure at all times to meet an ald friend with his ald face - You are now
almost the only correspondent that I have in Jedburgh and its neighbourhood.*

Except on business I have heard from none of my old acquaintances for nearly these two years past; neither George Scott nor James Anderson my old Assistants have ever condescended even to answer my letters to them. Shall I say that ingratitude is a sin that more easily besets many men than what is generally admitted? I will yet suspend my judgement for a little - I was lately introduced to Mr. Crichton who appears a shrewd, sensible, intelligent man. He informed me of the Falkirk Gentleman that had made the reported discovery of the Perpetual Motion, that he had seen him and his Machine which he had examined; but formed no great expectations from it; indeed, he seemed to think that it must just be ranked among as its pretensions reach little farther than former attempts. I shall request Mr. Buchanan to make the experiment as you require it, and inform you of the result in my next. - I am sorry to hear that my old shop is not as throng as formerly. - Many a days labour and nights thought was it to me to establish general Principles in my School; for, at an early period in my Profession, I perceived that the great defect in Parochial Schools proceeded from a want of arrangement and method; and I apprehended if this was first rectified the other department vir the branches of education would be easily executed if the Teacher only possessed moderate attainments; at the same time I perceived that while I was attempting to establish the former I must not altogether overlook the latter. - The one vir arrangement & method I had completely attained and had made considerable progress with the other at the time that I left you. I can with confidence say that if I had lived a few years longer in Jedburgh, I would have produced a Practical System of Parochial Education superior in method and efficiency to any that has ever yet been brought under consideration, and I regret exceedingly that the Plan has not been properly understood, and followed out by any of my Brethren in your quarter. The Plan will secure patronage and success wherever it is even imperfectly executed, for it is the result of upwards of twenty years experiment and observation. If I could only separate a few weeks from my Profession, I would give an analysis and a complete detail of all its parts; that I might yet have the hope of seeing it carried into effect and improved by persevering, ardent and diligent investigation...(torn)... and enterprising of my profession ...in my own lifetime - In my next I will inform you what I am doing, but at present for want of time I must conclude in which my wife joins in Kind Remembrance to you, your wife and Little ones

    I ever Am

      My Dear Sir,

        Yours sincerely,

          Wm. Lorrain

In 1821, it was decided that the school building needed to be replaced, partly due to the increase in Glasgow's population. The new school was opened in John Street. Three years later, recommended by Professors Robert Hamilton, John Glennie and William Knight, Lorrain was awarded LLD from Marischal College, Aberdeen. In 1830, he was made a burgess of Glasgow as merchant and teacher.

1830 was the year that William Chrystal died. On 7th June, while waiting at Helensburgh for the steamer to Gourock, he accepted a lift with two men in a small boat. There was a sudden squall and the boat overturned - all three were drowned. Mr. Chrystal's body was found floating in the river and was taken on board the same steamer he had been waiting for. He was not replaced at the school until 48 years later.

The High School building was still inadequate and one of the teachers, Alex. Dorsey, complained of unsuitable seating in his room while Lorrain's benches had to be remodelled. James Bryce's floor gave way, and William McKindlay reported that his benches were in a frail and ruinous condition. Over £800 was spent on repairs. The school operated as separate departments in one building, and several years later Mr. "D'Orsey" was advertising for 2 young gentlemen as Resident Pupils in his house, which was "commodious and beautifully situated within view of the Clyde, 2 miles clear of the West end of Glasgow where the pupils can enjoy open country, fresh air and regular exercise, with the use of a vehicle when requisite". By then there were 7 masters altogether in the school.

In September 1832, the Lorrains' son James Montesquieu Beattie died at Rothesay, aged 23. Dorothea Scott Lorrain, William and Dolly's only daughter, seems to have been of a religious disposition and wrote to "Francis Claude Lorrain" who presumably was her brother, born Francis Currie Lorrain:

"The believer has a perfect sanctification as well as a perfect justification in his Lord and Saviour. In his approaches to a throne of grace, he looks beyond both guilt & graces in himself pleading the Salvation of Jesus only. Spirit crucified is not the only source of peace, acceptance and humble boldness, but also of inward fruits and heart holiness. Sin cannot be mortified but by looking to him, who hung upon the Cross his atonement, and beholding the glory of God in the face, person, and

undertaking of Jesus is the only thing that transforms and changes the soul with the same image.

Christ is the tree of life both root & branch. The temple, the altar and the sacrifice. The giver and the gift. The all in all of a believer's dependance. Christ thus approached is the cause of holiness in the bud, blossom, and fruit. A perfect Christ is a cordial in times of fainting, a giver of hope in time of trouble & temptation. A healer of spiritual sickness, a setter of bones when broken by wilful sin or aggravated backsliding: a fountain, watering his own graces in the heart, an altar sanctifying every gift that is offered upon it.

In a word, the Spring of all happiness & peace, purity and holiness here and for evermore. Our sanctification in Christ is complete. Holiness in his child evidences the legitimacy of its birth, admits of different degrees, is of a growing nature here below and will be capable of increase, perhaps in the regions of Glory, where I trust we shall soon meet and be happy for ever.

26th March 1834
Dorothea Scott Lorrain.
To Francis Claude Lorrain, Esq.

By now, William Lorrain's health was failing but he refused to have an operation, being prepared to suffer pain for the rest of his life. When he retired from teaching, he was given an allowance of £100 and presented by his pupils with a silver jug and dressing-case.

The Lorrains had taken a house at Rothesay some time previously but still kept their Glasgow address. The son of their old friend, Rev. William Berry Shaw, was still visiting and in 1837 he sent Lorrain a note:

Glasgow Satdy 11th March ¹/₂ past 4 p.m.
My Dearest Lorrain,
I am just arrived at your house from Greenock and finished a harty dinner with Mrs. L. and family. I did not get your Note till I returnd today, having gone over to my Uncle's last night. I reachd Greenock about 9 o'clock & was much disappointd at not finding you there. I saw Mr. Ker but he seems quite fixed at his price namely 2,500 & says he will not sell it for one farthing less. I told him I considered £2,000 a fair price for it but that I wd divide the difference which wd make it 2,250 but he seems quite determined to stand his ground. I said that I would take

a few days to consider of it & would let him know the result. Let me hear what you have done at Rothesay. I have scarcely time to scrawl this as I go off in the Coach at 5 & it is hard upon it - Compls to William & Believe me

> *Dearest Lorain*
> > *Yours very sincerely*
> > > *George Shaw.*

Glasw 9 Jan 1837

Doctor Lorraine,

Dear Sir,

I feel greatly obliged at the interest you take about a servant. I have just this moment (12 o'clock) returned from Callander and it is quite impossible for me to say how I shall stand in regard to a successor for Mary as the one she had been training up for the last twelve months is still poorly and I cannot at present say what her own wishes are nor would I speak to her on the subject till she is convalescent. In that case I cannot ask the person to wait which you spoke of. Doctor Henry Robertson of Callander requested his best regards & is to be here at Peel's Dinner.

> *Yours truly*
> > *D. Hope*

[At this time, Sir Robert Peel was between two periods as Prime Minister - Ed]

Dear Sir,
> *Having Received on Saturday last by the Bearer Dun.n Marquis a charge for the Second quarter I beg you will have the goodness to let me know if there is no allowance to be made for the nine weeks he had been absent on account of Bad health which is to me equal to 9/- at least.*
Your atention to this will Much Oblige Sir
> *Your Most Obdt Sert*
> > *J.N. Marquis*

Springvale 30 Jan 1837

Saville Row

London

11 March 1837

Dear Doctor Lorrain,

The few minutes of leisure which my business at Glasgow permitted me to spend with you, have proved sufficient to revive those School recollections, which produce impressions that never are effaced. These recollections are as all your Scholars have felt, and expressed, of no ordinary character, & it is because I hope to have soon the opportunity of expressing them, that I write these few lines of apology for my hasty visit.

It is as you know part of my duty to superintend that branch of Medical Education that refers to Anatomy, & as Scotland has been added to my office, I shall, I trust, be able to shake hands with you shortly. The time is still uncertain, it will most likely be about April or May.

I had the good fortune to find some very choice Whiskey at Messrs. McMillans & Galloway in Nelson St. & should you be on any occasion near that part of the Town, it will, I doubt not please them, if you were to mention the treat it has proved to my friends. I have been quite mobbed for it, such is the estimation in which it is held by all who have tasted it.

I hope you have escaped the Influenza, & that your family are all well. Should you make up your mind to pay a visit to this huge City, you will find a hearty welcome from many of your pupils, & I need not say friends.

With kind regards to Mrs. Lorrain

> I am
>
> > my dear Sir,
> >
> > > Your most faithful
> > >
> > > James Somerville

Thomas Lorrain, William and Dolly's second son, had joined the City Bank in Glasgow. His friend John Robson sends a note:

Tuesday morning

My Dear Tom,

I am just up from Rothesay - and send a small parcel from Mrs. L. with orders that Mrs. Barclay is not to go down this week. they are all in their usual, down by. I am keeping the house today (got too much rum in Greenock last night) which is the reason of not delivering this.

> Yours sincly   John Robson

Thomas Lorrain Esq.,

City Bank

Glasgow

William Buckham Lorrain, eldest son of William and Dolly, was now 37 years old, but behaving in such an irresponsible manner that his father was distraught. William senior writes to Thomas:

Rothesay 4th Nov 1841

My Dear Thomas,

Mr. McTavish called today & Wm had some conversation about horse & I understand arrangements were that McT. was to leave his horse in Glasgow & Wm was to go up or send Dan with Jessie; but how he will do cannot say as he went out after dinner 2 p.m. & we have not seen or could find him after all Dan's search. God only knows what is to be the issue of such dissipate profligate conduct.

If your cold still continues better defer coming down. I still continue, I hope, to improve.

My Dear Thomas
Your afft father
Wm Lorrain

Thomas T. Lorrain Esq.,
City Bank,
Glasgow.

This letter was edged in black, possibly indicating that Dolly had recently died , and was written less than three weeks before the death of William Lorrain on 23rd November 1841. It was reported that he had died "surrounded by an affectionate family and in the home of a son who, with the name, inherits much of the character of his father".

Complimentary obituaries appeared in the "Dumfries Weekly Journal" and the "Glasgow Herald" which stated that "Few men have descended to the grave leaving a more honoured memory than that of Dr. Lorrain. Hundreds of young men, now scattered abroad in every quarter of the world and in every profession and sphere of life, regret his death and honour his memory".

Taken from the Progress Report of classes in the High School Glasgow during the year ending October 1, 1834. *By kind permission of the High School of Glasgow.*

DR. LORRAIN'S CLASS.
THIRD YEAR.

In Latin.

This class made two complete Revisals of Ruddiman's Rudiments, and, as on preceding year, a weekly Revisal of his Rules for the Genders of Nouns, and of Dr. Bryce's Prosody.

In LATIN PROSE—This Class read and parsed, &c. the Second, Third, and Fourth Books, and twenty-seven chapters of the Fifth Book of Caesar's Gallic War, and Mair's Introduction, from the beginning to the sixty-fifth Rule; parsing and applying the Rules of Syntax, &c. This Class also had Exercises generally three times a-week, in Latin Versions and Versifications, &c.

In LATIN VERSE—It read 240 lines of Ovid, the ten Eclogues, and 527 lines of the First Æneid of Virgil; Parsing, Scanning, and applying the Rules of Syntax, &c.

In Greek.

This Class committed to memory Tate's Grammar, from the Article to the end of the Conjugation of Verbs in $\mu\iota$; and made several Revisals of the same.

In English History, Geography, &c.

This Class read and was exercised from the beginning to the end of Goldsmith's Abridgment of Roman History; also upon Adam's Roman Antiquities, from the beginning to page 116; made its regular weekly exercises on the Scriptures; and executed Maps of various Districts and Kingdoms of Europe, &c.

Holiday Exercises.

1. For the most correct Revisal of Latin Rudiments and Grammars, Greek and Latin:—The Prize was, after a keen competition, obtained by *Thomas Gray.*

2. For a Revisal of the Studies of the Class in Prose and Verse:—The Prize was carried by *Thomas Robinson.*

3. For the most correct Map of Ancient Italy:—The Prize was adjudged by *William Findlay.*

The monthly Exercises which were prescribed on subjects suggested by the circumstances and studies of the Class, and the names of those Pupils who excelled in them:—1. An account of Pyramus and Thisbe. 2. Do. of the Contention for the Armour of Achilles. 3. A description of the Hebrides. 4. An account of the first Eclogue of Virgil. 5. A drawing, a description, and a model, of Caesar's Bridge over the Rhine. 6. A description of the Explosion of the Steam Carriage between Paisley and Glasgow. 7. A description and drawing of the Storm which Æneas encountered on his voyage to Italy. 8. An Elegy on the death of a distinguished Schoolfellow. 9. A Map of Perthshire. 10. Do. of Argyleshire. 11. Do. of the Hebrides. 12. Do. of Ireland. 13. Do. of Spain and Portugal.—*William Findlay, David F. Montgomerie, Thomas Robinson, Lawrence Gibson, John Reid, Archibald Graham, Thomas Turner, Robert Edmiston, Andrew Gibson, Robert Drew, Robert M'Gregor, Thomas Gray, Thomas Corbett, James Stirling Muir, William Gibson, Robert D. Alston, James Grey, John Monteath, James Roberton, Robert Pullison, James Stewart, William Balfour, George Fulton, Francis Frew, John Edington, Charles Hill, William Lochhead, Alexander Buchanan, William Greenshields, John Martin, James Reid, and John Roberton.*

LORRAIN OF OAKWOODHILL

Walter Lorrain = Mary Currie

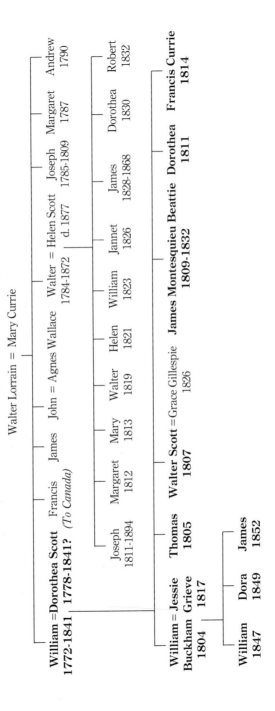

William =Dorothea Scott   Francis   James   John = Agnes Wallace   Walter = Helen Scott   Joseph   Margaret   Andrew
1772-1841   **1778-1841?**   *(To Canada)*   1784-1872   d. 1877   1785-1809   1787   1790

Joseph   Margaret   Mary   Walter   Helen   William   Jannet   James   Dorothea   Robert
1811-1894   1812   1813   1819   1821   1823   1826   1828-1868   1830   1832

Thomas   **Walter Scott** = Grace Gillespie   **James Montesquieu Beattie**   **Dorothea**   **Francis Currie**
1805   **1807**   1826   **1809-1832**   **1811**   **1814**

William = Jessie
Buckham   Grieve
1804   **1817**

William   **Dora**   **James**
1847   **1849**   **1852**

Chapter 5

LETTERS FROM HOME

*Great care has been taken in accurately transcibing all letters ·
errors in spelling and punctuation are as per original*

William Lorrain was a native of Dumfriesshire. His father, Walter
Lorrain, was a farmer at Oakwoodhill in the parish of Half Morton near
Canonbie and William retained an interest in farming throughout his life.
His mother, Mary Currie, does not seem to have enjoyed good health.

William appears to have been the eldest of the family; the birth dates of
brothers Francis, James and John are not recorded but they were followed
by Walter (1784), Joseph (1785) Andrew (1790) and sister Margaret (1787).

William married Dorothea (Dolly) Scott in 1803 and their first child,
William, was born in January 1804. This letter from Walter Lorrain
was written a few months later:

Oakwoodhill   May 3d 1804

*Dear Son, having this opportunity of andrew pattison being in this place
this Day I thought it very proper to send you a few lines to Inform you that
your Brother James is continuing still wors in a dazing condition to Everyone
that sees him   he lost his sensiess one Sobeth night So that we can get very
few sensable werds owt of him one Tuesday Night he wrestled the wholl
night Rasing up into his mother arms which owld have made the hardest
heart to lament his seatuation I come from him last night and we have tow
Docters atending him Docter Johnston in Ecelfecon and Docter heladay in
Lockerby we men to leve of Docter helady in Lockerby and to continue
Docter Johnston   Easter day Night whin I left him he was blistred in the
Brest and the tow arms and lickways his head shiven and a blister laid
theron I sent his three Brothers of this morning to see him as I Expect the
time to be very short that he shall be in thiss worold yowr poor mother is
very Destreed in her ledgss boath of them being so sor sweled and getting
so little Rest in the night I can give yow no acount how he is this Day
whether in time or not lord only knoth as there is non of your Brothers
Comed home yeet   give our kind complyments to your wife and hoping
thess lines will find you all well so no more at present from parants*

Walter Lorrain

*This day I went to longtoun
Expecting a letter from you but
got none*

William Lorrain's brother Walter appears to have admired and respected him, following him into the teaching profession. Walter left home for college in Edinburgh at the age of 20, staying with William and Dolly before walking to the capital.

Edinburgh Augt 29th 1804

Dear Brother and Sister

I got here about 6 oclock at night on the same day I left Selkirk and was very tired my feet is not yet altogether recovered -

I received your letter safe which you sent by the carrier last week in which you are wishing to know how matters stand with me. I think that there is none but what you already know and therefore I shall be happy to have your counsel in anything you find me deficient I shall endeavour to adhere to it to the utmost of my power -

I took brekfast along with Mr. Smith on Tuesday last and was mentioning to him about going to Scott for reading but he rather disuaded me from it, and told me that he charges at the rate of two Guineas per quarter when one enters by the month and besides he goes always away about this time and that he would think nothing of taking my fees from me and then going away as he has served others before, so I think I shall desist from him altogether and attend Wilson two hours in the day after this quarter is done -

My landlady was afraid that they would be informed of, an my comming back in so short a time, which gave me an opportunity to say that they should not be any fear of that for I would go and take another room imediately which I have done last night and am going to leave them this day on the afternoon, my room costs me one shilling per week more than this has done but it is far more comfortable -

You must let me have two pounds more by the carrier next week and I shall stay here as long as it holds out and then I shall return unto you if you think proper -

> *I remain,*
> *Dear Brother and Sister*
> *Yours sincerely*
> *Wr Lorrain*

P.S. Armstrong letter that he sent last week was to my landlady
> *W.L.*

It was at this time that William was preparing to move to Jedburgh, but it seems that he was intending to visit his parents beforehand. There is mention of brother Francis, or Frank.

Edinburgh Sept. 12th 1804

Dear Brother,

       I delayed writing you last week on account I thought that you would be gone to the South before that you could receive it - I am thinking of leaving this place on Wednesday 19th Currt. as it is the end of my third week in the room and to engage any longer it would but be throwing away time unless that I engaged with some different sciences such as Drawing or Fortification or perhaps both as I believe a knowledge of the former should be required before one engages with the latter. -

    I had the pleasure of supping with Mungo Smith on Sunday night he was on his way to Falkirk and left this place early on Monday morning he told me that you and Frank took brekfast along with him on Friday morning and was on your way to Dumfries.

    Mr. Bell your old pupil introduced himself to me I think it was on Wednesday or Thursday and I dinned with him the day following he left this place on Setterday last for his Fathers. Mr. Smith and I are expecting you in Town on the latter end of this week or the beginning of next - he joins me in love and affection to you and yours

I remain
Dear Brother
Your afect.
Wr. Lorrain

Francis emigrated to Canada in 1805. The next letter from father Walter gives news of Joseph, now 23 years old and seriously ill. Young Walter has finished his studies and is looking for a post at Half Morton school.

Oakwood Hill December 30d 1808

Dear Son, Your Brother John is going to Longholm this Day with a fat guse to com to you which I Expect you will Receive in a few Days your Brother walter has got Sir Johns voat very cherfully he sent it to Mr Martain So that Mr Martain we expect has the full pour in his own hand to Establesh him in half mortan in spit of all his foos but the old master is still keping on teaching tow or three Small Boys the laten in his own hous he has a few that is Counselling him to keep one teaching which will Disapoint your Brother of any Selery but hou it will End I canot tell you as yet but as soon as ther is annything more Don in it I will let you know

Your Brother Joseph is no Better He canot be put about with nothing that is fatigsum the rest of the family ar all well at present Blessed be god for it and houping that these lines will find you all in the saim

Dear Son our Markets is about asland at present we have plenty of good oatmell for three shilling per ston Barley for Sixten Shilling per Bushel and Befe and Mutten about sixpence per pound there is the aperance of grete plenty in this plece our gren pork has Ben all this time since martinmiss Six Shilling and Sixpence per Stone

you will write as soon as this comes to hand and let us know when you Receive your fat goos and how your family is all the family joins me with kind Complments to Mrs Lorrain So no more at present from your loving parants

Walter Lorrain

Joseph died on 2nd February 1809 and Walter expected a visit from his eldest son but eventually realised that he was unlikely to see him in the near future and sends a very moving account of his brother's last hours:

Dear Son,

We have wated this three weeks Expecting to see you acording in your last tow letters we Recd from yow but now we see the time is now past that we Expected to see you and god only knows whether Ever we shall have another opportunity or not as we are now boath very frail by Reson of age being all most up to the promised years that we are to live in this world wee feel to our Experience that we are fast Declening to the gave that bed of Rest for we most all Die and after Death we most all apear befor the Jugment seet of Christ ther to answer acording to Every Deed don in the body whether good or evell which ought to be a serious Consideration with Every on of us young and old to be zearnest in prayer to almighty at a thron of grace that he may prepair Each of us for his hevenly kingdom and glory

we are now left very single now as to our own famely your Brother walter went out from us into his own hous yesterday him living the hous and Joseph Being Gon which althow in a poor State of health yet he was a great Comfort to his parents for he was our lock and kee in our abecence hes Death is the weighty Dispancation that we have met within this world him being allways about his mothers hand the miss is very great yesterday hir Cheacks almost never Drayed throw the long Summer Day

    Dear son you write in your last letter that you wer not setisfied becaus I did not write to yow about Joseph last ilness But I thought it nedless as I Expected to see yow in a very Short time fess to fess and then converce with you about thess and many other things but I am now Disapointed Joseph was only about three weeks of his ordinar healt and in that time he still was able to walk out and in Beside his mother which toke great Delite In weting upon him all the three years and a half that he was in truble befor his Death the very last day of his Ilness in this worald he walked about looking for Docter wear, which came in the afternon to see him and about the Evening he grew worse we had verey litle siting up with him but sume few nights before his death which your mother sat one part of the night and I another that night he died your mother sat up till three of the Clock and she caled upon me so I get up and abut five of the Clock a caled the famely all up and when your Brother Walter com and spok to him asking him how he was he thought he was better the stiches was all left him and he bid him Reed to him a pairt of the sermon he Red to him one the sabath night and so he begin to Reed and his mother was siting beside him at the bedside and he beholding his Brother Redind looked about to his mother and caled to his mother to give him a Drink and she turnd about to the table to lift the drink and in a moment his head droped down and she was anabled to lay his head on hir arm and deperted this life with a Brething or tow no strugle was for Death but I trust fell asleep in Christ

    Dear son your uncle James has got a letter from your Brother francis and they are all very well when he write to him your Brother walter write to him at his Brothers Death but he speks nothing of Receiving it in his letter we have at present a very great rains this three weeks which is hurting our crops very sor our markets was very hy oatmell was 4s pr ston but is now down 3s-4d corn aboll 10s pr Bushel and Barley 18s pr B. and bef and mutten from 6d to 8d pr pound and Backon is very hy 10s pr Ston for flacks and 12s for hams and Butter 1s pr pound your mother has now one half firken of Butter Redy to send to yow I will take the first opportunity in geting it to yow If you had the one half regaird for hir she has for yow yow ould have payd hir a viset at this time if in a state of health your Brother John and his famely is all well we have all caus to Bless god that we are anabled to wak out and in and serve our god and non to make us afried

I houp you will send us a few lines when this comes to hand to let us know how you are all in helth at present I have louked for a letter from your hand this last week to let us know what had Disapointed yow but non com to hand as yet the famely joins me with kind complyments to Mrs. Lorrain so no mor at present from your loving parants

Walter Lorrain

The next letter from Walter concerns the farm which is rented by John Lorrain from Sir John Shaw Heron Maxwell, 4th Baronet of Springkell Estate, who was M.P. for the Dumfries burghs 1807-1812. William has been involved in calculating a fair rent but his advice has not been adhered to:

Oakwood Hill Novr. 3day 1809
Dear Son,

I wish to inform you that Mr Estain and I had a Silee Converssation about the Catgillhead ferm he ould wished that Sir John ould have given your Brother John abetement of the ferm of Catgillhead for sum few years that he could be able to Improve the said farm buy Building housiess and liming and Diching making fencess on the said farm but he was afried to spek of it to him lest he should Refuse to alow it to be don the last tim he was at home he was speking to Mr. Estain abot the ferm Conserning a letter that you sent to Mr. Estain about the ferm that yould send a man from Jedburgh to work the ferm and Joine him with it Mr. Esten let Sir John See the letter so that Sir John is depending much on your word for asistance with your Brother John thiss letter you sent to mr. Eastin before the ferm was taken N.B. So I told Mr. Estain that we sent a letter to you of the miserment of the ferm and you sent a letter to your Brother John Saying that he should not give above a hundred and twenty or therty pounds ster for the said ferm of Catgillhead or it ould not pay as far as you could see at present but we took the ferm far above what you thought it to be worth so that you wer offended at us for taking it so high and told me that it ould Ruing us Boath as far as yow Could see at present not withstanding you ould lend him a few pounds to help him to set forward althow you see no (chance) of geting it again this you had don Expecting never to geet it again
  I wished yow know what past betwext Estain and me about the ferm that you might know how to answer him when he writts to you about the ferm for he told me that he was going to write to yow about the ferm Mr. Estain ould do annything lays in his pour for your Brother but unless Sir John be

willing there can be nothing don in the way of abeatment of the Rent Mr. Estain said if Sir John Could be persuaded to let him have it for a hundred and therty pounds for sume few years but he was afried that ould not be don Sir John has now apointed a baran Court at Sprinkell and has summond all the Back gon tenents to apear and either to pay up all begon Rents or give ther Bill for the sam and sends the Bills indto the Bank and in three months time the most be payed but he never asket no such thing at your Brother John he wen into the Court and he asked him when he thought he could get him apairt and he told him that he ould have him sume as soon as posable now if so be that a letter comes to hand you will know how to answer him as I have warned as far as I can and I houp you will send him a Discreat letter for Sir John will be very Disirious to see it not Ingaging your self in anny payments Concerning the said ferm

In your writing to him that you had sume thoughts of Joining him with the ferm but it was taken at such Rak Rent that you did not wish have any consern with it you have taken a peace of ground which will serve yow at present yow may write faverable Concerning your Brother in that you houp he will answer them Better in a few years when he had got in a full stock I houp these lines will find you all well at present as we are Blessed be god for it   the famely Join me with kind Complyments to Mrs Lorrain so no mor at present form

Your Loving Parants   Walter Lorrain

William Lorrain's friend, Rev. William Berry Shaw, was presented by the Duke of Buccleuch to the parish of Langholm and part of his duties covered the little church at Half Morton *(below)*, where he was to preach every 4th Sunday.

Oakwoodhill   July the 29 1812

Dear Son,

We are very glad to hear from you that you and your famely is all well and that under kind providience I houp there is now provided for this parish of longholm a nouble precher of the Gospale of Christ by the Caricter you give him to me   In this place ther is many to say to the Contrery holding him to be a very haroniouss precher but I tak no head to what is said among us as we are such a divided Sect of peaple and thinks ourselves very wise to know all things and Insted of this I louk upon us to be a peaple very Ignerant and knows very little about the gospall at all for the most part in this place is dead to pracktill Deulyes which gives a trew Evedence that they know litle of the gospell and has no trew love to Christ Tit was said in our place that he was to preach in longholm last Saboth but it was a fals Report for he was not ther he has ben long an Itimate aquientence of yours I hop in a short time I shall have an opportunity to hear him preach the gospall friely from the heart Standing dint of no man as he is Ny to you you may perhaps see him and if so be that you see him befor me you will give my kind Complyments to him and tell him that I ould be very glad to see him when he comes first into this place if I can hear when it shall hapen -

Dear Son, we have great Skercity of Breds in this place very hard to be got for money oatmell is Six Shillings pr Stone and Barley mell five Shillings per stone and very hardly to be got   it dos apear to be good Crops in our place but bakward

Dear son, your parents is now well growing in years and Decelining fast to the grave Espechaly your mother She is very few days without som truble last night she murned the one half of the night with pains in hir legs and thays and yet Blessed be god for it She is this Day waking about and making Redy our Vituals your Brother Johns wife has got hir Bed and has a Daughter abou ten days ago and them and the Rest of our famelys is all well at present Blessed be god for it we are living in the Expation of seeing you when you give up the Scholl in harvest if convenience serve but you will write to us befor that time and let us know whither or not

Houping thess lines will find you all in the saim state of health as you wer when I Recd your last letter   So no more at present

from your Loving parants

Walter Lorrain

This is the last existing letter from Walter Lorrain. By this time Walter junior was married to Helen Scott and had a son, Joseph, and daughter Margaret.

Oakwood Hill, 21st Oct. 1812

Dear Brother,

I have longer delayed writing you than I intended; but as you said in your last, that you would be here in the course of a fortnight, I put off in expectation of seeing you about this time. Our Mother has been very poorly all this harvest, and is indeed getting every day worse; she has various disorders to cope with, and I realy think that if she does not get better in a short time, her life will be dispaired of. I saw Mr. Patterson in Cannobie on Friday last, and he wishes to know when the second Edition of your Collection will be published, as he is going to introduce it as soon as it is ready. Mr. Easton has nearly finished the repairs of the tolbar house at Cadgil, which I am to remove to in the course of a week or ten days, & I understand Sir John intends me to lift the toll money; for which I expect to be allowed 4 or 5 pounds a year besides, the farm of Cadgil is out of lease this year, and I have some hopes of getting at a reasonable rent as much land as will keep a Cow in the summer. Write on receipt. Compts to Mrs. L. in which my wife joins me

> *I am*
> *Dear Brother*
> *Yours Sincerely*
> *Walter Lorrain*

P.S. You need give yourself no uneasiness about our Mother as nothing shall be wanting that is in my power, and if any alteration takes place to the worse, I will write you immediately.

> *W. L.*

Mrs. Lorrain senior was still alive in June 1813, for Rev. William Shaw mentions that she is still complaining, just as his own mother is! Shaw appears to be attempting to intercede on Walter's behalf *(p.196)* to obtain the schoolhouse for him, but the letter of December is addressed again from Cadgil.

Dear Brother,

I have long ago received your favour of October last, and the parcel of books for Shaw and Bell I have also received and sent them them accordingly - I had James Bell one day all day shortly after he had been with you in Edinburgh and he was informing me all about your procedure there - I should like very much to attend this meeting, which if circumstances permit, I am resolved to do next Autumn -

I have not yet procured a lease of my park, but as soon as Sir John comes home I expect to obtain one: yet I am under some doubts, as I have this year refused to collect my Salary from among the tenants and have sent my account to Mr Easton a few days ago, demanding payment of last years Salary and all arrears, at Candlemas next - You were speaking of an old fowling piece which you had by you, and for which you had use, would you send her to me you would greatly oblige, as I must either have one this year, or give up my Crop altogether to my neighbours hens - Mr Easton would perhaps tell you when you were here, that he is fully determined to leave Sir John at Whitsunday next - with Compts to Mrs. Lorrain and family, in which my wife joins me.

> *I am,*
> *Dear Brother,*
> *Yours Truly,*
> *Walter Lorrain.*

P.S. I have almost forgot to mention that I have got another daughter [Mary - Ed.] added to my family about six weeks ago - Wife and child and all other friends here are quite well.
> *W.L.*

Walter was ill and unable to teach for some time during 1814 according to Rev. Shaw. However, he made a good recovery and in his next letter he is optimistic about getting a new house built for him.

Dear Brother,

Your favour of a late date Father has received, and sorry are we indeed to hear of the distress in your family, however, I sincerely hope that it will not turn out infectious - Did our Father say anything in his last respecting his views of building? he is purposing building a house this Summer which is to be put up in my name and under my superintendence - And I am going to endeavour to raise about £20 and add to the sum which he thinks a sufficeiency, and make it a little superior to any in its neighbourhood - We are not yet sure on which side of the road it will stand, as I have some hopes of falling in with Sir John which if I do it will stand on the North side somewhere upon the farm of Cadgil, and if I do not I daresay I will fall in with James Dickson, and in this case it will stand upon the South side somewhere between this and Chapelknow - James Dicksons lease is I believe about 80 years to come; but if I fall in with Sir John I will have it 99 years.

It is a terrible bad season here it rains a great part of every day, and has done for about these five weeks past; all business in the field is at a stand and Uncle James, Dick o' the Mains etc are standing gaping for the Markets rising every day - I understand Mr. Easton leaves us this Whitsunday, and it is reported here that he has taken a house in Langholm, and is the Surveyor of the High-roads in this County. Let us hear from you again in a short time, as our mother is anxious to know how the boy is, and if the fever seems to be infectious.

I am,

Dear Brother,

Yours truly,

Walter Lorrain

No further letters from Walter are extant, but he lived until 1872, having been a schoolmaster for 64 years. His wife survived another five years. Of their 10 children, Joseph became a minister at Caerlaverock and died in 1894; James died aged 40 in 1868 at Wellington, North America; Walter (b. 1819) became a missionary.

SCOTT OF NETHER BONCHESTER

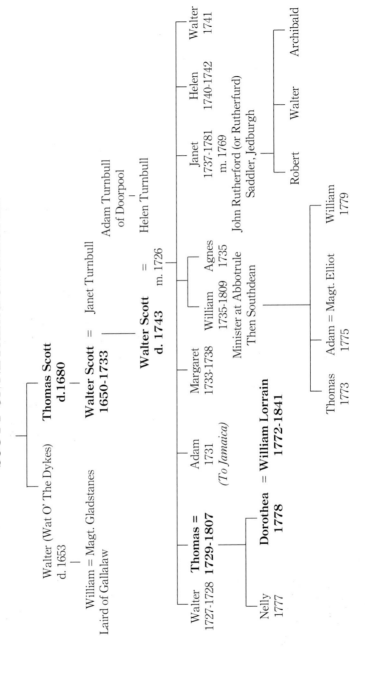

Chapter 6

THOMAS SCOTT

Great care has been taken in accurately transcibing all letters -
errors in spelling and punctuation are as per original

Thomas Scott, father of Dorothea Lorrain, was descended from a branch of the Scott family of Nether Bonchester. Walter Scott - "Wat o' the Dykes" - bought the estate in 1632, with Kerr of Abbotrule as superior. Wat's son William, Laird of Gallalaw, disponed the lands in favour of his uncle Thomas, whose son Walter inherited in 1680. Walter's son and namesake married Helen Turnbull, sister of the minister at Abbotrule. Their eldest son Walter died of smallpox and Thomas, the second son, (Dorothea's father) succeeded his father in 1750, although to do so he was obliged to obtain a writ from his superior in his favour.

Thomas Scott decided to grow forest trees and set aside a couple of acres known as "the Nursery" for this purpose. Despite being very successful in his venture, he got into financial difficulties and had to place his affairs in the hands of trustees, who put the lands up for sale. In 1779 he moved to a farm on the Bowhill Estate, rented to him for a nominal sum by Henry, 3rd Duke of Buccleuch, head of the Scott clan. Thomas Scott seems to have been caretaker of the house at Bowhill, which at that time was a plain hunting-lodge with two wings.

Little is known about Scott's wife but they had two daughters born at Nether Bonchester - Nelly in 1777 and Dorothea in 1778. Thomas seems to have been a widower at the time of Dolly's marriage to William Lorrain. His younger brother William Scott became minister of Abbotrule and then Southdean.

Letters to his daughter and son-in-law began after their move to Jedburgh.

Bowhill Aprl 15 1805

Dear Dolly
I Received yours yesterday I am sory you and william has been ill, it is a common trouble in this part a sor throt, I am now so well that I went to Selkirk upon Shankins nagey yesterday and was no wors of the Jurney, mr kier is gon after Staying two week, Peggy was much greved

as she could get non Spun; they wold have had it all dun befor whitsunday if he had not com, She thought to have had it befor the term she wants to bring it over to see william mr kier found everything right, and was well pleased with Peggy I had little opportunity of Speaking with him by himself but never saw him kinder, with Stevens he was not so he never asked him to brekfast nor super he never was here at Dinner, Stevens and pattison had a sor out cast at Selkirk fair, pattison cam next morning to mr kier and entred a great Complaint mr kier was very angrey Stevens went away to longholm very sulky I think it has ben Stevens that told him about the Coals, we have got a nice lassey She has ben a year and half with *archbald Park they wold not pairted with hir but they had no use for hir this Summer Let me here if you have got all your maids yet you have the worst luck ever was, I wold keep non of them, they were not quite so dear at Selkirk as was thought, 5£ was about the Common wages, I am to get Tam Brown to work with me at whitsunday the man that I have is little wiser than Simey was, this Comes with Som coming to the Circut is their any trayls this year, I wish much to see you all but the weather is so Cold I cannot think of seting out Peggy wants to know what way you will have the yarn Boiled their is no lee Ashes to be got good they Burn all kinds of wood which makes them good for nothing, I forgot if I told you that you mrs Park had given over bet Basley and that she goes to the toun at Hawick, I have no other news worth writting Let me hear all your news I hop John Renwick is now got Stout again Peggys Comts to william. I am with Comts to mr Lorrain and william and to any that asketh for me, your affectionat father

Thomas Scott

[*Archibald Park was brother of Mungo, the explorer. - Ed]

Bowhill House in 1812, from an architect's sketch
Courtesy of the Duke of Buccleuch

Bowhill may 23 1805

Dear Dolly

I received yours with Robert Emen you spok of another which I never have seen as to Sending the yarn to yarr we cannot get it dun nor do I think it right Emen is to be at Hawick on the term thursday he will bring it saf and send it with a certain hand to Jedburgh, I am quite happy down in our little house mr George is com and a man cook at two Guenys a day they brought on maid with them and got another from Hobsburn they could do nothing without Peggy mr George says she shal have no hard work, the two lasses says they will do all the hard work. their is two Landry maids coming they slep in the Stable loft the bed in the back room at the Stair head is taken away and the childrens beds put up in that room all the housemaids sleps in the garets, I do not see they can put them all up, *Leadey Dalkeath comes on Saturday, I can say no more about them at present, you say mr Lorrain is to be at mr milns house heating he will be too late for it is this day, mrs miln sent here for some things out of the garden, I have no news to write you you shal hear from me with the yarn Peggy gives hir kind love to william She thinks he has forgotten hir now as he had no word to hir in your last .....

This with Comps to mr Lorrain ....

affectinat father

Reverse:
20 slips
9 slips and 6 cuts
4 slips and 6 cuts
11 slips of thirtey cut
16 slips of lint yarn
15 slips lint yarn

[* Lady Dalkeith was Harriet Townsend, daughter of Viscount Sydney, who had married Charles, son of the Duke of Buccleuch, in 1795. - Ed]

Bowhill may 26 1805

Dear Dolly

I Received yours of the 20 only yesterday I was vexed at them coming Just when Peggy was coming away I spok to Robirt emen who is to be at Hawick on the term thursday I packed all the yarn in a box and marked every kind as Peggy Directed me, on of the kinds I was obliged to put is loos the other was all bound he is to send it from Hawick

with a certan hand, the large Bundel is the yarn of the lint that cam
last and contains 34 Slips and the cuts about the lint that was here
befor is 22 Slips and the cuts about it Peggy says you must make woft
of it as the lint was not good the lint which Peggy Spun is 20 Slips
and the cuts about it the cours is 5 Slips and one Slip unboiled I hop
it will com saf to hand, Leady Dalkeath cam here last night hir and
the governour and the governess with three children cam into me last
night and asked how I had ben all winter and Asked for you and how
your Son was thriving She Said the garden was in good order She
Said hir Son and Daughters wold help me to weed, they have Speds
and rakes and two watering pans, I saw *Lord Scott as they call him
this morning in the garden with the governour he says he will help me
tomorow their is three bairns maids three landry maids a cook two
other maids and Peggy they could not want Peggy but mrs Pover is
very kind to hir She will let hir do no hard work She makes mr Georg
Submit to what she says, their is four Stable groms a nursrey footman
and Leady Dalkeath footman mr George and the Cook Peggy and on
of the bairns mades sleps in mrs abercromby bed two more in the
other bed the little tent bed is put up in general mckays writting room
one sleps in it and on in the Settea every bed in the house but one was
full I here nothing how long they stay we are in hops they will soon
tayer Lord Dalkeath is not com from London yet the cook maid that
cam from hobsburn has a brother Gardiner at weens and is married
to mis miller that was in falshop and oakwood mr miln house was
het on thursday they hild it out till Sunrising Lord Dalkeaths birthday
on friday mr George was at it he was hom at eleven, I get Tam
Brown to work to me he gets a house built in the west side of the
planting near the Scor head. - I thought it wold be better to send the
yarn in case they stay long and I had such a good hand to send it with
it wold have ben troubelsom for Peggy to have careyed it, She Says
She will com and see william and you if they were gon if She can find
the way to Jedburgh I here bett ritchey is Just at the doun laying I here
nothing of Nanny angus, Leady Dalkeath went over every Corner of
the house and said it was all very Clean after She had Seen it all She
said She wold come and See how I was put up, mrs Pover will not let
Peggy do any hard work She has hired a woman to do all the hard
work Such as Scoring the grats and washing the flors they all ways
asks me to denner where we keep up high life belostairs the Nursrey
woman dines with us and the Coock who is a desent middleaged man
Nanceys husband wold not let hir come if they were fairly settled we

*will do very well, let me hear from you son   how is williams foot now
I here no news worth writting, this with Comts to mr Lorrain and
william   your affectinat father*

Thomas Scott

*P.S. I was very much Disapointed when Letham ....Burnfoot Called here
that night, mr George and .... was to com, no other two can com that I
like so... to see had it ben but a night sooner*

[*Lord Scott was George Henry, eldest son of Lord and Lady Dalkeith,
who died at Eton College in 1808. Lady Dalkeith found solace in reading
the newly published "Marmion" written by Walter Scott, a friend of the
family. - Ed]

The next letter is addressed to William Lorrain and mentions a law-suit
which is being handled by Alexander Park, another brother of Mungo,
who is a solicitor in Selkirk:

Bowhill June 21 1805

Dear Sir
*   I Received yours and am glad you are all well I am very well at
present and doing very well now when we are all setled I am seldom at
the big house Peggy is very atentive to me She comes and see me get all
dayels and makes my bed the little Lassey doth all things very well
according to Peggys Direction they go all away in a month befor the Leth
races, Lord Dalkeath is not com from London yet, the Leady is going to
Selkirk kirk on Sunday, the Leadys of Fowlshiels and the two miss vetches
is drinking tea with mr george and mrs pover this afternoon.
   as to my Law Suit their is nothing dun in it I went to mr Rodger he wold
say nothing to it as he is doing for Braydin I went to Park and Showed
him the Sumons, he says Dollys oath and mine cannot be taken it may be
Selkirk law but I see no other way to prove it, we were both certain that
they were gon when they cam to Selkirk
   I intend to take the advocats advice next wednesday tell Dolly not to
make hirself uneasy about it, I hop to see you at Jedburg the end of next
month as I am very well at present and able to ride I got very little
Speaking to his grace Leady Dalkeath was always with him mr miln Saw
him but I have not seen him Since he is to be here again Soon when I will
make it my busines to see him, tell Dolly mis millers husband is bet Shawes
Cusen Peggy henderson Still works all the work She has no maden careys*

in the water as She did befor write me soon and let me know how you all
are I hear no news in this place, I am now well off Since I got tam Brown
he works all the work which keeps me easy their is a terable death amongst
the bees in this part almost all the bees about Selkirk is dead Dollys is
both dead and two of mine william lader saw them in may he said wer all
very strong this cold weather and maney young bees they have had no
meat, my Comts to Dolly and william
    I am der
     Sir yours Sincerely
     Thomas Scott

P.S. I saw mrs Buckham on wednesday she was not very well She was
wishing mary wold com hom as son as you can want hir.

Thomas Lorrain, named after his grandfather, was christened in
Jedburgh on 30th June 1805.

         Bowhill oct 19 1805
Dear Dolley
I Recd. yours of 11 only on wednesday I am glad to hear you are all
well as I am at present our family is all gon but mr George and the
landrey maids which goes away this day if I can get away I hop to see you
the end of next week but cannot set the day as we have our potatos to
take up and many things to put right mr George has had no person here
since they went away he has ben at som of their houses but has had no
drinking here he has ben very good this time I have had no trouble this
time I think of Staying all this winter as I have Tam Brown Closs so I
ned do nothing as he can do all the work, I supos Peggy will Stay as She
has taken the car of every thing from mrs pover and they hath given hir
as much as any of the other maids, mrs pover says She Could not have
dun without hir so I supos She will Stay all this winter but I never have
spok to hir about it as I seldom see hir Since I got your Letter Lord and
leady Dalkeath comes here next month in their way to longholm only for
one night and one night as they return the leady sent all hir childer to see
me befor they went away and brought me a kind of Shirt to wear in cold
weather it Sems to be knit like Stokens walter henderson is sory for their
going away he had mr Georg dining with him of thursday mr camble
was looking at the ministers garden the mrs has left nothing in it every
gren and leek is gon all the Bushes and box hedges is gon mr Robisons

friends gets nothing She gets all I here nothing Strange to tell you as I hop to see you soon mrs Buckham and hir daughter gives their Comts to you they are well I am in hast so this with my Comts to mr Lorrain and Thomas Robson william and all friends I am your affectinat father
                                    Thomas Scott

                                                      Bowhill mar 15 1806
Dear Dolly,

I Received yours of the 8 I am glad you are all well and that william's hand is got better I am still well but this cold weather makes me take great care of myself for fear of cold. I have had a slight cold but not ill I am almost better. Lord Dalkeath was to have ben here last thursday and Leady Dalkeath and hir family was to ben at Hawick last night in their way to longholm for to stay a month or six weeks for Change of air as the Children has the chingcough I got a letter to tell me they cannot set out untill better weather, we here they will not be at Bowhill this summer Peggy is very much vexed as it has stoped hir spining to get the house all Clean. She hops to get it dun in good time to get it wrought. I will boile it according to your orders She cannot tell when she will have it ready as yet She says she will not hire without she gets a good place as she is not able for hard work with the pains. Marrey tait is gon to longholm with mr George for a few weeks but hir mother is coming over to mrs Elliots on munday and will bring this with hir if she canot com she will put it in the post, I cannot say how she will answer mrs Elliot I rather am affraid of hir but you ned not say any thing of hir Peggey wishes she had such an easey place as she is not able for a common place. I supos you will here no more of Jenney Robson is she still at the Shaw I heard of the marage you spok of, if you thing two women will do your work it will save a good deal as the wages is so much the women at Pebles fair was getting 5..10sh and six pound for the half year P says she wold like very well to com to you if it was not hir wother and she is not able for the washings walter amos brought me lethams letter how is mis Balentyne Husband, Selkirk news James Rodgers property was all sold this week the House was bought for Carsar of ormistone who comes to it soon his Daughter is going to be maried to Holalie and to com to ormiston house the andisons Bought the tanage Doctor Anderson bought a smal park Bailie williams is to be sold on the 26 of this month, I winder they had not sent Thomas Scott to Jemaica he will do no good at london, I am Glad to here Robert Elliots wife is better Jenney whitson and Cud is to get a house built at

Howford She is for a Carpet and all fine furnitor mr Curie howford
kepes Company with non but whitson Cud and a mool catcher. write me
a few lines with Nelley Laidlaw if she comes over P Compts to you and
W my Compts to mr Lorrain and Thomas Robson and all friends. I am
Dear Dolley your affectinat father
Thomas Scott

Bowhill Apr 24 1806
Dear Sir,
        I waited all Saturday and Sunday in hops of seeing you here I
hoped to have seen william with you on sundays night I got your Letter
I am sory to here of poor williams illnes, I got your other letter yesterday
at Selkirk and this morning I got yours of the 23 I am happy to hear that
william is in hopes of geting better and hop when I here next the fever will
have left him, I did not see mis Joan yesterday it was late befor she cam
home but a man at work here brought me your letter this Comes with
John melros who will bring me Certain word I hop of williams being
better he will call on you freidays morning and let you know where he
puts up so that you may send me a line or two with him. I am sory to
here that mr Robison is so ill he was a good peceable man, his grace was
at haining tuesdays night in his way to london he did not Come here, we
here non of the family is to be here this Summer. Their is nothing but
bersreling about members of Parliment. I hop to here from you on
Saturday, whin I hop william will be better and I will write more news,
this with best wishes to Dolly william Thomas I am Der sir yours afety
Thomas Scott

Dear Dolly   Bowhill may 21 1806

    I Received yours som days ago I Can Send a Cart to meet you any day
you mention, I wrot you the day befor I got yours let me know by a line
what time you will be at melros so that you may not have to wait, our
family goes all away on Saturday Leady Dalkeath told Peggy that she
might go to Sea bathing for it had Cured hir   this is the best time she
Can go as hir Cusen takes hir with hir and keeps hir in her house all the
time she is their the leady is speaking of Coming back in august, we
Cannot do without a Lassey, but we have not got on yet you may bring
your lass with you and william but we will not keep hire after you go away
we here of a lass but has not seen hir yet   if she Can run about with

116

william she will do I am Sorey for mrs Renwicks Daughter and Doctor
wood, I will not say any more as you are so soon to be over P will stay
until the monday after you Come so that you may look over every thing
if I here no other word from you, a Cart shal be at melros on thursday
foornon, our great people has ben very good this time they spok of only
staying two days but they have Stayed a week, P Comts to you and william
my Comts to you mr Lorrain and the Lads   I am Dear Dolly
your afectinat father
Paid 1d by post   Thomas Scott

This is the last existing communication from Thomas Scott. He is
said to have died in 1807 and is buried in Hobkirk kirkyard.

[Lord and Lady Dalkeith became Duke and Duchess of Buccleuch
and Queensberry in 1812 and Bowhill was rebuilt between that year
and 1814. Duchess Harriet did not long enjoy it, for she died on 24th
August 1814. Her husband, the 4th Duke, died in Lisbon in 1819. - Ed]

Chapter 7

THE CENSUS

Great care has been taken in accurately transcibing all letters -
errors in spelling and punctuation are as per original

In 1811, William Lorrain was involved in drawing up a Census for the
town of Jedburgh. This followed a pattern of Statistical Accounts begun
by Sir John Sinclair in 1791, but unfortunately these were not as detailed
as the Census dating from 1841 and give limited information about the
population as individuals.

Prior to drawing up the account, Lorrain was summoned:

To the Schoolmaster
of the Parish of Jedburgh

Jedb 24 April 1811

The Sheriff hereby requires your attendance in the Court House here on
Saturday the 4th of May next at 12 oclock midday for the purpose of
receiving instructions with regard to Carrying into execution in your
parish the new population Act of Parliament.

Will Oliver jun.

[William Oliver succeeded his father, William Oliver of Dinlabyre, as
Sheriff of Roxburghshire. In 1834, he succeeded to the estate of his
uncle, John Rutherfurd of Edgerston, and became Oliver-Rutherfurd. He
died in 1879 aged 90. - Ed]

Population of Parish of Jedburgh in 1801	3,834
in 1811	4,727
Increase in population since 1801	893

Census of Town & Country parts of Jedburgh 1811

The increase of population in the Burgh of Jedburgh of nearly 600 since the taking of last Census in 1801 may be attributed to the many manufacturies in Cloths, Flannels & Hose etc. which have been increased and enlarged within the last ten years and the liberality of the Police of the Burgh.

The increase of population in the Country part of the Parish of nearly 300 is owing to the highly improving state of Agriculture, which has and daily is employing more hands in proportion to the increase of provision and the spirit of Improvement. It has been stated that the reducing a number of small farms into one has had a tendency to diminish the population. This may be the case in grazing farms which I should even feel inclined to contradict; but the reverse is the case in farms under tillage in this Parish & I am apt to believe will be found the case in all parishes similarly situated, under the last Census. Men are often led by appearances than fact. In surveying a County and seeing the onsteads reduced, the natural conclusion is that the population must be also reduced in the same proportion or nearly so. But this is a very falacious mode of procedure, as it generally is the number of families, and not of onsteads or Cottages in a parish or Country that affects its Population. In the present improving state of Agriculture each farmer upon an Improving lease has in his employ ten or fifteen Hynds more or less, & these Hynds must all be married persons, and of the strictest sobriety and industry, to entitle them to the profession of a Hynd, who generally have very numerous families the effect of their sobriety & industry. These Hynds are more comfortable and more numerous than the families of the little crouching vassals or tenants which they have supirseded. It is therefore in the present state of agriculture to this Class of men that the population of the Parish in the Country owes its increase, perhaps I might attribute the whole increase sparingly. It has often occured to me & I believe every Clergyman will agree with me, that there is not under his charge a more virtuous sober & industrious Class of men than Hynds. It is their sunburnt and heath blasted sons that keep the battle far from our gate.
"Proud of his laws, tenacious of his right,
And vain of Scotias old unconquered might." - Leyden. -

CENSUS   29th July 1811

JEDBURGH	Town	Country	Total
Inhabited Houses	323	346	669
By how many families occupied	715	358	1,073
Houses now building	5	4	9
Houses Uninhabited	2	17	19
Families chiefly empl. in Agriculture	107	292	399
Families chiefly employed in Trade	369	36	405
Families employed in none of preceding Classes	239	30	269
Males:	1,354	876	2,230
Females:	1,473	1,024	2,497
Total	2,827	1,900	4,727
Deducting French Prisoners of War	72		
Deducting Local Militia	201		273
Population by the Act			4,454

*   *   *   *   *   *   *

	Town	Country	Total
Persons employed in Trade or Handcraft	594	130	724
Persons employed in Agriculture	139	392	531
Persons employed in none of above	2,094	1,388	3,482
Children under 14 years of age	889	598	1,487
Persons between 14 and 50 years	1,508	1,013	2,521
Persons above 50 years	430	289	719

*   *   *   *   *   *   *

	Town	Country	Total
Males:	1,354	876	2,230
Deducting Prisoners & Militia			273
			1,957
Females:	1,473	1,024	2,497
		Total	4,454

Mr. George Scott of Lilliesleaf was in charge of collecting the data and appeared to be so impressed by Lorrain's submission that he recommended to Walter (later Sir Walter) Scott that he be entrusted with revising the census manuscript:

Lilliesleaf 3d March 1812

Dear Sir,

I duly received your very welcome letter, with the Population Tables & poor rates.

I cannot express my sense of your kindness in thus forwarding my designs but I assure you I am duly sensible of the favour. Your communication concerning the Jedburgh Jougs is very acceptable.

I would have written you sooner, but I was disappointed in not getting it forwarded to you last week, and was also waiting the answer to a letter I had sent Mr. Scott (Sheriff of Selkirk) on the subject. As your communications were so very friendly, & as you seemed so much disposed to give me all the assistance in your power, I took the liberty to propose you to Mr. Scott as a fit person to undertake the revision of the Manuscript before being sent to press, & Mr. S. informs me, that, as he has not time for that task himself, he thinks you a very fit person for that purpose.- You may then (unless you send orders to the contrary) expect me at Jedburgh in 4 or 5 weeks with the manuscript which I hope you will be so good as revise, & correct, or propose correction, of any mistake.

The work I have undertaken is divided into two parts. The first contains a general description of the County - viz. Name, Situation & Extent, Seasons soil & climate, Surface, Hills, Rivers, Minerals, Vegetable productions, Animals, Population, Towns & villages, Trade & Manufactures, Agriculture, Schools & education, Antiquities, Civil Establishment, Civil History (Border History) in 3 Sections, 1st Local History of the most important districts, 2d Historical Anecdotes, 3d Manners & customs of the ancient Borderers, - and lastly, a short sketch of Ecclesiastical History.

Part second contains the Statistical Account of each parish, corrected, enlarged, & abridged from Sir John Sinclair's work of that name, with the addition of the different original communication from the respective Schoolmasters.

The first part is also chiefly selected from Douglas' Survey, Chalmers Caledonia, Scott's Border Minstrelsy & Lay of the Last Minstrel, containing everything of importance, on the subject, that is to be found in the works of these authors, & arranged in a systematic plan. - I have not, however, confined myself altogether to the above authors, or rather I should have said, I have intermixed the above selections with remarks of my own, & have taken every necessary liberty with their words & sentiments, inserting, occasionally, several paragraphs, & even whole sections of my own - so that this work is partly Original & partly Selected.

Among the former may be reckoned the article on Schools & Education. I have not gone very fully into the subject, but shall be glad of a few hints from you which I shall add to, intermix with, or adopt instead of my own.

It has cost me a great deal of labour, but have now got so far through that I have only the blanks to fill up with the communications of the Schoolmrs. &c. & several alterations to make. After which, as already said, I shall lay the whole before you. - I have ventured to write a few lines to Mr. Rutherford whom you mention, & shall take it kind of you to deliver the same. I shall be glad of his help, "Antiquities" being a favourite study of mine.

I have returned your very correct Population List, which does great credit to the head & hand that penned it.

I might inform you that, in the article "Schools" I have not gone into any historical details, but have confined myself to a few remarks on the smallness of our incomes &c. As to stating the number of Scholars, though it might tend, in some instances, to gratify the vanity of some teachers, it would, in others, be rather a matter of delicacy, where the teacher has not been successful. As to the interior of a schoolroom, it is a matter of little consequence as long as the exterior is so shabby. In short, everything respecting schools must be, to the public, a matter of indifference, as long as those who conduct them are kept in a state of poverty & consequent contempt. The workshop of the mechanic, is at least as respectable an apartment, as any (country) schoolroom in Roxburghshire.

I should like to hear from you before I venture to make my appearance at your house, (but shall expect a few sentences on the subject of Schools), and am, Dear Sir,

> *Yours respectfully*
> *Geo. Scott*

Excuse this paper, we have no better in town. As for the M.S. I shall not affront you by asking your excuse for it.
N.B. Leave yor letter with Mr. Thomson.

Lilliesleaf 22 Oct. 1812

Dear Sir,

Excuse me for troubling you with these few lines. I have my intended publication in such a state of forwardness as to be ready for taking in the names of intending purchasers. For this purpose I intend being at Jedburgh some day soon, - probably next week - & I would take it kind of you to make out a sort of list of the gentlemen in, and about Jedburgh who, you think, might probably take a Copy - and I shall take the liberty of calling upon them when there.

I have sent a copy of proposals to Mr. Oliver Selkirk, and if you should happen to be there on the 31st of this month, I hope you will second a motion, (if any be made) for promoting the subscription among the brethren that may meet on that day - I shall also send you a subscription paper. In the meantime I am

Dear Sir your M.sevt

(The price is 12/-)   *Geo. Scott*

Chapter 8

MILITIA

Great care has been taken in accurately transcibing all letters -
errors in spelling and punctuation are as per original

In July, 1797, when the threat of imminent French invasion was alarming the government, an Act was passed (37 Geo. III cap 103) authorising the raising, by ballot, of 6,000 militia in Scotland. Lieutenants of Counties were to order schoolmasters to draw up lists of all men aged 18-23 in their respective parishes. These lists would then be fixed on church doors, intimating the days on which Deputy-Lieutenants would meet to hear claims for exemption. When the lists were amended, the King in council would determine the quotas for each county and the regiments into which the men would be distributed.

Those eligible for exemption included men serving in the army, or on half-pay; University professors; clergymen; schoolmasters; articled clerks; apprentices; seafarers; all those with two children born in wedlock. Anyone chosen in the ballot could provide a substitute, or could pay £10 to be excused, but would appear on any subsequent list. Eventually an Insurance Society was established and, by paying three guineas, those liable to be balloted could obtain a substitute.

In order to make the recruitment more attractive, it was agreed that the militia could not be ordered out of Scotland and its members could not be drafted into the regular army. Militiamen could engage in any trade in any town, without paying dues - which might benefit them up to £50.

This was the first time there had ever been militia in Scotland and it was a very unpopular measure. In some areas, lists were torn down off church doors and parish registers were taken by force from the schoolmaster's house. In Selkirk, a mob from Galashiels and Melrose drove Mark Pringle and other deputies out of town, and in Jedburgh some rioters ended up in the jail. As schoolmasters were naturally peaceable, even timid men, they found it difficult to stand up to mob pressure and in most parishes the lists were amended accordingly.

By appealing to the patriotic spirit of men, and reminding them that England had raised 90,000 militiamen, their resistance was overcome.

In 1802, the regiments of Dumfries, Roxburgh and Selkirk were amalgamated under the command of the Earl of Dalkeith as Lieutenant of Dumfriesshire.

The schoolmaster at Oxnam submits an account for work carried out in connection with the Militia lists:

1805 District of Jedburgh County of Roxburgh
Account due to John Scott Parochial Schoolmaster
of the Parish of Oxnam for executing the Acts relative to
the Militia in Scotland.

Date		No. of days	Sum £	s	d
August 4	For filling up and delivering Notices to Householders, at 5s per day of 8 Hours	6	1	10	0
August 18	Making out 2 Copies of Lists of Names, consisting of 4 Folios, and each Folio containing 60 Lines, at 1s per Folio	0	4	8	
September 26	Attending Meeting of Lieutenancy, held at Jedburgh on the Dates mentioned in the Margin at 10s per day	0	10	0	
	Stationery Ware	0	5	0	
		2	9	8	

Oath

I the said John Scott do hereby solemnly certify and swear, That the preceding is a just and true Account of Business performed by me, for and in Behalf of the Public Service, according to the Manner therein set forth, and agreeably to the Regulations of the Court of Exchequer, dated the 4th Day of February 1805: That I was employed during the full time therein stated, and that the Sums claimed, as disbursed by me, were well and truly paid out, in conformity with the said Regulations. And this is Truth. So help me God.

District of Jedburgh County of Roxburgh
Account due to John Scott Parochial Schoolmaster
of the Parish of Oxnam for executing the Acts relative
to the Militia in Scotland

Date		N°of Days	Sum		
			£	s	d
August 4	For filling up and delivering Notices to Householders, at 5s per day of 8 Hours	6	1	10	0
August 18	Making out 2 Copies of Lists of Names, consisting of 4½ Folios, and each Folio containing 60 Lines at 1s per Folio		0	4	8
September 26	Attending Meeting of Lieutenancy, held at Jedburgh on the Dates mentioned in the Margin		0	10	
	Stationary Ware		0	5	0
			2	9	8

Oath

I the said John Scott do hereby solemnly certify and swear, that
the preceding is a just and true Account of Business performed by
me, for and in Behalf of the Public Service, according to the Manner therein set forth, and agreably to the Regulations of the
Court of Exchequer, dated the 4th Day of February 1805: That I
was employed during the full time therein stated, and
that the Sums claimed, as disbursed by me, were well and
truly paid out, in conformity with the said Regulations.
And this is truth. So help me God

TABLE of ALLOWANCES to Schoolmasters,

by Order of the Right Honourable the Barons of Exchequer.

1*st*, For delivering Notices to Householders, *Five Shillings* per Day, confisting of Eight Hours.

2*d*, For making out Lists, *One Shilling* each Folio, confisting of 60 Lines.

3*d*, For attending Meetings of Lieutenancy, *Ten Shillings* each Meeting.

4*th*, For delivering Notices to ballotted Men, *Five Shillings* per Day.

5*th*, For Stationary Ware, *Five Shillings* per Annum.

> *N. B.*—The Account of each Schoolmaster must be accompanied with a Certificate from at least Two of the Deputy Lieutenants under whom he acts, bearing, that, to the best of their Knowledge, the Business could not reasonably be performed in less Time than is stated in the Account; and he must likewise swear to the same before a Magistrate, in the precise Words of the Oath subjoined hereto.

OATH *above referred to.*

I   *Schoolmaster, acting in the District*

of   *in the Shire or Stewartry of*

do hereby solemnly certify and swear, That the preceding is a just and true Account of Business performed by me, for and in Behalf of the Public Service, according to the Manner therein set forth, and agreeably to the Regulations of the Court of Exchequer, dated the 4th Day of February 1805: That I was employed during the full Time therein stated; and that the Sums claimed, as disbursed by me, were well and truly paid out, in Conformity with the said Regulations. And this is Truth. So help me God.

Sworn at

before

this   *Day of*

And William Lorrain submits his for 3 consecutive years:

1805 Lieutenancy of the County of Roxburgh Dr. to Wm. Lorrain
     Schoolmr. of the Parish of Jedburgh.

Sept. 30th   To Militia List put on the Kirk Door
                of Jedburgh, containing 1220 Lines Folio   £1 . 0 . 4

"   To a Copy of the above List delivered to
                the Lieutenancy of said County containing
                1175 Lines Folio.   £ 19 . 7

"   To 10 Days in writing out 900 Notices and
                receiving them; each Day being 8 Hours. £4 . 0 . 0

"   To 1 Day attending Lieutenancy.   10 . 0

"   To Stationery.   5 . 0

                                                  £6 . 14 . 11

"   To Mungo Glendinning, Constable in
                assisting the said Schoolmr. Wm. Lorrain
                in delivering and receiving Schedules -
                fifteen Days Eight Hours each.   £3 . 0 . 0

                                                  £9 . 14 . 11

28 Oct. 1807 This day received of the above Acct
       £6. 14. 11 no allowance being made for Constable by Turner -
                 horrid   horrid !

Holograph Copy was given into Mr Riddells office upon 1st Janr. 1805

1806 Lieutenancy of the County of Roxburgh Dr. to William Lorrain
     Schoolmr. of the Parish of Jedburgh.

		£	s	d
Septemr 29	To Militia List put upon the Kirk Door of Jedburgh, containing 968 Folio Lines.		16	1
"	To a Copy of the above List delivered to the Lieutenancy of said County containing 939 Folio Lines.		15	6
"	To 19 Days in writing out 1000 Notices and receiving them; each Day being 8 Hours	4	15	0
"	To 2 Days attending Lieutenancy first on the 11th March, and second on the 29th Septr 1806.	1	0	0
"	To Stationery		5	0
		7	11	7
	To Mungo Glendinning Constable, in assisting the said Wm. Lorrain Schoolmr. in delivering and receiving Schedules 151/2 Days eight Hours each.	3	2	0
		10	13	7

Oct. 28 1807 This day received of the above Acct.
7 11 7 no alowance being made by Gardner *(a horrid imposition)*
Given in to Mr Riddell's office upon this 1st Day of Novr 1806

		£	s	d
Nov 18	To thirty days and a half day in preparing, delivering and receiving 950 of Schedule A to and from House-holders of the Parish of Jedburgh for the Militia List for the year 1807; each day being Eight hours	£7	12	6
	To Militia List for the Kirk Door partly filled up from Schedule A but stopt before it was finished containing 260 Folio lines		4	4
	To thirty three days in preparing, delivering and receiving 1000 of Schedule C to and from the House-holders of the Parish of Jedburgh for the Militia List for the year 1807: each day being Eight hours	8	5	0
	To Militia List for the Kirk door filled up from Schedule C containing 1230 Folio lines	1	0	6
	To a Copy of said List delivered to Lieutenancy of the said county of Roxburgh containing 1160 Folio lines		19	4
	To three days attending Lieutenancy at 10/-s per	1	10	0
	To two days in delivering Notices to Balloted men at 5/s each day being Eight hours		10	0
	To Stationary		5	0
		20	6	8

"Dr." appears at the top of the money columns.

A Copy of this Acct. was attested and delivered at Mr. Riddells office into the hands of Mr. Geo. Scott Clerk to the said Mr. Riddell upon Wednesday the 27th Janry 1808 by me Wm. Lorrain.

Jedburgh 11 Janry 1813

Dear Sir,

By the Fly on Saturday I received Mr. Gardner's report on the Militia Accots. transmitted to Exchequer in Nov last and as he has made a deduction from your Accot. for 1811 I think it right to intimate the same to you in case you should wish to write Mr. Gardner on the subject.

The amount of your account transmitted was	£11.17.6
Mr. Gardner says allowed as formerly	£10.17.4
Disallowed	£ 1. 0.2.

I am, Dear sir
    Yours sincerely
        Geo Scott

Once the war was over, Mr. Scott wrote:

Jedburgh 19 Augt 1814

Dear Sir,

The men serving in Dumfriesshire Militia for the County of Selkirk were disembodied yesterday and the Berwickshire Militia are to be disembodied tomorrow. You will therefore discontinue payt. to their Wives and families from those days.

Jedr. 20th Augt 1814

Dear Sir,

The Kirkcudbright Militia is to be disembodied today you will therefore stop payt. of the allowance to Jean Dunlop from this date -
    I am
        Dear Sir
            Your most obdt
                Geo. Scott

This was followed by a meeting to identify defaulters:

Excerpt from the Minutes of a
General Meeting of Lieutenancy
held at Jedburgh 2nd November 1814

Inter alia   The Clerk stated to the Meeting that the Schoolmaster of Jedburgh had given in a List of persons, occupiers of Houses, who had refused at least neglected to make out and deliver to him the Schedule to the Act annexed marked A; which had been left at their places of abode by the officer he employed for that purpose.   The Meeting having taken this matter into their consideration were of opinion that the provisions of the Act ought to be strictly enforced and therefore required their Clerk to call upon Mr. Lorrain and the person he employed in delivering the Schedule and upon their being willing to certify that schedules were delivered to any of the persons mentioned in the List to cause such person be summoned before the Justices of the Peace of the District of Jedburgh for the Statutory penalty or such part thereof as the Justices may think proper to impose.

*   Extracted by Geo. Scott   C Gen*
*   Tax Office*

Jedburgh   3 Nov 1814

Dear Sir,

I hope it will be convenient for you to attend here on saturday first at 1 o'clock with the person you employed in delivering the Schedules to give me the information wanted in execution of the prefixed Excerpt.

*   I am   Dear Sir,*

*   Your most ob Sert*
*   Geo. Scott   C Gen*
*   Roxrshire*

Jedbr 13th Febry 1815

Dear Sir,

*   Before sending the Officers to the people who did not return their Militia Schedules to you it is necessary to be informed of the date of the Schedules and whether they were dated on the day of delivery Be so good as give me this information any time today   I am*

*   Dear Sir*
*   Your most obd Servant*
*   Geo. Scott*

The following correspondence relates to an appeal for exemption:

Sir,

I James Paterson, Student of divinity late in the Parish of Shots presently in Selkirk finding my name included among the names of those liable to serve in the Militia would be glad to have my name still continued in the column of exemption for the following reason.

After knowing that my name was enrolled I immediately wrote to the Parish to which I belong for a certificate testifying that I would answer there, but because of the distance of the place, & shortness of the time an answer is not yet returned. I therefore desire as a particular favour that my name be continued as aforesaid - I am yours etc.

Jas. Paterson

1807 Aug. 25 Selkirk Militia Certificate

This is to certify that Adam Millar from Howecleugh has an evident contraction of the tendons of the fingers in his right hand and of 2 fingers in his left. Says also that several years ago he got a strain in his left Ancle which gave him considerable pain when he walks any distance.
Thos. Anderson, Snr. Surgeon

1807 Oct. Memorandum of Meeting, Robertoun Parish
Robert Lun, plowman of Borthwickbrae Burnfoot appeared and produced John Wilson as his substitute, whose height is 5'8", dark hair, blue eyes, ruddy complexion, 30 years of age. Born in the town & parish of Penrith & county of Cumberland and by trade a weaver and who was sworn in the terms of the Act of Parliament and ordered to join the regiment without delay.
Certificate of Fitness signed by Robt. Douglas, surgeon, Hawick.

The list of those who seem to be exempt from service from Lorrain's previous parish of Selkirk may be of interest, particularly as it includes the name of Walter Scott at Ashiesteil.

MILITIA LIST, SELKIRK c. 1807

Name	Address	Occupation	Remarks
BALLANTYNE, Jas.	Whitehope	Servant	
CLEGHORN, Wm.	Whitefield	Shepherd	4 children under 10 and not worth £50
COWAN, Jas.	Catslacknow		son to Wm. Cowan
DALGLEISH, Thos.	Catslacknow	Mason	In a bad state of health
COWAN, Samuel	Mt. Bengerknow	Plowman	Paid penalty for Militia 1803
COWAN, Robt.	"		Has been long unhealthy
BRYDEN, Walter	Tinnis	Shepherd	1803 Procured a substit for army of reserve
SCOTT, Francis	Eldinghope	Tenant	Yeoman
BLYTHE, John	Kirkhaugh	Cooper	Constable
STUART, Andrew	Gilmansc-leughburn	Weaver	Unable with an inward complaint 4 children under 10
SCOTT, Mungo	Dodhead		In a bad state of health
TAIT, Wm.	W. Fauldshope	Servant	Vol. in Peebles. Infantry
LAIDLAW, Robt.	Crosscleugh	Servant	Balloted for Ettrick Parish Rejected. One blind eye.
TAIT, John	Howford		Hath been in a bad state of health since Jan. last & appears no better
SCOTT, Geo.	Ettrick Bridge	Labourer	Volunteer, Par. of Wilton
SCOTT, Walter	**Ashisteil**	**Yeoman**	**Lame**
BELL, Thos.	Galashiels	Stocking weaver	Dull of hearing
DOBSON, Geo.	"	Weaver	Paid the Penalty
GLADSTONE, Arch.	"	Dyer	Blind of an eye
REA, Jas.	"	Labourer	Below size
CLAPPERTON, Andrew	"	Clothier	Deaf & Dumb

François Espinasse

Né à St Germain en Laye le 1h. 8bre 1788

poil ch.

taille

fils de Augustin

Claude de lagrange — marié à

demeure à ... des Drappiers Mr. Anonime.

Nº 302.

α 15.

François   Espinasse

Né à St. Germain en Laye le 1h. Octobre 1788

poil

taille

fils de François augustin Espinasse
et de marie claude de la grange

Nº 132.

Nº Cl.

1er Decembre
1806.

French Naval Certificates of Registration

136

Chapter 9

FRANCOIS ESPINASSE
1788 - 1870

Great care has been taken in accurately transcibing all letters - errors in spelling and punctuation are as per original

Francois Espinasse assisted William Lorrain as a teacher of the French language for a short time during his captivity as a prisoner of the Napoleonic War. A warm friendship seems to have developed between the young naval lieutenant and the Lorrain family, resulting in considerable and ineresting correspondence.

Born in St. Germain-en-Laye, near Paris, on 14th October 1788, Francois was the son of Augustin Espinasse and Marie Claude Delagrange. On 22 May 1804, he joined the French naval service on the corvette "l'Etna" under Captain Rousseau. He transferred, in November 1806, to the frigate "Junon" as a second helmsman under Captain Lambour and soon gained the rank of midshipman, first class. He was a Lieutenant by the time "Junon" and all her crew were captured on 10th February 1809. Taken first to Halifax, Nova Scotia, he and his compatriots were transferred initially to Crediton, Devonshire and arrived in Jedburgh in March 1811. Within a few weeks, Espinasse was assisting Lorrain *(p.52)*

At the end of 1811 French prisoners were removed from Jedburgh under the impression that they were being transferred to France. Instead they were taken to the camp at Valleyfield, near Penicuik, apparently as a reprisal for a similar action towards British prisoners by Napoleon. The former paper-mill held 6,000 prisoners, 300 of whom were interred there.

(in English)   *Valley-field 16th November*

Sir,

I am at last arrived at our new habitation, and my first care is to write to you, this is I assure you so great a pleasure to me as to solace me in my present situation: could it be otherwise? When I recall to mind that you loaded me with all those particular marks of esteem and benevolence which honour him upon whom you bestow them, and force him to accept of them as if this were the most sacred of his duties. by what means shall I ever be able acknowledge what you have done for me - no words can be the interpreter of my sentiments of gratitude, for what can I say which would not prove inadequate to what I feel. -

What a difference from this place to Jedburgh which will always be the object of our regrets. When I inhabited the Later, I lulled myself with the sweet idea that my misfortunes were at an end; methout I had entered a footpath leadind to happiness which was to be crowned by my return to my dear native country. - how much I have been deceived this last event shows it.

We have been treated all along the Way with the regard due to unfortunate officers. We are going to have a room for ourselves. they give us to hope that before another month we shall be returned to our former quarter; but I dare not trust it. We are about 30 Navy officers among whom there are two who are Lieutts lately promoted. We are all the three equally unfortunate for not having any certificate to ascertain it, but the letters of our friends which informed us of it. We shall apply anew to our friends to have such useful a paper as this sent to us. I wrote a letter to Mr. Montvaillant, to write also about it to my Mother; in order if one of my letters is lost another may get over. I have sent to Montvaillant the money which I owe you.

I beg of you Sir to honour me with your Letters believe that they will be next to my mothers the greatest consolation I can enjoy in this circumstance - Mister Gallois charges me to offer you his best compliments. Our respects to Mrs. Lorrain.

Excuse me for my writing be so good as to send me an old cesarii commintari for I will resume to study the latin Language

I have the honour to be Sir, your most humble

Servant

Espinasse

Shortly afterwards, the entire group of prisoners were abruptly ordered off, chiefly to Sanquhar in Dumfriesshire, as a reaction to the anxiety of a titled lady in the neighbourhood. She had become frightened at the idea of so many of H.M. enemies being allowed to be at large in the vicinity of Neidpath Castle, where the arms and ammunition used by the Militia were deposited. Her alarm was communicated to the War-office, and an order was immediately issued to disperse the prisoners. The hasty departure of the French officers caused considerable financial difficulties for local traders, as a number of them had contracted debts which they had no time to settle and some insolvencies took place in consequence.

Francois and his friend M. Gallois were transferred to Lauder and his next letter to Lorrain is in French:

Lauder 30 December 1811

Monsieur

    It is with the greatest pleasure that I inform you that I have received your letter, and the items which accompanied it, but I will not seek to describe the contentment which it brought me, because it is beyond all expression.

    Your expectations were not disappointed; we arrived here without accident: and we beg you to accept our thanks for the interest you have taken in us on this occasion.

    You say your letter is so short it will be of little importance (which matters little) compared with the length of that of my friend: if only you knew how much all that comes from you is dear to me, you would think otherwise. It is true that you lavish kindness in a manner so noble, so delicate, so disinterested that you lose count: but I who have reaped the fruit, I will remember and never cease to honour.

    I have not yet received news from Edinburgh on the subject of my removal, that gives me little hope of success. I have written again today to Mr. Same. If I have not received any response by the end of the week, I will make a last attempt writing to My Lord. If I am so unlucky as not to be recalled to Jedburgh would you allow me to write to you from time to time; this would be a great consolation to me.

    Mr. Gallois wishes me to convey his respects to you. My Compliments to you and your wife.

    I have the honour to be
                Your very humble Servant
                    Espinasse
We are staying at Mrs. White's

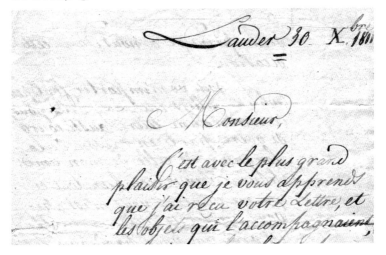

The Government agent in Lauder, responsible for dealing with the prisoners and finding billets for them, was Mr. John Romanes, the Town Clerk. He was allowed 5% commission on his disbursements and 5/3 per month for stationery. [In later years Espinasse taught French in Edinburgh to Mr. Romanes' son and greeted him with the words "Ah, your fader had me - now I have you", his hands indicating "under the thumb". When Mr. Romanes senior called on a visit, M. Espinasse seized and embraced him, shouting excitedly "Mon agent, mon agent!"] The Lauder Town Hall bell was tolled daily by James Thomson to enable the prisoners to be mustered and counted, and for the 8 p.m. curfew. The prisoners gave little trouble and there was no occasion to lodge any of them in the Tolbooth, although one did make his escape from the town.

(In French)   *Lauder 8th January 1812*

My Dear Sir,

I have just this instant received your note and the parcel which were destined for us by your kindness: we thank you with all our heart.

I received today two letters from Edinburgh telling me that the moves which have been made for our transfer have been unsuccessful.

I have enclosed the letter from the agent in charge of the prisoners addressed to Mr. Somerville.

Mr. Gallois and myself beg you to request that Mr. Bell writes in our favour to the transport office to obtain our return to Jedburgh; for the success of our request depends entirely on him.

You see Sir, that we have no other hope than what you are willing to do for us with the Agent, but this hope is so well-founded that I flatter myself in advance that it will be realised.

Please be assured of our respects to Madame your wife.

I have the honour to be, and you know my feelings, your very humble servant,

Espinasse

I am sending you the names of the two Frenchmen who wish to exchange with us: M. Lateste - Officer of the Corsaire
M. Thomelet - Surgeon.

My Dear Sir,

Your letter, the pleasure of having seen and spoken to the amiable young ladies to whom you entrusted it; a letter which I received last Sunday from my good and tender mother, all these circumstances united to produce such an effect on me, that I am relieved of boredom.

My dear mama, all my relatives and friends are well: the date of the letter is the 20th December. I am expecting to receive soon the value of the money orders which I sent to France through the good offices of Mr. Somerville to be sure of a pension.

I am thus able to hope to pass less sorrowful days awaitng the happy moment when I will return to my country & my family, since thanks to your generous care you give me the greatest hope of seeing you again as well as my good friends.

With what pleasure I will see Jedburgh again and its charming surroundings; and I will enjoy repeating my walks on the banks of the Jade when Flora rejuvenates the countryside, either to abandon myself to quiet reflection or to contemplate the fields and neighbouring hills which nature, assisted by the industry of the labourer, enlivens and makes so fertile, that I often delude myself to believe I was on the bank of the Seine where I was when I saw the light of day. But cold reason recapturing his empire destroyed very quickly my imaginary games; my happiness was very short but how much charm it had for me!

You must write to me in French; please give me that satisfaction as soon as possible; you can be sure that your letter will not be the object of my derision, I would consider it, on the contrary, as a mark of your confidence in me.

I send you a straw picture and beg you to accept it. In order to conserve the colour, it is necessary that you put it behind glass.

Mr. Gallois sends his regards. Our respects to madame your wife.

Your very humble servant

Espinasse

Dear Sir,

Do I not presume on my abilities in your language to write to you in English? I beg you will connive at my presumption, when you see I aim at nothing else but setting before you an example in order to incite you to comply with my request. Were you willing, dear Sir, to get the better of your timidity, I really think you could write to me in French in such a manner as to afford me much pleasure.

Mr. A. had the goodness to call for me Wednesday last and delivered to me your letter.

As to Mr. Anderson, I am pretty well acquainted with him. I am very much indebted to you for your having been so good as to recommend me to him, for just after his return to Jedburgh he gave himself the trouble to call at my lodging, invited both my friend and me to go and breakfast with him the next day, so that since that time I have paid him frequent visits. I enjoy myself very much in his company. He is a very good scholar, his conversation is both engaging and instructive: he is the only acquaintance I have in this place, the dullest place I have ever lived in since I was a prisoner of war.

Your last letter revived my hopes of getting back to Jedburgh, they begun to fail me, in expectation of that pleasure, I must remind this saying: a good Pilot is best tried in a Storm.

I have got a good set of French books from Edinburgh: I have as many English ones as I can wish for, through Mr. Anderson's favour. I study mathematique, Latin, indeed too many things at once to be ever proficient in any of them, but as my intent by so doing is to amuse myself, it is for this reason I do not attend to this useful maxim de Mr. de Voltaire:

"Ayez de l'ordre en tout: la carrière est aisée
Quand la règle conduit themis, phebus, mars,
La regle austere et Pure est le fil de thesee
qui dirige l'esprit au dédale des arts".

I do advise you again, not to let your straw picture without a glass over it, for fear it should lose its colours.

Mr. G. charges me with remembering him to you and both join to beg of you to give our best compliments to Mrs. Lorrain.

I am dear Sir,
your humble Servant,
F. E.

(In French)   Lauder   (written 15th Feb)
My dear Sir,

I was this morning at the Black Bull Inn when the "fly" arrived, hoping to get some news from you, but I returned home very despondent, not to be favoured. I am wrong, I admit, I know that you are fully occupied, and if you have some leisure moment to spare, it will be too

142

much of a nuisance to use it continually to answer my letters. All these reasons are right nevertheless the more letters I receive, the more I want to receive.

Did you receive the letter I wrote to you in bad English, 8 days ago today? Let me know in your next and above all it should be written in French, because I can't wait to judge your progress and have the pleasure of congratulating you.

I have a favour to ask you to hand on to my friends M. & C. a few lines that I address to them on the second page of your letter.

Mr. G. sends kind regards. My respects to madame your wife
Your very humble Servant
E.

To my friends Montvaillant and Caillet.

For a long time I haven't had any of your dear news. To what do I attribute your silence? It is not indifference, I would like to persuade myself; it is not illness, I would have been informed. It is not only lack of opportunity because they are frequent; it is perhaps because you have nothing to say to me. Ah! well write to me that you have nothing to write about. At least tell me in your next: We have received your letter, we are well. I absolve you from the rest, it is all your friend needs. You think that I jest, no, I am in earnest. Do this, I'll be happy. Our amusements consist of entertaining ourselves and to distract ourselves with our books. I said us, because you should know that our dear friend has become studious, even something more, but because I am the soul of discretion, I will keep it to myself.

You see that if we stay here (something far from my wishes) we will be able to become perfect models of wisdom. One of our young companions in misfortune was about to join the dead, to see what's happening there, but thanks to the care of some good people of this town, his visit is deferred, and we hope he will not soon embark on that again.

Tell me what you are doing. I suffer so much not knowing.
Look after yourselves
I embrace you
your faithful friend
Kind regards to everyone we know.   *E.*

(In French)   Lauder Wednesday 19th Feb 1812

I have received, my dear Sir, this letter which I impatiently awaited, written in such a way that if I were egocentric it would make me hesitate in future before daring to offer my services as your teacher of the French language: for I can assure you, you gave me today convincing proof that you don't need one any more. This modesty with which you conceal your talents becomes you well. It prevented me, it is true, from enjoying sooner the favour you accorded me on this day. But I can't admire it enough. Modesty is to virtue what perfume is to flowers. I can't count any longer on the request which was made to have me in Jedburgh again: because six of my comrades have left here for Dumfries on the request of the authorities of that town: and it was only ten days ago that the petition was sent off supported by Sir Jam. Mongomery. Such a contretemps would not surprise me as good fortune has always been against me since I left France.

Yesterday I tried the last resort: I wrote to Lord Ancrum. I am sending you some parts of the letter which I sent to him. If I am not successful I will do no more, but I will never stop thinking of the good people of Jedburgh.

A Monsieur le comte d'Ancrum
My Lord,

It was a great honour for me to be called at your request to help two young lords with my meagre talents in the French language; but an august favour is a good thing only if it is deserved, and I am not persuaded that some artless lessons are sufficient qualification for me to dare to beg your protection at this time. But I dare to hope, my lord, if you deign to read my letter that I can arouse your interest in my painful vexations, even if the little merit I have might not inspire you ....

...after having expounded all the reasons which call me to Jedburgh, I finish in this way...

...you, my lord, whose unique happiness is to contribute to that of others, please honour me again with your kindness, by taking an interest in having me recalled to Jedburgh with M. Gallois, my best friend and my companion in misfortune since I was made prisoner. A blessing which I would cherish forever!

Deign, my lord and my lady, to allow me a greater favour than that which I request by accepting the respect I show you........

My respects to madame your wife: please thank the Misses Bannerman for their best wishes. You will infinitely oblige
your very humble Servant
I shall write soon to my friends - excuse my scribble

(In English)   Wednesday   Lauder, 26th February, 1812

My dear Sir,
It is with real pleasure that I hasten to let you know that yesterday I received a very flattering letter from Lord Ancrum, in response to mine, in which he told me: " I depart tomorrow for London, and there I will do everything in my power to have you recalled to Jedburgh"; so you see, my dear Sir, that I have more hope than ever that I will soon return to you: you can also see that as far as my request is concerned, I should have started where I finished.
I am counting on seeing Dr. Somerville today, who, according to what I have heard, will be returning today to Jedburgh.
I will never forgive myself as my thoughtlessnees, my heedlessness, made me forget to thank you in my last letter for your good advice concerning milord. The only excuse, but the most sincere I can give you, is that the omission was not in my heart.
Our respects to madame your wife and also to the Misses Bannerman.
Your very humble Servant,
E.

(In English)   Lauder 14th March 1812

I have only time to tell you that I have received your letter and that I have very little hope of returning to Jedburgh; for I have just this moment learnt that Lord Ancrum left for Ireland as soon as he arrived in London. What should I do in these present circumstances? Please help me with your advice: I await this to find a way of overcoming this new setback.
Your very humble
Servant

A few prisoners were transferred to Jedburgh and it is possible that Espinasse was among their number. At any rate, there are no more letters from him until his return to France in June 1814. Napoleon capitulated on 6th April 1814 and was taken to Elba. Louis XVIII (brother of the deposed Louis XVI) took the throne of France.

Writing from Le Havre (In French):

My dear Sir,

I arrived here a week ago - I don't need to tell you how happy I was; what my feelings were on seeing again, after six years absence, the sky of my native land, my mother and my friends: your good and sensitive soul will feel it better than I could express it. What gave me the greatest satisfaction was to find again, in perfect health, all who are dear to me. I spoke to them of you, my dear Sir, as well as of your good wife: I told them of all the good things you had done for me: they bless you, and they will never stop cherishing you. How sweet it is, how fine to rule over hearts because of the good one has done!... you wished to be liked and in this you have succeeded.

Everything is quiet in France; even if opinions are divided about the new state of things. The young people, and above all the military, are not satisfied by the change of government: the former, because a career of glory and fortune is closed to them; the latter, because they have to leave these behind!!... But the artisan, the labourer, the merchant, the only true supporters of the state, are content and happy to think that soon, under a legitimate and protective government, they will be able to profit from their industry and to see the rebirth of plenty and of prosperity... They will no longer see their sons snatched from their arms before the age when the heart and spirit are formed, to be made both the instruments and the victims of a grand ambition; on the contrary, they will see them grow up before their eyes, they will be able to teach the principles which inspire virtuous feelings; finally, they will see them become the comforters and not the disgrace of their old age.

The bad financial state does not allow the government to accord half-pay to those officers who are being discharged: for the same reason, the double taxes and reconciliation duties etc etc have not been abolished. The business treaty is not yet known; as a result, the country is still in a state of inactivity. All of this is distressing, but what's to be done? The law of necessity determines it. We have endured, with great patience, for twenty years and more, blatant humiliations, sorrows unparalleled in other nations; we should, it seems to me, suffer the present misfortunes without complaint, since they will be of short duration, and followed by good fortune which we have not known for a long time. We must hope that, however difficult and painful our good king's task may be, he will, by moderation, goodness and noble efforts, reconcile all the various interests. - I will wait four or five months, to see what turn the affairs will take, and then I will know which side to take. I will soon leave for Paris. I would have written to you sooner if the opportunity I was counting on had transpired. As the letter post is safe just now, I prefer to use it to write to you. -

Of the three allied monarchs, the Emperor Alexander is the only one loved and respected by the French: his name is almost as dear as that of Henri the fourth. When this immortal and virtuous Emperor went out, all the people showed their gratitude with loud and sincere acclaim; while all was silent for Frederic of Prussia; and the most outrageous sarcasm rained down on Francois II -

I beg you, my dear Sir, to give my respects to your wife, to send my regards to your children and Messrs. Scott and Laidlaw. - I have written to Dr. Somerville - Tomorrow I am going to have published in the Rouen Gazette, what you said to me about a French teacher, for such a man as would suit you is not to be found in this place.

Farewell, my dear Sir, write to me as soon and as often as you can, and oblige
Your very humble and obedient servant,

F. Espinasse

Mr. Blackie of Edinburgh, who is here upon business for Mr. Walker of Leith, is to carry to you a parcel of french black lace, I intend for Mrs. Lorrain, which I beg her acceptance of, by her kind condescension she will add one favour more to the many she has already honoured me with.
F.E.

[Note: Alexander, Emperor of Russia; Francois II of Austria
Frederic-William III, King of Prussia - Ed]

(In French)   *Le Havre, 25th July 1814*
My dear Sir,
I wrote to you about a week after my arrival here; that was about a month ago and I have not yet had your news. Perhaps my letter has not reached you; because of this uncertainty I could not blame you for your silence. As I am assured that this one will reach you, I allow myself the hope that I will soon have an answer. I dare to anticipate that

you will inform me that your dear and worthy lady, your amiable children and you yourself are enjoying the same good health and happiness as when I left you. This thought fills me with joy; may I not be mistaken in this expectation. If your duties allow, my dear Sir, please give me all the details about the fine town of Jedburgh. We always like to hear about that which has been dear to us.... France is still in the same state as when I last wrote to you. The oppressive taxes of the last reign have not yet been abolished; the military have not stopped complaining; business is not good and that is because we don't understand the fundamental principles; but the greatest evil which we are suffering from, and the cause of all the others, is the total exhaustion of our finances. I repeat it for you, the majority of the nation is content and happy to see again, and to contemplate being back on the throne, the descendants of the great Henri. If the virtuous aims of Louis XVIII are supported by those surrounding him, peace and tranquillity will be reborn among us; our France will no longer possess vast riches, since it does not have the means of acquiring them any more, but it will enjoy an honest affluence which will produce more virtues and benefits than all the treasures of the continent locked up in our coffers have produced in the way of misfortunes and calamities.... We don't hear any more about Bonaparte: I believe that you English know more about the subject than the French. I am going to wait several months before I decide which state I should embrace; in any case I must await the result of the solicitations being made on my behalf - we are afraid that the nobility and the clergy will regain their former power. - However, I don't think we yet have substantial reasons to fear this.

I have asked Mr. Blackie of Edinburgh to hand over to you a parcel of black lace which I beg Mrs. Lorrain to accept; in responding to my plea she will add a new favour to all those which she has already accorded me. - I am transcribing for you a few lines of verse written here, to mark the entry of the Duke of Angoulême [nephew of Louis XVIII and last Dauphin -Ed] *into Bordeaux on the occasion when this town was taken by the English. The people were happy to know that one of the Bourbons was in France; but they did not dare to show their satisfaction openly. A person of this town, bolder than the others, wished to make his feelings known by putting the tyrant of the French off the scent; he did so in this manner:*

"Long live the Emperor of the French.
The royal family is unworthy of life;
Henceforth let us forget the branch of the Capets,
The Imperial race must survive forever,
Let us be a strong support for the proud Napoleon:
Cursed be the soul of the great Duke of Angoulême,
It is to him that this punishment belongs,
The honour of the crown has its just merits."

Later:

I am sorry, my dear Sir, to learn, at the very moment of Mr. Blackie's departure from havre, he cannot take charge of the lace I intended for Mrs. Lorrain, without his running great risks - Mr. Blackie will give you all the particulars about this disappointment of mine

havre 28th July   *Your sincerely devoted*
                   Servant
                     fr. Espinasse

Espinasse didn't stay long in Le Havre, for in February 1815 he is writing from Edinburgh, where he has set up as a teacher of the French language. He evidently had no problem in attracting pupils, for Elizabeth Grant in her "Memoirs of a Highland Lady" notes that in 1814 her father, John Grant, Advocate, engaged tutors for his daughters, including M. Espinasse for French. The Grants lived at 4, Heriot Row, which at that time had no laid-out gardens to Queen Street, only a long strip of unsightly grass and a green used by washerwomen. When John Grant and his wife were out, Elizabeth's brother William held clandestine parties, which however had to be over by eleven o'clock, and M. Espinasse was among the guests. Each visitor brought fruit and cakes, and tea (nothing stronger) was provided. The following year, when Elizabeth was unwell and confined to the house, M. Espinasse visited as a friend and passed pleasant hours there, helping to keep the governess, Miss Elphick, in good humour.

Miss Martha Somerville is returning to Jedburgh next Saturday: she very kindly offered to be my messenger, so I am taking advantage of her goodwill. Therefore she will deliver this letter to you. I received today yours of the 13th of this month. In it I find renewed proofs of your friendship: I believed it to be already at its peak; but I see, through the gentlest and rarest experience, that real friendship is infinite in its works - A real friend is a truly sweet thing! I have often said it, thinking of you; but I am too well-rewarded not to keep repeating it. I am always very busy: 10 or 11 hours per day. I will tell you that my brother has left for Guadeloupe. He is a Master's mate on board a 74 [gunship] - He has intellect, knowledge, talents, goodwill, good behaviour, amiability, and fifteen years, with all that he will be able to make his way in the royal navy, although career prospects are shrinking - If my success continues, I propose to bring over my youngest brother, to keep him at a boarding-school for 2 or three years, to learn English perfectly and to send him home again to his mother, as he is destined for business. He is also a very fine fellow, very diligent and easy-going. - How are politics in Jedburgh? Is the barometer for peace or for war? What do they think about Prussia and Russia? Are they not monopolising too much land and too much power? Tell me your opinions on the subject. Would it not be strange to see, one fine day, France and England united in restoring, by use of arms, the balance which still seems to be missing in Europe? How gauche I must seem to you in the matter of politics! I speak so little about them at present that I daren't express my feelings on this topic; I am afraid of revealing my inexperience. In the meantime, I read the Paris gazette every day, and the newspaper (called Correspondent) of Edinburgh three times a week, and that keeps me up to date with political events - Good evening, goodnight, adieu: I must finish, it is almost midnight, and I have almost no candle left, my respects to Mrs. Lorrain, and remember me to Mr. Laidlaw -

*Believe me, my dear Sir, with all the
gratitude I owe you, your devoted servant*

Espinasse

[Napoleon returned to France on 26th February 1815, ending the "100 days" reign of Louis. Waterloo followed on 18th June 1815 - end of Empire. - Ed]

I beg you, my dear Sir, to do me the favour of accepting the parcel which I am sending to you - It is a comical offering, I know, but it is the French way - I have to tell you that, among the linen that my mother sent me recently, there was a shirt which she only had time to baste. I spoke of it to a very kind lady, who was happy to see that it was made up. It is so well made; it has been admired by so many people, that I thought it was worthy of being presented to you - I have added one of the cravats which I received at the same time - this makes it quite a pleasing ensemble.

Adieu, my dear Sir, time is pressing - Write to me, as soon as you can, give my respects to your wife, and believe me your devoted and grateful servant

Espinasse

In October 1819 Francois Espinasse married Janet Cruikshanks and eighteen months later their first son, William Augustin Robert Duncan Espinasse, was born. A daughter, Mary, followed in 1822 and a son, Francis, in 1824. The family income was supplemented by taking John Grant, then aged 18, as a boarder while he attended college in Edinburgh in 1825. Elizabeth Grant describes M. Espinasse as "a clever Frenchman", but is less kind about his wife, who is dismissed as "very absurd".

By the time of the Census in 1841, the family was living at 8, Royal Terrace and had grown to include Frances (Fanny) and Jane, then aged 11 and 7 respectively. Francis, the second son, had moved with a servant, Isabella Thomson, to 42 Frederick St. which was listed as an academy in the Edinburgh Directory.

Ten years later, 1851, Francois was a widower living at 1, Hill Street, Edinburgh with daughters Frances and Jane; Isabella Thomson was housekeeper and the housemaid was Hannah Divine from Roxburgh. Frances was first a governess and then a teacher; in 1880 she moved to 27, Nelson Street where she died in 1925.

M. Espinasse's French classes became famous, not only for language training but as "a school of philosophy and moral training". One of his pupils, Mrs. (Admiral) Dunlop wrote: "He taught me to know and to love France; he explained to me the charms of her social life; and to him I owe the never-ending enjoyment of her literature". Every year, M. Espinasse visited his mother's grave in France, calling on Scottish friends in London en route. His son, Francis, became a literary historian working on the staff of the "Imperial Dictionary of Universal Biography". Francis was acquainted with Mr. & Mrs. Thomas Carlyle and did not at first dislike them as his father did. However, on one visit to London, M. Espinasse was delighted to hear Francis admit that he had changed his mind and was no longer blind to Mr. Carlyle's great and many faults. Thanking Heaven for "a saved, inspired offspring", M. Espinasse pulled out a five-pound note and gave it to his son. Towards the end of his life, Francis lived in a club called Charterhouse and died on 3rd January 1912.

M. Espinasse was made a Chevalier de la Legion d'Honneur and was known in Edinburgh as "the Chevalier". He admired the qualities of the British people and said of the French "We have too much heart, which carries us off balance". (See "The French Character") Before his death, he asked that the following words might be engraved on his tomb: "Mon coeur a ma patrie, et ma reconnaissance a l'Ecosse" ("My heart to my country and my gratitude to Scotland"). He died in Edinburgh on 4th March, 1870.

THE FRENCH CHARACTER
(Translated from the French)
= = =

Of all nations, the French is the one whose character has changed least over the years. In the French of today the Crusader is still to be found and similarities with the Gauls are still perceptible. This nation has always been lively, cheerful, brave, generous, sincere, presumptuous, fickle, conceited, inconsiderate. Its virtues come from the heart; its vices are only in the mind, and its good qualities correcting or balancing out the bad, all come together perhaps equally to make the French perhaps the most sociable of nations.

The great fault of the Frenchman is to be forever young, and almost never adult; consequently he is often more amiable, and rarely certain; he has almost no age of maturity and passes from youth to decrepitude. Our talents are shaped early on; we neglect them through long-term dissipation, and no sooner do we wish to make use of them than their time has passed; there are few people amongst us who can have the support of experience.

It is the only nation whose morals can be depraved, without corrupting the heart and distorting courage, which allies heroic qualities with pleasure, luxury and indolence; its virtues have little consistency, its vices have no roots. The character of Alcibiade* is not rare in France. The dissoluteness of morals and imagination does not affect the frankness and natural goodness of the Frenchman. Self esteem helps to make him amiable; the more he thinks, the more he pleases, the more he is inclined to express his love. Frivolity which harms the development of his talents and his virtues at the same time preserves him from dark and premeditated crimes. Perfidy is alien to him and he is ill-at-ease in intrigue. If sometimes he has been responsible for odious crimes, they have been erased more because of the national character than the severity of the laws.

M. Duclos

....

The English are public-spirited, and we have national honour; our fine qualities are more the gift of divine favour than the fruits of political education: like demi-gods we belong less to earth than to heaven.

M. de Chateaubriant

....

[*Alcibiade: Athenian General (450-404 BC) Pupil of Socrates Chief of democratic party. Made an expedition against Sicily (415 BC) Accused of sacrilege because of the mutilation of Hermes' statues. Fled and lived for some time in Sparta. Assassinated in exile. - Ed]

EBENEZER CLARKSON
(1759-1844)
Clarkson was said to be the original for "Gideon Gray" in
"The Surgeon's Daughter" by Sir Walter Scott.

Chapter 10

EBENEZER CLARKSON

Great care has been taken in accurately transcibing all letters -
errors in spelling and punctuation are as per original

Ebenezer Clarkson was a surgeon in Selkirk during William Lorrain's time as rector of the High School there. The warmth of their friendship is evident in Clarkson's decision to send his son Ebenezer to Jedburgh Grammar School to board with the Lorrains when they moved and in his support for Lorrain during his application for the post at Kelso Grammar School *(p.36)*. Ebenezer Clarkson was born in Dalkeith but moved to Selkirk and set up medical practice there. His original house was in the centre of the Market Place, among a group of buildings which was demolished in 1803, after which he occupied a property facing the Town House. *(p.10)*

Clarkson was a great admirer of Robert Burns, who visited Selkirk on a very wet day in May 1787. Burns and his companion arrived at Veitch's Forest Inn where Clarkson was drinking with some friends and the landlord was sent to ask if the travellers might join them. Clarkson formed a poor impression of the new arrivals who looked like "twa droukit craws" and although one had the air of a gentleman, the other appeared to be a drover. They were turned away. A few days later Clarkson learned the identity of the "drover" and never recovered from his remorse.

In 1791 he married Mary Burnet and they had two sons, Ebenezer and James. Ebenezer obviously gave his fond parent cause for concern.

Selkirk Mondy Morning

Dear Sir,

I wrote you a line yesterday informing that Tibby would not pine This is principally for Mrs. Lorrain - have sent a box of the Ointment as before for the Boys Head to be used not eaten - one of the powders to be taken at bedtime, twice a week - there is a small box too of the Ointm. for Eben for keeping his hair free of nits which he asked for - in the outer box are some Partridges for Mrs. L. which require no directions -

It is all nonsense your Spanish and Italian -, Much learning will make thee Mad - 'twas shabby not to have left your Coach at Galashiels and taken a trip over when so near us - We could have got you wafted over some way -

I sometimes spoke gravely to Eben when hear about the situation he held in his Latin Class - He imputes it to his want of practice in making Versions - Now as he only makes one Version in the week I urged him never to allow himself to play till it was finished properly - I told him I would write you to enforce this - I know how naughty he is - but I am sure he does not want abilities to learn anything, and I am afraid if he loses the spirit of emulation (which he once possessed) of being high in his class, that he will lose something very essential to his respectability in life - the Man is going - I am ever

Most sincerely yours
E. Clarkson

Selkirk 29th Oct 1808

Dear Sir,

In consequence of a threat in your last, I expected for some mornings past to have been roused prematurely from my slumbers - but no you could not come - Will you try it yet? - Many thanks to Mrs. L. & you for the *pears - they were very good & afforded some very sweet morsels to myself & some friends -

The principle intention of this is to apprise you that the Boy (Brayden) I formerly hinted to you of, proposes being put under your care in the beginning of Next Week - he is to begin Latin etc. - If you have any new ones starting at this time he wont I hope be too late; - How is Eben coming on now? Does he continue to pay more attention? I wrote him lately but have not heard from him since tho Mr. Rodger told him he would be some hours in Jedburgh - We last night finished the Insp. and mustering of our Troop - I feel somewhat solitary today when they are all gone. We were very happy - my house was just the Coffee room -

With best Compts to Mrs. Lorrain
I ever am verily yours
E. Clarkson
Give my love to Eben and tell him to write E.C.

---

* Pears were renowned in Jedburgh from the time of the monks and in 1822 the following varieties were listed:

Grey Longueville; Green Longueville; White Warden or Monk's Pear; Grey Warden; Drummond (grey and red); Monk; White Achan; Grey Achan; Pound; Grey Goodwife of Glasgow; Rob Hynd; Worry Carle; Bell-tongue; Scots Bergamot; Crawford or Ballencrieff; Lady Lamont; Grey and Red Honey; Douglas; Mother Cob; Fair Maid; Pitfirrane; Bon Aretien; Lud; Buchanan; Cranstoun.

Selkirk 11 Janry 1809

Dear Sir,

I dare say that you will be thinking that I am playing the fool very much in keeping Eben so long here - I too regretted it, but the weather, roads, & a lame horse forbid his going over sooner today we avail Ourselves of the opportunity of Dickson's Cart going - I have had some very serious discussions with him respecting his being still at the bottom of his Class - I am truly concerned on this acct as it must materially damp that spirit of emulation & ardour to excell, so essential a requisite for a Boy who has to push his way thro' life - I'll be greatly obliged to you to keep him sharply at his task, Nor Allow him any indulgence at play, or amusement untill he shows more convincing proofs of attention in this respect; for a Boy quietly to be satisfied with remaining at the bottom of his class for so long a period, appears to me to be horrible - and the effects of it I fear will be evident thro' life, this I shudder at - I know he has abilities - and if he does not exert them, 'tis his fault - I have placed the subject in so clear a point of view to him, as being so ruinous to himself - and totally incapacitating him from ever making a respectable figure in the world, that I really believe he is now sensible of the impropriety of his inattention, & will now double his dilligence - I shall be glad to hear from you that this is the case - and with best Compts to Mrs. Lorrain & sincere wishes that last year may be the worst of many returning happy ones to you and yours I ever am

> *Yours most sincerely,*
> *E. Clarkson*

Selkirk 23 July 1809

Dear Sir,

I was duly favoured with yours announcing the day of your examination - on which day I hope to be with you in proper time - Mr G. Brayden is here today. My plan is, that he should be here the night before, and that we breakfast at Woodhead & so be with you in time

As I have just heard that Mr. Rodger is to send to Jedburgh tomorrow I seize the occasion to send this - I think I'll take a bed with you after your Ball rather than take Eben home so late as last time - Why did not you tell me the secret? - You'll forget it before year time I doubt, - is Mrs. L. confined yet? you give her no rest, - I heard you was preciously drunk when H. Dun was over, a pretty Elder faith - have only time to subscribe myself

> *Verily yours   E. Clarkson*

Best Wishes for Mrs. L.'s well doing
Jamie writes Eben - if not closed I'll add a line or two - but am just going out to dinner.

Clarkson's first wife died and he remarried in July 1810 to Agnes Henderson. He became Chief Magistrate of Selkirk and was a close friend and physician to the Sheriff, Walter Scott.

Clarkson's sons both entered the medical profession; Ebenezer junior joined the East India Company and became medical Aide-de-Camp to King Oude, while James remained in the Borders, settling in Melrose.

In July 1815 William Lorrain wrote to Clarkson seeking a reference to support his application for a post at Glasgow *(p.81)* and was appointed. His old friend expresses his pleasure:

Selkirk 21 Augt 1815

Most sincerely do I congratulate you my Dear Sir, on your success - you will hardly believe the interest all in this house felt in your affair - Your letters particularly that of yesterday, which I had this morning by ¹/₂ past six - We were all quite happy at its contents as many of your friends have been today - Oliver bids me say he most sincerely congratulates you on the occasion - When are we to see you here, I hope soon - You have nothing else now to do - excuse haste being all bustle with the Fair. All join in best wishes for Mrs. Lorrain & family   Ever yours
E. Clarkson

P.S. My father bids me say he expects to see you and Mrs. Lorrain here for some days before you go West   Give my best Compts to Mrs. L. -

Your most obd servt
E. Clarkson junr

Ebenezer Clarkson remained medical adviser to Sir Walter Scott and in 1831 persuaded him to consult a "mechanist" called Fortune in Edinburgh about a splint for his lame leg which was troublesome. Scott did so and found temporary relief. The following September, 1832, James Clarkson attended Scott on his deathbed, closed his eyes and performed an autopsy the next day.

Chapter 11

REV. MARK AITKEN

*Great care has been taken in accurately transcibing all letters -
errors in spelling and punctuation are as per original*

Mark Aitken was born in Crailing, Roxburghshire, in 1787. His father, Robert Aitken, (1760-1840) was the parish schoolmaster. Mark was educated at Jedburgh Grammar School and may still have been a senior pupil when William Lorrain joined the school. He attended Edinburgh University and his first letter to Lorrain reveals a puckish sense of humour...

Edinburgh 24th Decr. 1807

Dear Sir,

With pleasure I received yours this afternoon. The hurry in which it appeared to have been written renders it more agreeable. We are all tinctured a little with vanity, & flattery has the greatest charm when it seems not intended. I am but a bad moralist & shall quit the subject. But still it pleases me to think that probably you have left a select company, or put a stop to your more important duties, to write a foolish boy, an acquaintance of not above a half years standing. Pray don't put me off the belief of this. It would mortify me sadly were you to say I forgot till the carrier was almost going - I am afraid the coffee is not as good as was expected. I am sure it cannot equal, by much, my wishes. A curious phrase this! But it means, I wish it had been much better than it really is, better than any coffee ever was, or will be. I am glad to hear John is doing well. Probably it would have been better had he fallen for a Militia man being insured. I enter a French class as soon as the holy days are over. Mr. Smith & you seem to agree with regard to Mr. Moffat and he is my man if he will accept of me. I am attending the 2d & 3d Greek classes & Natural Philosophy & studying very hard at Mathematics and Algebra in my spare hours. Indeed I have no time for private teaching were such a thing ever to occur. -

I have paid three visits to Madam Louis. But as yet all my schemes have proved abortive. I took a friend with me from Northumberland & his tongue put aside all suspicions, for you must know, we posed as Northumbrian gentlemen, our names Thomson & Gray. These chance directed us to assume. On our first visit Miss Robertson her oldest daughter made her appearance. From her we could learn nothing. I was curious to see the glass blown; even this could not be done, her Brother being from home. So taking two thermometer tubes, we took our leave, notering we would soon be back to see her Brother perform. Accordingly out we set and Miss R. ushered us into the presence of her Brother. A fine sensible young fellow about seventeen yet knowing very little of the world. He went through several operations with great skill, and although not very talkative, he completely showed us the art of his business. Still I could learn nothing concerning my main pursuit, my only resource was whisky. We therefore after much persuasion adjourned to a Tavern & the second & third glasses loosened his tongue. Then question & answer followed in succession. Where do you come from? I asked. From Hawick. Was it your sister that we saw? Yes. Have you only one? I have three, but Sally & ... are in the country. What do you call this one? Betsy. By this time he was getting very talkative and as good luck would have it, one of his acquaintance was in the same room. I still continued my interigations glancing always on Sally. & his friend nearly as tipsy as himself aided me greatly & launched out in the praise of Sally. I prevailed upon Mr. R. to set me away a little and learned that Sally and her sister were in the country on a visit. None of them were married, Sally was very pretty and they were expected home on Saturday. He said Sally's features were good, but they were far inferior to her other accomplishments. This from a Brother? He must indeed be a nonsuch. At parting, he desired us to come back on the Tuesday following and we should see some other of his performances. Out we set a third time, but Sally was yet in the country, owing to the badness of the weather I believe. However, we saw the mother & had a little chitchat with her. If she is as bad as we suspected her, she is a most consummate hypocrite indeed. After this do you think it safe for a young fellow who has a heart to lose, to venture in sight of Sally? But curiosity is upon the stretch, it must be satisfied & I shall take the earliest opportunity. Her Brother I understand was very ill with the dose of spirits we thrust in him.

I shall probably call on Mr. Smith tomorrow as we have no class. I hope the little ones have got free of the chincough. I shall be happy to receive a letter from you whenever you can find it convenient. I am rather inconscionable in this respect. With my best respects to Mrs. Lorrain & family   I am , Dear Sir
Yours sincerely M. Aitken
P.S. Miss B. might probably make a very pretty little wiffie. But do you know I am already married! This was among the first news I received from my friends at Edinburgh. The newsmonger was a gentleman from

this place. Don't you think I should call on him and have the honour of shooting him through the head! Marriage I could have forgiven, But he likewise reported that I had given myself out at Jedburgh as a gentleman who had finished my studies & just in expectation of a Kirk. However I am as yet unacquainted with my wife's name. Any news from Jedburgh are interesting since I became one of its inhabitants. I don't know how it is but I have always a pleasure in thinking of that little happy place. It must proceed from the respect I bear for some of its inhabitants. M.A.

["Miss B." was probably Eliza Bannerman, who married Mark in 1817. -Ed]

Edinburgh 21st Jany 1808

Dear Sir,

 It is now so late & I feel so very sleepy, that I certainly should not have troubled you with my nonsense tonight, if I could possibly get it done tomorrow. But the mornings are so short & the forenoon being spent in attending classes, I must either write tonight or not at all. At any other season of the year, I should have thought you were very unkind in not writing me. Indeed I was going to make a great many complaints both upon my own account and on that of some others who expected to hear from you long ago, but I recollected Christmas & New Year are scarcely over. I hope you have spent the time merrily. Or are we Brothers in misfortune, for I have seldom been more dull. The only pleasant time I had in the vacation, was when I transplanted myself into your fireside at Jedburgh, talked with William and Thomas and paced up and down the room floor with Walter in my arms. and I was often sorry to recollect that I had only been dreaming & surprised to find myself at Edinburgh whilst I thought I had been at Jedburgh. I am going briskly on with the French. Indeed they flatter me if I am not doing well & speak falsely if I am not doing very well & I likewise think if this is not the case, my own judgement deceives me, in I have only been three weeks at the class and can translate Telemagne pretty well. I started with a young officer in the 94 Regt. who had formerly learned some French at Canterbury. But I did not like to march with his heavy armed infantry, so off I set and left him to accompany the rear guard. I expect in a fortnight or three weeks to enter into another class. I understand our Old Friend Tibby has been at Edinburgh lately, paying a visit to her new friends. By this marriage she is now a 2d 3d or 4th cousin of mine. I am not a good hand at counting genealogies, but I think our relationship subsists somewhere in this series of numbers.

I expected to have seen Misses Harkness & Misser here before this time but none of them have put up their appearance. George Pott has been very poorly with the measles, but is now attending his classes. It is he who expected you to write him. I have not yet unriddled the mystery concerning Mrs. Loui. You will receive by the carrier two pounds of coffee. I hope it will be better than the last. With my best respects to Mrs. Lorrain & expecting to hear from you soon.

> *I am*
> > *Dear Sir*
> > > *Yours sincerely,*
> > > > *M. Aitken*

P.S. I should have filled up my paper, but my fire is gone out and I am almost shivring with cold - .

During 1810, Mark spent a short time assisting Lorrain at Jedburgh before obtaining a post as tutor to the Hogarth family at Lennel, near Coldstream, where he remained until 1814.

> *Lennel-hill, 7 Decr. 1810*

My Dear Sir,

But what shall I say! - This thought or saying (I don't know which) very unfortunately occurred just when I had determined to write you - for, would you believe it, there has been a sad contest between laziness & inclination. The former urged delay, and among a great many frivolous arguments in favour of her purpose, produced this very substantial one - namely, that I had been very throng all day, & felt myself of course, a little fatigued. But this as well as the others inclination over-ruled, & exulting in her conquest, proceeded to write - but, what shall I say - immediately put a stop to her proceedings and laziness exulting in her turn, - Ay! what will you say? - Shut out from the world, - almost a stranger to the place of your abode & its outlandish inhabitants, - what entertainment can you give to Mr. Lorrain! - Self love, you may be sure, was not a little piqued at this, & Egotism coming forward promised to furnish materials for a page or two - Good luck likewise insinuated, that should I write nonsense (a very probable case) it would only cost you the trouble of reading it, - to begin then - I arrived here ten days ago very wet & dirty, for it rained from morning till night & the roads were execrable. But for a very good horse, I should not have been able to accomplish my journey - a kind reception, a good room & a blazing fire, you know are excellent restoratives & in a short time I found myself quite well- The family here are good beyond my expectations, & should I continue to feel myself as comfortable & as much at ease as I have yet done, I may justly say the lines are fallen to me in pleasant places - Hours of teaching & everything regarding the children was left entirely to myself - But there is an art (could it be hit upon) of getting one's own way, by referring the matter to our employers - I luckily hit upon this & of course Mr. Hogarths opinion and mine perfectly coincided - & I teach a little more than four hours a day - from nine till eleven, from twelve till one, & from half past two till about four - I see the children can learn & I hope to have firmness enough to make them learn - You will conclude that I have a great deal of time upon my hands, (I believe that is the phrase) but I confess I have very little to spare. The true method of killing time, I find is to be very busy - I therefore never allow myself time to weary. I have my regular tasks to perform, like any schoolboy & although imposed by myself they are strictly attended to - so that I have scarcely had a spare moment since I left Jedburgh even in the school hours I endeavour to make myself as throng as we used to be at Jedburgh - by this means, time glides smoothly & imperceptibly along — I should like soon to hear from you. I hope my successor in office acquits himself well - Should the weather be favourable, I expect to see you at Jedburgh about Christmas. Should I not be in time to dinner, on Christmas Day I shall breakfast with you perhaps some day soon after. I was much pleased to observe in the Kelso Mail today, that Mr. Shaw has published his sermon preached at Ashkirk. This will serve for a desert, when I see you - Give my best respects to Mrs. Lorrain & family & Misses Bannerman - I am

My Dear Sir,

Yours sincerely

M. Aitken.

I scarcely think Tweedside so pleasant as the banks of the Jed, - Perhaps an impartial judge would give the preference to the former -

Lennel-Hill 13th April 1811

My Dear Sir,

I feel much at a loss in what manner to proceed with our Review. A new employment like a new coat is generally accompanied with uneasiness until custom has reconciled our shoulders to the precious burden. But the office of Critic is so foreign to me, that I have not as yet been able to imitate the manner, & far less to equal the matter of my honourable, respected & redoubted Brethren. With a little practice however & on a proper occasion I may learn to snarl with the best of them. In the meantime I have sent you a Specimen, in order that the Critic may be criticised in his turn. [see p.222] I am by no means pleased with it, but if you be in no great hurry, perhaps I may proceed no further until I see you. I had lately an opportunity of seeing some English reviews, but they were equally barren of this kind of criticism as the Edinr Monthly Magazine & Review. I had therefore to depend upon myself, & not till after two or three attempts could I produce even the enclosed. - So soon as seed time is over (& this will be in the first few good days we are favoured with) I intend heating up your quarters, when we will concert a better Critic. I have been very throng for some time past, & have only got the institute glanced over, I think independently of your Notes I could have guessed the Dramatis Personae. The institute or institution made a great noise when I was in Edinr I made some enquiries concerning the wonderful phenomenon, and was told a fine gentleman had instituted Public Lectures for the instruction of the Public. But I had no idea, that I was so nearly connected with this honourable body, although I still imagined myself a member of the Philomathic Society. I indeed heard some time ago from one of the Brotherhood, that they were about to make some new arrangements, but little did I think their scheme was to comprehend universal science, or that they would degrade themselves into common quacks.

You ask for all my news - but you may as well expect to get a certain part of dress from a highlandman as news from me. I have somewhere heard or read of a gentleman, who wrote an account of the empire of China, its curiosities, learning etc., while confined in prison for debt. 'Tis true he never in his life was fifty miles from London, but by this ingenious device he found means to procure his enlargement & at the same time to impose upon the credulity of his friends, for his long journey sufficiently accounted for his long absence. Now had I a portion of this gentlemans ingenuity I might amaze my friends with sketches of the most distant Countries, with perilous voyages & hair breadth escapes, without ever stirring from the fireside. But as it is the occurrances of a day may answer for those of a month, & those of a month for several years. I shall keep the copy of the Academic & mark any mistakes that occur on looking over it. Can you excuse my officiousness! 'Tis a fault I owe to nature, and this kind of fault is not easily rooted out. Will you make my compts to Mrs. L. & family and to Misses Bannerman. If Andw Rutherfurd has got to Jedburgh will you tell him I have forgot the day on which our Society is to meet -

I am

My dear Sir,
        Yours sincerely,
                M. Aitken

My Dear Sir/

    I am favoured today with Mr. Buist's answers to our Queries, - but had they been more favourable than they are, I could not now have availed myself of your kindness, the time being so very short.   It would require more than the activity & speed of Ajax, to transport myself from this to Faukland in thirty six hours.   -   Mr. B. says "the number of Scholars in the School here, has varied for these several years past from 100 to 160.   -   The rate of school fees as fixed by the Heritors is 2/- 2/6 & 3/- per Quarter for reading, reading & writing etc. & from 4/- to 5/- pr qr for Latin.   The Salary consists of 20£ paid by the Heritors & £ 3. 6. 8 by the Burgh. - When the Schoolmaster is appointed Session Clerk, & Kirk Treasurer, he is allowed from £10 - £15. -   There is no house nor garden & the present allowance for them is very small.   -   I have made some calculations, & strained the matter as far as reason would allow, yet I cannot make out £100 a year. - The average number of Scholars, say 120 - & 50 at 2/- 40 at 2/6 & 30 at 3/- & suppose 12 at Latin, at 4/ - the whole amount will only be about £68 which with the Salary will make £91.   The other emoluments are doubtful & will by no means make up for the want of a house & garden. - In point of profit & ease, my present situation is certainly the more preferable, - but to breathe the free air, - & to taste the sweets of independance, what would we not sacrifice: - Liberty, although attended by poverty, is far more desirable than .....howsoever it may be ameliorated by all the luscious sweets of plenty. Were I to speak in this manner to any one who had not experienced the like situation, I daresay he would think Bedlam my proper place of abode. - But I have often said it, & I cannot yet alter my opinion, - that Tutors as they are called, who would experience happiness in a Gentleman's family, must sacrifice every independant principle, & forget that he is a rational being - he must think and act not as he ought, but as his employers do, - or than the family in which he resides must be "one of a thousand". - He who can be happy otherwise, may thank Heaven for his natural dullness & stupidity. For my own part, I have every reason to respect Mr. & Mrs. Hogarth. They have used me more like a friend than a hireling - yet I should be contented to leave them. - The time may come perhaps when I can do so, to advantage. At all events, I shall be my own Master before this time twelvemonth, - & should nothing better occur, I intend to winter in Edinburgh. -

    Thanks my Dear Sir, are a poor equivalent for your kindness on this as well as on former occasions, - but such a beggar am I, that these are all that I have to bestow. Were I less sensible of my obligations, I might say more, but this is a topic on which my pen refuses to act its part. - Whatever fortune may have in store for me, I must always retain a grateful sense of your favour, & will always recollect with pleasure the many happy days I have spent with you & Mrs. Lorrain at Jedburgh. May you see many new years, & always enjoy that happiness which you have so often imparted to others. - Had I delayed writing till tomorrow, you might have had a more coherent epistle but I thought you would be anxious to hear the news & perhaps I might not have had an opportunity of sending my letter to Coldstream, but when I tell you I had only twenty minutes, I hope you will excuse this scrawl. With compts to Mrs. Lorrain & family, I am

> *My Dear Sir,*
> > *Yours sincerely,*
> > > *M. Aitken*

As I have not time to write to my Father will you tell Bob, that I don't go to Edinr till Feby - they will understand by this how the business has gone

> *Edinr. 16 Decr 1812*

My Dear Sir/
> *I once more have the honour to address you from the Metropolis, where as usual at this season all is hustle, splendour & gaiety. I have had my share of the former, but as to the latter I may say, I yet only know them by report. I know not however if I can with justice claim any degree of praise for what necessity has in a great measure imposed upon me. But for a severe cold, perhaps by this time I might have experienced that pleasure does not always please, and that gaiety is not always the attendant of happiness. In a few days more, I am in hopes, that my self denial, will be in consequence of the sober dictates of reason, and not the necessary effect of bad health. - From an individual who leaves his room, only upon the call of business, you must not expect much local intelligence. I believe however I can furnish you with some news, - at least with something new in the History of the Divinity Hall of Edinr. - This is nothing less than an actual Insurrection headed by a Mr. Ross who was supported by Mr. Wm. Turnbull of Lanton. Ross I understand has all along been a turbulent fellow - he is very clever, & having given in all his discourses & obtained his Certificate from the Dr. imagined I suppose, that he had nothing to fear. - He wished to reinstate us in the privelege of criticism, which very fortunately has been done away since Ritchie became Professor.*

- He made a very clever, but a very imprudent speech just when the Dr. was beginning his lecture and accused the Dr. of injustice, oppression &c. After the lecture he again began & as soon as Ritchie had left the Hall there was a complete uproar. This happened on Thursday and he pledged himself to renew the business on the Tuesday. The friends of the Dr. met on the Saturday & drew up some resolutions expressive of our approbation of the conduct of Ritchie while under his tuition & disapproving of the proceedings of Ross. On Tuesday he again came forward after being summoned to attend the Senatus Academicus & behave with all his former imprudence. The Senatus Academicus meet to consider the business today, & I am much afraid expulsion will be the consequence. Turnbull has likewise acted a very improper part & it is said Ritchie talks of representing his conduct to the Presbytery. I will not finish my letter until I hear the decision of the Senate.

I have been so stupid as to forget the author of the Church History you were recommending. I will thank you to mention it, I am at present reading Morheim & find him truly tedious. - Dr. Murray our new Professor of Hebrew is going on very briskly, & is universally liked as a Teacher & as a man. I was with him a considerable time a few days ago, & was not less pleased with his unassuming but polished manners in private, than astonished at his learning when in the Chair. Hebrew as yet seems a dry study, although he does everything in his power to make it entertaining. But we begin to translate tomorrow & I am then in hopes of getting more fond of it.

I have seen a great many of your old Scholars & you will be pleased to hear, that in general they maintain a very respectable character in their different classes. Stavert I met with frequently & have fallen in with Eben Clarkson & John Bryden who appear very attentive to their Studies.
-

Tuesday 22nd Decr

I was in hopes of sending this last week by the carrier, but Ross' business was only determined yesterday. The Senatus Academicus met again on Saturday & were occupied in examining witness for four hours & a half. They again met yesterday, & unanimously agreed that the charges against Ross were fully proven, & the sentence of expulsion was passed. - Dr. Ritchie read it in form, today in the Hall & erased his name from the Hall records. It was a most solemn scene. - Alas poor Ross - although almost everyone reprobated his conduct & thought that he deserved punishment., yet I believe everyone was sorry to see the sentence put in force. - He is a young man of very superior abilities & with a little more

167

prudence could have been the first in almost any Society. - Although I must blame him, - I cannot but admire his strong and independent mind. - His punishment however will secure the tranquillity of the Hall, while his boldness will render the Dr. a little more cautious in his criticisms.

I will expect to hear from you soon, - and if you should stand in need of an agent in Edinr., I surely need not say that I hope you will apply to me. With compts. to Mrs. Lorrain & family & wishing you all a canty Christmas, I am

My dear Sir,
Yours sincerely,
Mark Aitken
Will you make my compts to Misses B.

Edinr. 5 Feby 1813

My Dear Sir/

Without mentioning what I ought to have done, I will only tell you what I did, & I trust you will excuse me for not doing so sooner - I delivered all the parcels to the care of the different Carriers in a few days after they arrived, - & I hope they have all got to their respective destinations, as I took the precaution to Book them. - I thank you for your Essay - and am pretty ambitious to have it in my power to make you a compliment of the same kind, - but I have been & continue to be so much occupied, I am afraid May will be at hand before I have fixed upon a proper subject. I intend however to make the attempt, - & should some propititious moment produce a proper introduction, - the rest will follow of course. - - I sometimes fall in with Mr. White, he tells me he has got a copy of the Essay, - but I have not had an opportunity to hear his opinion - & Wilson the Bookseller has I understand, disposed of a few copies, but I have seen no Critic upon it. -

Since the expulsion of Mr. Ross the business of the Hall now goes on pretty smoothly. Good sometimes proceeds from evil. For the Students are not only much more quiet, but the Dr. himself is much milder with his Criticisms. - It must be something very ridiculous that rouses his anger. I only wish his good humour may continue until my fiery trial be over. - I have not yet forgot what I thought my unmerited thrashing, & I look forward to the 26th of this month with not a little anxiety. It is then I expect to get quit of all my Discourses, - but whether with honour or disgrace, - time will determine. Of the three, not one is finished, - but I have yet nearly three weeks, & if the itch of writing would only seize me, perhaps three days would be sufficient. - We are going briskly on with *the Hebrew, & translating ten or twelve verses every day. I am very fond of it, but it is a great waste of time & the Dr. must have every lesson prepared, - otherwise the sharpest rebuke is given in the bluntest manner, with "I am determined you shall not trifle so long as you're with me " - in spite of his severity however, he is universally admired and respected. - I was in hopes, I should have been able to give you some account of Mr. Gray's (of the High School) discourses - but he has disappointed us two or three times. - I have no news, but such as relate to the College and these in general are so trifling they hardly deserve notice. -*

With best compliments to Mrs. Lorrain & family
   I am My Dear Sir
    Yours sincerely
Will you be so good
as give the enclosed to Robert   *M. Aitken*

Mark Aitken was licensed to preach by the Presbytery of Chirnside on the 28th of December, 1813. However, he did not immediately find a charge and returned to the Hogarths at Coldstream, with occasional opportunities to preach as an alternate to the regular ministers.

        Lennel-Hill 17th Augt 1814

Dear Sir,
 I was favor'd with yours on Friday, & I believe immediately resolved, should I even be but tolerably well to trouble you with my presence on the 25th. I am something in doubt, that by this time I am out of the Drs books, as he had reason to expect a day from me some months ago - if however he should again ask me, I have no objection to make good my promise, on the Sunday after the Sacrament, - although I am in hopes he will think of officiating on that day himself. - He desired me to let him know some days before, when I intended to visit Jedburgh, as he might then embrace the opportunity to see his Friends. - But he will not be absent from the Examination, so it is of no consequence whether he know or be ignorant of my intention. -

 I have just arrived from Coldstream where I had the pleasure of seeing your old Friend Mr. Wm. Hume. - The whole regiment is there in order to be disbanded on Saturday. Mr. H. enquired when I had heard of you, - I told him, he was just going to be set at liberty in time for the Ball on 25th & he desired me to mention that he would certainly be with you & perhaps a day or two before - He looks extremely well I don't know whether you have seen him in his soldiers dress, - but I assure you he looks much more like our ideas of a Soldier, than the greater part of his Brother Officers.- Neither his profession, nor his jaunt to England, seems to have made him forget himself, - and this in my opinion, - is the highest proof not only of his goodness of heart, but of his good sense. - We have also got Mrs. Flintoff at Coldstream, in as dancing a humour & as dancing like as ever I saw her.- She likewise talked of the Ball, - but there still seems some demur, between inclination and interest. She would like to be present, but then she must leave her School for some days. - From what I can guess, hoever, inclination will prevail. - She is in great hopes of a good School having already mustered about twenty.

The result of the long pending law suit, - would indeed be a terrible thump to Mr. Thomsons family. I feel for Joseph*, - he certainly expected a very different issue, - but perhaps some other parts of the family may not be the worse for it. - But has not the Dr. asssumed a little importance on the occasion? -

We had a gentleman from London a few days ago, who was curious enough to attend a gentleman in London who professes to make anyone write not only legibly, but well, in the course of half a dozen lessons. - He was at that time attended by some of the first Gentlemen in the Kingdom in order to improve their hands. - The principle on which he proceeds seems very simple, substituting angular turns for oval or round ones, - & in order to give a little more freedom to the hand, nothing but the little finger is allowed to rest upon the paper, - I mean that neither the wrist nor any part of the arm rests upon the paper. - His first Lesson is this

Indeed in doing this well, the whole art consists, - as from these, all the letters of the Alphabet may be easily formed, thus

Writing finished in this manner is beautiful and as it is much more easily done, I have little doubt, but it will soon supersede round writing. - The gentleman gave me two or three specimens of his writing but I cannot imitate them. It is rather small and something in appearance to this, -

*This last is line is something like. - What think you of the plan? - Wishing
you a joyful conclusion to the labours of the season, and a month of pleasure
as well as of liberty, with best respects to Mrs. Lorrain & family,*

    I am,

        Dear Sir,

            Yours very Sincerely,

              Mark Aitken.

[*The reference to Joseph Thomson would appear to concern the son
of Jedburgh's Town Clerk, who was licensed to preach in 1814. He was
presented by the Prince Regent to Ednam and was involved in a libel
case against a Roxburgh schoolmaster. - Ed]

This is the last letter from Mark Aitken in the Collection. After a spell as a teacher in Sunderland, he was ordained in 1816 to Robinson's Lane Presbyterian Chapel there. A year later he married Eliza, daughter of Gilbert Bannerman of Banff. Their son Robert was born in 1818 and a daughter, Mary Ann, in 1819. Robert died at sea in 1841.

Mark Aitken became minister at Dyke in Morayshire, but took part in the Disruption of 1843 and was obliged to move to Forres, where he stayed for 10 years, his wife dying in 1850. In 1852, Brodie of Brodie gave a site for a new Kirk, and a Manse was built the following year.

In 1855 Aitken's health broke down due to stress and he was eventually "laid aside". He went to live in Brighton with his daughter and her husband, Rev Peter McLaren, originally from Lossiemouth. Mark Aitken died there on 20th June, 1869.

Chapter 12

THOMAS ROBSON

*Great care has been taken in accurately transcibing all letters ·
errors in spelling and punctuation are as per original*

Thomas Robson appears to have been related to William Lorrain for he mentions "our uncle James"; he apparently acted as assistant to him before taking on the school at Newcstleton, a village 20 miles from Hawick and 5 from the historic fortress at Hermitage. Roads in the area had been primitive or non-existent; for 16 miles it was necessary to actually walk in the river on a path known as "Watergate". There were no bridges and a traveller had to cross the river on foot 24 times in 16 miles. Produce for market in Hawick or Langholm was carried on horseback through bogs and marshes with real risk of injury.

Two miles from the settlement at the "Castle of Liddell", which gave its name to Castleton, a new village was constructed in 1793 on the farmland of "Park" by Henry, Duke of Buccleuch. It was laid out in a regular pattern, with large squares and straight streets and was literally a "New Town" when Thomas was appointed to teach at the school which had capacity for over 100 pupils.

William Lorrain wrote Thomas a reassuring letter:

Addressed to Thomas Robson in Lorrain's handwriting

Jedburgh 16th Janr. 1808

Dear Thomas,

*Yours of 20th Decr. last came duly to hand - I think you are perfectly right in making a choice for yourself of the Books which you think proper for School - Murray certainly stands high in the list of school authors and would have rendered himself more universal and useful had his prices been proportioned to the work or even merit of his books. He has exhibited judgement in the selection and interpolations of all his works in his Gram. learning and criticism - but in his French recueil these abilities dwindle gradually into avarice. In a situation like yours and mine there are many circumstances which frequently if not totally prevent us following our own judgements and choices viz. our own popularity and the purse of our employers and in not a few instances the want of a timely propriety in mingling our Sentiments too with theirs that our conduct may seem more from a deference to their opinion than our own choice. In this way we always have our own choice & make theirs subservient - I dare say you will see the propriety of not entirely and at once adopting any new book but by degrees. - You will find Walkers Dictionary a real Treasure. We have been labouring at it for a good while now and its effects are already aparent.(sic) What a pity that there are no small copies of it for the use of Schools! Since I saw you had a conference with a Stationer in Edinr. upon this want in Schools and the consequence I understand is likely to turn to good acct. - *Mrs. Flintuff is very anxious to try her fortune in shaking her foot at Castleton. Do you think that a School could be made there for her? Would you advise her to make a trial? She hopes your support and waits for your opinion.*

I am happy to hear of the increase of your School and hope soon to see my first Ideas of your situation realised - if I fail in them I would have you to blame and not your Situation -

Do you ever hear from Cannobie how Mr. Russel the Minister is? It being the place where my Father worshiped a word on it now and then would be acceptable - Your friends and acqs here are all well - My sons have been very poorly ever since you left us youngest rather alarming in symptoms but a Fathers fondness frequently always hopes the best. - My wife joins in wishing you all the Compts. of the Season and many happy returns - Let me hear from you soon.

I am

Dear Thomas,
Yours sincerely,
Wm. Lorrain.

[*The name Flintoff appears several times. Mr. Flintoff had a theatre in Selkirk in 1804 *(p.20)*. Here is Mrs. Flintoff - his wife? - giving dancing lessons in Jedburgh - at the Grammar School? *(p.33)* Mark Aitken mentions that she has a dancing school in Coldstream in 1814. And in January 1816 a baby girl, Margaret Flintoff, daughter of John, is buried in Kelso churchyard. - Ed]

Castleton 23d Jany 1810

Dear Sir,

    I suppose you will have heard long ere this that the bees are again got into my head - If you knew the reasons why you would not blame me, but these to you would not at all be interesting and are far too tedious for a written detail - I would have written you much sooner but matters have always been, & still are, in an indeterminate state - A fortnight however or three weeks will now resolve the business - Whether I go or stay - I only intend to stay upon the condition that I may attend the College, if the Heritors refuse this I mean to give in my resignation & set off for Liverpool & London at both which endeavours have already been made for a situation & have a promise of one in the latter in the course of a week or two provided I were upon the spot - I shall not be more particular till I can speak with greater certainty - I am not certain but I may have to pass your way to Dryburgh in about three weeks to Mr. Riddell, the Duke's Chamberlain - but if not shall write you - Please communicate the above to my Uncle James - But say you not a word of my two pounds all this time - It is certainly high time it was returned either by bringing or sending, which I intend shall be the case in the course of above mentioned time with 20% of thanks upon it - Indeed the principal reason for delay since Martinmas has either been the want of a proper conveyance or the neglect of it when it occured - With best respects to Mrs. L. & little ones

    I am Dear Sir

        Yours respectfully,

        Thos. Robson

P.S. Have been unwell some time past but got quite better - Have had two diff. letters from brother Jas. lately who is in Ireland.

[James Robson was in the army, probably training for Wellington's forthcoming battles against Napoleon - Ed].

Dear Sir,

    Now that I have got a little time to recollect myself & form some idea of matters here, I sit down to do myself the pleasure of conversing for a moment with an absent friend. The subjects of discourse I fear will be but trifling & contain little information or novelty consequently not much entertainment - but coming from an old acquaintance & fellow labourer, may not be altogether unacceptable. From the time of leaving you at Jedburgh, till the present, shall briefly mention a few of the occurrences which have intervened. I arrived in Liddisdale on the Friday Night hastened through my business & left it on the Monday night, reaching Carlisle about seven next Morning. Then took a seat in the heavy Coach setting off at 6 oclock P.M. same day & arriving here on the Wednesday (day following) much about the same hour. But such a voyage as we had between Carlisle & Lancaster I never had before & wish to God I may never have again. At Carlisle four Jolly Tars took a passage upon Deck, having first taken their grog pretty freely. Not an opportunity upon the road of taking in fresh provisions (Grog) but was embraced contrary to all that could be done, swearing they would have their grog In spite of the Devil & his Father too. One of them at last fell overboard & was left in the passage as also another who had taken too much of his dose. This gave us some relief. Every moment I expected we should be upset. So long as we kept straight, we in the Cabin might have done very well but for a (I had almost said damned) drunken guzzle that tormented us perpetually & kept himself so by fresh supplies from his pocket. I could have seen the old Devil at his proper abode - of those in the same end of the Coach he made a resting Couch alternately, & of those in the opposite end spitting boxes. We at length taught him better behaviour by a few solid shakes & squeezes. However they say it is seldom an ill day when followed by a good night. Here I now am in Liverpool, safe & sound wind & limb. My agreement at present is only temporary & to be allowed what is thought reasonable until a more permanent agreement be made. That I daresay will not be more than at the rate of £50 per An. neither, from what passed the other day, do I suppose he is inclined to allow more in time coming - thinking within himself, as I am convinced that he has me entirely at his mercy. In this I shall shortly undeceive him as I have the offer of another situation in which I can have £65 per An.: liberty in the meantime to accept of a better situation; & interest used to procure it. Even the £65 pounds will barely afford maintenace as I find that it requires all my economy & frugality to make 20/- a week cover my board *washing & lodging. All these are very high in Liverpool - the last I pay 6/ - a week & find myself very comfortable. My employment so far has been entirely upon the books which were fallen very much behind. This however I consider as an advantage to me. The leeway I have now nearly brought up. But I find I must stop short at present. Ere long will write you again. Please let my Uncle James know that I am well & if anything particular happens with him have the goodness to let me know. With respects to Mrs. L.*

I remain Dear Sir,
Yours sincerely,
Thos. Robson

at Messrs. G. & J. Blake's,
  Soap Boilers,
  Blundel Street,
  Liverpool.

Liverpool 16th Sepr 1810

Mr. Lorrain,

Dear Sir,
I wrote you about a month after my arrival here, which I trust you would receive, & intended to have sent the second ere now but have scarcely had time to do so. I mentioned in my last that it was uncertain if I remained in my first situation. It is now certain that I have left it & have been with Messrs Geo. & James Blake Soap-Boilers since the middle of May- Men from the Neighbourhood of your native - they deal very extensively in that line. We have two travellers who sell by commission & one of the Mastermen frequently out himself. I have now made three excursions, the two first only two or three days each the last ten days over into Yorkshire as far as Leeds Wakefield etc. Travelling I by no means relish in the way we take it. Our hours at home are from 6 a.m. to 9 p.m. with half an hour to breakfast and an hour to Dinner. Notwithstanding that I have had my health very well which I attribute chiefly to the stirring about, my department being to send the goods out, also to attend goods coming in. To assist in keeping the Books & to make out the Journey Accts. etc. for the difft travellers - . For a man to get forward in the world without either friends to aid, or means to accomplish his aims is a very difficult matter indeed. A judicious plan early laid down & steadily pursued is certainly most proper. Happy the

man who has been directed in one way or other to such a choice. For my part, I seem to spend a precious part of my life in learning how to spend the remainder. But it is now my Maxim "whatever is, is right"

When I forwarded Walker's Dictionary to Mr. Renwick I directed him to pay the price to you. That I trust he has done. Perhaps the 10/6 from Erskine of Melross is not yet recovered. I am sorry I have it not in my power at present to return you the balce of what I recd about a year ago nor will I be able for some months to come. Please write me on receipt of this & say if you have recd these sums with all news & particulars. How my Uncle James & Wife are & how he now stands with regard to his pecuniary embarrassments etc. I should wish to hear how he is going on from time to time. Be so good as let him know that you have recd this - I shall expect your letter every week & with best repects to Mrs. L. I remain

>Dear Sir,
>>Your mot Obed y
>>Thos. Robson

P.S. Saw my brother Jas. here on the Regt. landing from Ireland.
Please Direct at Messrs. G. & J. Blakes, Soap-Boilers
>>Blundell Street
>>Liverpool.

>>>Liverpool 18th Feb 1811

Very Dear Sir,

>I have only time to give you a hurried scrawl without descending to particulars. Your esteemed favour was handed me on my return home the beginning of last month. Its contents both pleased & surprised - who would have thought that the seemingly extinguished old love of R.R. & J. Renwick would have rekindled. What have you made of Miss Tibbie Renwick, whose accomplishments for the agreeable companion & bosom friend are not surpassed by any. Has she entered into the solemn league & covenant with Mr. Mates fm Edin - how does Wm. come on - & is Jno yet the Bachelor - I am really sorry for Bailie Robinsons family, but should hope they are not left in indigence. At any rate they are left among those who, I doubt not will be friendly to the fatherless & widow - Have you got your big house for administering Jeddart Justice & other improvements completed or yet carried into effect.

>I have heard from my Brother the other day. The Regt is under orders to embark for Portugal but not yet gone. He is quite recovered in his health, a piece of news I did not expect. As to his going abroad (if he

should go) I consider it upon the whole favourable. There are matters both for & against, but the former I think considerably overbalances the latter. Concerning myself, this is just me & like the Wife I am just where I was. Did I mention the promise I have got of £20 advance in salary for next year. I am nominated for a South Journey through Stafford, Warwick, Leicester, Derby & Nottinghamshire. The Accts are made out, but perhaps one of the partners may yet go himself. One of them has prematurely returned today off the Yorkshire Journey not having finished it, & as I suppose out of consate with himself not having succeeded well. The other partner is very clever. We are closing last years Accts & are engaged almost night & day - Things are in a deplorable state here. Failures to a heavy amt take place almost every day some said as far as £300,000. Hundreds of Clerks altogether out of employt - If things do not speedily take a turn it is impossible to say what may be the result. I am this moment informed the wind is turned & will blow me north instead of south. I set out tomorrow or Tuesday & will be as far as Dumfries - I will not however have time to come & see you. Have you the name of Miss Billerwells Beau - I am sometimes at Huddersfield - Please give Uncle Jas what information this supplies & remember to Mrs. L. - J. Veitch & all enquiring friends. Verily I say unto thee I should like thy ans

    Blunders, blunders, blunders - farewell
          Thos. Robson

P.S. Direct at Messrs Blakes Soap boilers
      Blundell Street
      Liverpool

                    Liverpool   21st July 1811

Dear Sir,
      Were it not to grant the request of my answer contained in your last I really think I should be culpable in putting you to the expense of Postage, so barren of any thing in the least interesting do I foresee this to be. It is almost impossible to select one distinct Idea from my muddy stock today, my head being filled with ill nature & the tooth ache. For the latter I have had my face tied up this week past being so much swelled, but am a good deal better. -

    I rejoice with you that you have now got room to reel in, & as to my reeling with you this season I think there is little probability that I shall.

Had I continued traveller I probably might have had the pleasure, but it was only yesterday that I was asked to take the sole direction of the Books, together with that of the Cash, in consequence of their nephew who kept the latter, having formed the resolution to return to Scotland. This I accepted in an indifferent sort of manner of course for the time being though I do not consider any great preferment in the first instance yet it may lead to it, or prepare for it, in some other quarter. Being Cash Keeper is certainly attended with considerable anxiety & also loss in some instances, both our late Cash Keepers having fallen considerably short. They are debited with the deficiency one to the amt of £30.

I am happy to hear so good a report of our Uncle James, - I take for granted you will remember me to him first opportunity, - I have not heard from my brother since Feby I think. The Regt is now in Portugal under Lord Wellington & as I expect my brother with them. I see by yesterdays Courier that one of the Troops belonging to the Regt sent forward as a picquet were pushed too far & surprised and taken. It is not his troop unless his Captain has been changed. Would you be surprised to hear of me becoming a soldier? A friend has offered to make application for an Ensigncy if I sincerely wish it & doubts not but it will be obtained. Were it not that I fear it will require more pecunia than I am master of I do not know but I shall urge the matter. What do you think of it? I imagine I hear you saying, "Oh Tam Tam! still the Bees are in your head" This however has cost me a good deal of thinking lately & if I thought I were to be a Clerk for life, I should certainly use every exertion to attain to the above mentioned. However I am not uneasy. Times were never worse, & I comfort myself that as I can fight my way now, I shall do better when they mend.

Should like to hear from you before I determine upon the abovementioned, whether I shall pursue the idea or not, as it will not be long before I must say either yes or no.

With best respects to Mrs. Lorrain
I am
Dear Sir
Yours respectfully
Thos. Robson

P.S. Direct as before viz at Messrs Blakes.
Excuse blunders.

For some reason, William Lorrain kept a copy of his advice to Thomas:

Jedburgh 29th July 1811

Dear Sir,

Your favour I received a few days ago & was happy to hear of your health & prosperity. You wish me to state my opinion with regard to the proposal which has been made you respecting the Life of a Soldier which it is not in my power decidedly to give unless I were acquainted with the will & ability of your Friend who has made the proposal. He might easily obtain for you an Ensigncy but will he also advance 60£ or 100£ to fit you out for that situation? Will he abide by you untill you have served the Regular time for a promotion & during that time will he advance at least £30 per an? Will he have Interest, Means, or Inclination, to patronise your promotion after you have served the legal time? If your friend does not undertake more than a part of the above queries it would not be very safe to make an experiment which though not principally yet most entirely rests upon supposition. In our present situations we see all the fors & againsts but from a want of experience the livelyness of our own imaginations which dwells more upon the againsts than the fors makes us not unfrequently fly from the ills we have to others that we know not of: gives us an Ideal picture of other situations by drawing conclusions from the charming prospect of the successful individual which generally the unprominent figure of the unfortunate individual buries in oblivion his sufferings. Such I may term the moral stratagem of Humanity, but this the author of our nature seems to have implanted in us for good purpose if we fairly reason from experience & analogy - My opinion candidly is that you should not be too prompt to act or too decided in your opinion and if possible discover the motives which induces your Friend hence you will better judge of the desirability and extent of his Friendship. You will also remember that you are now at that time of life which should settle your views in one way or other - Could you not form a prudent Connexion with some fair hand and good heart that might secure you a comfortable life either by Stock or Interest? A good address, genteel manner, a clear head, and an affectionate heart might I think secure your comfort and success in life much easier than by powder & shot. Friends here are all well.

I am

Dear Sir

Yours most faithfully

Wm Lorrain

Liverpool 10th Novr 1811

Mr. Lorrain
    Dear Sir,

       I duly recd your favour but cannot promise to relinquish altogether the scheme mine mentioned, but of that no more at present. Whatever line of life providence may allot me, shall, & must be considered as the best. Yet still my inclination is near equally divided between that above alluded to & the life of a country Farmer. To jeer poor Tom Dame Fortune has, though the desire is so strong, denied the power of obtaining the object, & seems to have doomed me, in one capacity or another, to be a Quill driver all my days. But whether in that or in any other capacity, with contentment (philosophers say) a man may be happy, but to complete the happiness I begin to be of Mr. Lorrain's opinion; that he must first take unto himself a Wife - & in domestic comfort find his object most easily attained. But the World & its customs now positively declare that money is an essential ingredient in the composition. Now here is the rub, as that is yet very scanty with poor Tom. But "stand out my shin" as I become cash keeper & Commander in chief over the Books tomorrow & enter to £100 Salary with the commencement of the new year. The recollection of having advanced from £60 to £100 in less than 2 years when times are so peculiarly adverse, bids me hope for something handsome, should they resume their former prosperity, & says "up higher yet my bonnet". Of myself enough - now for others. How are all your good family - yourself, your Wife, & Callans, & how monie hae ye now? My Uncle James & partners I think you have not said since Whitsunday if he remains or is removed or what. I take for granted he still continues in his ordinary state of health, not having informed me anything to the contrary. Please remember me to him & partner first opportunity & say I am well & should be glad to hear from him. From my sisters in Tyne & Redwater I suppose you will hear oftener than I do. I heard lately from two of them at which time all were well. I have not heard from my Brother since I wrote you. The Regt was much engaged in the affairs of the 25th & 27th Sepr and suffered considerable loss. Whether he was or is amongst the survivors or not gives me great anxiety to know. I have since wrote to him but cannot yet expect an answer. So soon as I receive one if ever shall suppose you so much interested as to wish to know. To hear from you, with me, is to hear good news from a far Country. I suppose you understand me.
    I am

      Dearest Sir,
          Yours with true regard
          Thos. Robson

P.S. As I send the M.S. hope you will excuse corrections & blunders. The labour bestowed on your M.S. on Book-keeping & pouring upon Mayor, now brings its reward. One useful lesson never to be idle. How are Mrs. Renwick's famy   T.R.

Liverpool 2nd Feby 1812

Mr. Lorrain
   Dear Sir,
            *I duly received your esteemed favour, the conclusion of which requested me to write soon. Unless something had intervened I think I should have had nothing to write. Short as the time is since its receipt, it has brought me the intelligence, that I must sustain the irreparable loss of an only Brother. He is now no more. By Wednesday's post (the 29th Ult) I received the disagreeable information, given by a Serjeant of the Regt & of the same Troop. I suspected something was amiss as I had wrote twice without receiving any answer though sufficient time had elapsed. The latter the Serjeant very properly & kindly opened & explained the silence which sickness & Death had caused. You may perhaps recollect it being mentioned in the Papers that the Regt (11th Light Dragoons) was one of those particularly engaged on the 23rd & 25th Sepr. These affairs he survived. But he whom the sword had spared was not to escape. Death had marked him as a Victim & on the 26th the day after the engagement, by sickness struck the fatal blow. On that day he fell sick of an ague & fever _ a complaint of which he says hundreds, nay thousands, have died there lately) was sent to the Rear to the general Hospital at *Castella Branco, & on or about the 10th Decr last paid the debt to nature which we yet owe.*
   He is not the only relation I have lost, nor yet the nearest, having already lost the best of parents. For their loss I trust I felt, & also still feel, a proper sorrow. But his loss is attended by circumstances which makes it grievous indeed. By his folly, at that time a blameable folly, he brought himself into a life of hardship & sorrow, for which he repented every day he was a Soldier. As a consequence of it he was doomed to visit that country "from whose bourne he shall never return", & is most likely against his choice. When I consider these matters, & that he is now gone, I can only pity, not condemn, his conduct. That from the 26th Sepr to the 10th Decr wearisome days & nights were appointed him, & not only among foreigners & strangers, unattended by relations or friends on the bed of death, & perhaps, nay very probably, not one that would

administer even a cup of cold water to cool the burning thirst of a fever, or support the tremblings of an ague, but the refusal might occasion the loss of a sinecure place - When I consider these I feel all the bitterness of grief & begin to charge myself with a want of brotherly affection that I did not use more endeavours to effect his liberation by some means or other. But this to you may perhaps appear foolish at any rate, must be gloomy & tiresome. With it however my letter at this time must be chiefly or wholly occupied. The News of the day seem unimportant neither am I in a mood to collect, or rehearse them. With myself there is nothing new.

You will please intimate my Brother's Death to Our Uncle James & tell him I intend to write him soon. I have wrote to all my sisters, the unpleasant news. Please give my best respects to Mrs. L. & to Mr. Wm Home when you see him & ask him what he thinks of the Army - Yours always calculated to cheer, would be acceptable at this time - therefore hope you will write me in a few days. In good health, though but in low spirits.

I remain Dear Sir
    Yours with true regard
        Thos. Robson

[* Castelo Branco is in the Portuguese district of Beira Baixa. - Ed]

                  Liverpool 25th October 1812
Dear Sir,
      The information your last favour conveyed of your domestic tranquillity & flourishing state of your School gave me real pleasure. May the clouds of adversity never interrupt the calm & prosperous sunshine. That I do not write you oftener is not from want of inclination (as I hope our correspondence will never entirely fall away so long as we can write letters) but from the monotonous sucession of time & events with me for some time past. This being the case, makes me loath to make you spend money for that which satisfieth not.

I was very happy to hear of Mr. Shaws succeeding to Langholm Kirk. It is a preferment which he has for a long while deserved. - At the same time I was sorry for the sudden death of Mr. Martin. He was certainly a good man. Laying private friendship aside & viewing only the ministerial abilities of the two, the Parishioners of Langholm need not regret the change. More happy may they be that the Successor was not our Dr. Kirkpatrick Minister of the Scotch Kirk here if everyone estimates him *for a Minister & preacher as I do. I have been informed that he was a Candidate. He was twice down in Scotland about the time. From this circumstance & being unpopular here I credit the report.*

Perhaps the Annals of election, whether Parliamentary or local, do not record an instance of a more obstinate contest, than has been lately witnessed for the representation of this Borough. The Candidates, as you are probably informed by the Newspapers, were Mr. Canning (lately prime Minister) & General Gascoyne one of the late representatives, supported by the Town & what may be called the loyalists, or ministerial party, & a Mr. Brougham, a Cumberland man & a Mr. Creevy a Native of Liverpool but now residing in Norfolk, both Lawyers, supported by what are termed the opposition here. The Election lasted nine days, but finished with the strong Majority of 500 in favour of Canning & 400 in favour of Gascoyne. General Tarleton the other late representative offered himself but could not poll more than 7 votes. Canning is I think the finest public speaker I have yet heard. He addressed the electors each night, & so great was the crowds that they have been reckoned on some instances at 30,000. Brougham is a man of abilities but a factious turbulent dog - ..(torn)..at present agitating a fresh agreement with my employers. So soon as able will communicate the result. You will be good enough always to remember me to our Uncle James & to let me know how he is when you write. That habit of his whether natural or acquired is so interwoven with the man that I believe they must live & die together. With best Compliments to Mrs. L. & such as you think merited by enquiring friends, if any, I remain Unfeignedly yours

> *Thos. Robson*

Liverpool, 29 Decr 1812

Mr. Lorrain
> *Dear Sir,*

It is now some time since I had this pleasure & I think longer since I had the pleasure of receiving one from you. When I begin to disclose the chief object of this you will be thinking (& perhaps justly) that it is more interest than pleasure that has prompted me to address you at this time. Some time ago I spoke to my employers respecting the terms to be allowed for the ensuing year. I then asked permission to do business on my own account & though the permission was not granted it was not denied. This I construed into a tacit consent. I have now an opportunity for clearing a very handsome profit upon a certain article

*but want a small capital to begin with. From £20 to £25. Might I count
upon your assistance for this sum. I should be able to return it I hope by
the latter end of March with interest & if ever I had it in my power to make
a proper acknowledgement either to you or yours it should not be wanting.-
The scheme is in conjunction with the Traveller. We are certain of a profit
of £30 p. Cent and no risk. If you can venture that amount & will send it
in a Bill at 40 days or 2 Months it will be a favour that would not soon be
forgot. I intend to be with my friends on the borders so soon as the days
get to a tolerable length & should then return you the pecunia.*

*There is no news here of importance. The capture of the Macedonian
causes universal regret. No hopes are entertained here of a settlement
with America.- This is unfortunate for many in L'pool & your hble servt
amongst others. I intend writing my Uncle in a short time please give my
compliments to him - & to all friends & acquaintances in & about Jedburgh.
I accidentally stumbled upon *Miss Somerville's marriage in the papers
the other day to His Majesty's late Consul General at the Island of Madeira
- This I should suppose will meet the Doctors approbation & flatter his
vanity not a little - Please write me in a post or two & say whether I may
expect the Needful or not. With respects to Mrs. Lorrain*

     I am
        Dr. Sir
           Yours in sincerity
              Thos. Robson
P.S. Just going to bed . T.R.

[*Miss Janet Somerville, daughter of Rev. Thomas, married Joseph
Pringle in Jedburgh on 8th December 1812. - Ed]

                                 Liverpool 6th March 1813
Dear Sir,
     *This will be handed you by Mr. Archibald Blake a near relation of
my employers. He is a young man of prudent conduct and good abilities,
& one with whom, you will naturally suppose, I am pretty intimate - any
attention you will be pleased to shew him will be considered a favour
bestowed on your humble servant I.*

     *By him I shall expect you will return the compliment (if mine will bear
the appellation) & send me the news of the day &c. About the latter end
of April or beginning of May I propose shewing my Phiz. amongst my
border friends & will probably have the pleasure of drinking a nogging of
Jeddart whiskey with you. In expectation of this I shall forbear particulars*

at present & for Liverpool news refer you to my friend Mr. A. Blake.

With the foregoing leaf he was so good as to furnish me, which he procured from the designers & proprietors having been a Pupil with them twelvemonths. As it contains the terms of a brother in trade, I thought it might not be altogether unacceptable & that its perusal might afford a transitory - Amusement -

Expecting by him to hear from you I remain

   Dear Sir,

       Yours with respect

          Thos. Robson

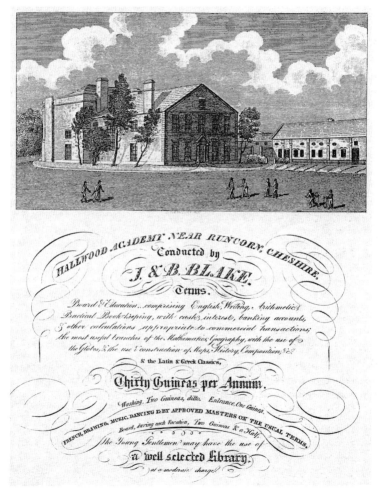

HALLWOOD ACADEMY, NEAR RUNCORN, CHESHIRE,

Conducted by

J. & B. BLAKE.

Terms.

Board & Education...comprising English, Writing, Arithmetic, Practical Book-keeping, with cash, interest, banking accounts, & other calculations appropriate to commercial transactions; the most useful branches of the Mathematics, Geography, with the use of the Globes, & the use & construction of Maps, History, Composition, &c.

& the Latin & Greek Classics,

Thirty Guineas per Annum.

Washing, Two Guineas, ditto. Entrance, One Guinea.

FRENCH, DRAWING, MUSIC, DANCING &c BY APPROVED MASTERS ON THE USUAL TERMS,

Board, during each Vacation, Two Guineas & a Half,

The Young Gentlemen may have the use of

a well selected Library,

at a moderate charge.

Mr. Willm Lorrain

Dear Sir,

As intended I called at Chesters yesterday upon our Uncle whom I found in his ordinary way - I also fulfilled my intention in suggesting the propriety of changing the mode of managing his ground if he continued to hold it & also mentioned that I thought it probable he would be much more comfortable without it altogether - with respect to a change in mode of management he readily admitted the reasons to be just, but with respect to quitting it he seemed reluctant though I am persuaded our joint urgency would prevail with him in that too - only it will be necessary I suppose to hold it till next year at any rate - I find several of his intimates have signified their readiness to assist him in procuring another Galloway but are apprehensive you might put in a nugatory claim for it when obtained. This apprehension I took upon me to assure him was groundless - you will as you mentioned find what they are disposed to do - & if they are only promises they intend to give you may advance two or three pounds & charge it to me which with 25/- I left with him should amount to half the expense or thereabouts of buying such a Galloway as he wants - I also mentioned the Earthenware of which as to the success he seemed very sanguine. I shall write you again so soon as I return home & by that time or immediately after expect to receive your favour giving me all particulars - In good health with best respects to Mrs. L. I remain

Dear Sir

Yours unfeignedly

Thos. Robson

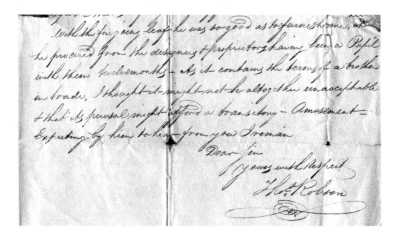

Chapter 13

WILLIAM BERRY SHAW
(1776-1856)

*Great care has been taken in accurately transcibing all letters -
errors in spelling and punctuation are as per original*

William Shaw was born in Abbotshall, Fife, the son of Rev. George Shaw. He studied at St. Andrew's where he shared a room with Thomas Chalmers, who in 1843 was one of the leaders of the Disruption of the Church of Scotland.

In 1801, Shaw was appointed assistant minister in the parish of Roberton near Hawick, where the Rev. James Hay, the incumbent minister, was ill.

Roberton 5th Feby 1803

My dear Lorrain,

> *As there is a Selkirk man to pass this way today I take the opportunity of sending you a few lines. I am surprised you did not write me an account of your jaunt with Mitchel to Howford. The report most prevailent here at present is that you are just on the top of your marriage. So that I am daily expecting a call to Selkirk, and have a grand form prepared for the occasion. My best respects to the dear object - I had hopes lately of my Rider's speedy dismission from this mortal state. He was in such extremity, that his friends had lost all hopes of his recovery: no less than three physicians were called, and Dr. Douglas sent for express from Galashiels; and I am informed by one who saw it, that he had thrown up an incredible quantity of bloody matter. I have heard no further accounts for two weeks. There must be something particular in his complaint known to Douglas: for you may recollect I mentioned to you when last at Selkirk, the latter told me that the state of Mr. Hay's health was such that he should not be surprised if he were called to Edinr suddenly before the end of January.*

> *The following anecdote may not be unacceptable to a lover, and I can safely intrust it with a friend. About three weeks ago in the forenoon I came over the hills from (you need not be informed) where. By the way I recollected having come from the same place one evening in August last, and could not help reflecting on the different aspect of the scene with the no less different state of my mind, which formed a curious contrast.*

*That evening was calm and pleasant, the moon peeping over the summits
of the hills, and sometimes hiding her face behind their dusky shade, as if
in sport, while her mild beams discovered the surrounding landscape.
But my mind was agitated, and clouded with gloomy melancholy. The
late forenoon the cold was intense, the hills white with snow, the wind
blew boistrously, and the hail, every time I looked up, threatened to blind
my eyes. Yet my mind was placid, chearful, and serene. This shows how
little our happiness depends upon external objects; at least, how little it is
often affected by their immediate influence, and what ascendancy a
virtuous attachment has obtained over my heart. Then jealous of my
Eliza's constancy, and deprived of the usual smiles of her countenance,
in vain did Nature display her beauties to my view; all appeared a dreary
waste, the moon shone but not for me, the song of the Nightingale sounded
harsh in my ear. Now happy in my Eliza's affections, I feel not the
piercing cold, I can laugh at the fury of the storm, and rejoice amid the
desolations of winter. - But the man is come and in haste, so I must have
done. I shall be in Selkirk the beginning of next month - hope to hear
from you and ever remain*

*Your sincere and affectionate friend
Will B. Shaw*

The "Eliza" who was being so ardently courted by Shaw was one of
two sisters who are thought to have been Scott's inspiration for the
characters of "Minna" and "Brenda" in his novel "The Pirate". Margaret
Scott of Deloraine was Brenda - "serene and lustrous as a summer day"
- while Eliza was Minna - "dark and stormy as an Oriental night".
Margaret married Dr. Thomas Anderson of Selkirk.

Roberton 6th March 1803

My Dear Lorrain,

*I have continually occasion to complain of a bad memory. Your
wine decanters and sugar box never occured to my thoughts on Thursday till
I had reached Borthaugh. I remember however that there was a time, and at
no great distance too, when the epithet attached to the former would have
prevented such stupid forgetfulness. But now every thing is absorbed in the
vortex of love. I had almost forgotten today that I had to preach, and was
sitting a little before kirk-time busy making verses to my mistress. I came
from the dear place yesterday.- Mr. Stavert tells me today that he had a letter
from Edinr. which was written on Thursday last mentioning that the doctors*

Eliza Scott of Deloraine

had then no hopes of Hay's recovery; and that Dr. Douglas was in the company. Heaven in mercy send relief to the distressed!

You may depend upon my procuring the above articles on Tuesday, and they shall be sent with the Fly on Wednesday. You mentioned a silver thimble, but as We both forgot the measure, I cannot venture to bring one. You may depend upon my being back before the first Sunday of April. I wrote out the form last night. Would that somebody were writing one for myself!

My love to the dear object.   Yours always
Will B. Shaw

The next letter is written from his father's house:

Abbotshall 30th Octr 1803

My Dear Lorrain,

I had yours this afternoon, and am much obliged to you for your particular attention to my interests.   Having mentioned my sermon to Clarkson at Traquair, I ordered Armstrong the printer, in a letter I sent him from Edr to send Clarkson 2 score copies, the one at 6d and the other on somewhat finer paper at 1/-. I mentioned that as several of my acquaintance had observed that 6d was too cheap, he would better cast off 300 at that price, and 200 on finer paper at 1/-. I will be obliged to you to give a copy of the latter to Mr. Pringle, Haining, with my compts and if you think proper, another to Yair.   But alas! there is nothing but vexation in this world.   I found yesterday upon looking over my scrawl copy (for I preached it here today) that in the hurry of writing it over I had omitted a principal paragraph; which I beg you will write on the bottom of the page of the one you deliver to Mr. P. It comes in near the end of the 2d head, after the peace, safety, and prosperity of the united kingdom.   If the inhabitants of Great Britain be thus true to themselves; if, in the fear of God, and in a due subjection to the higher powers, they be unanimous and steady in their own defence, (and I feel confident in my persuasion that they in general will) they have little to fear from the threats or attempts of a foreign enemy; they may set the whole world at defiance; they may be annoyed and invaded, thousands and tens of thousands may fall in the painful struggle; but the nation never can be conquered or subdued. Who would not disdain the thought of seeking his personal safety in the hour of danger at the expense of honour? Who would not hazard everything and valiantly stand forth, and fight to the last drop of his blood in defending himself, and all that is dear to him, from the ignominious, the inexpressible horrors of French Tyranny? Who would not prefer a glorious and happy death to a mean and wretched existence? Who would not court an honourable grave amid the ruins of his country? If I forget thee, O my country! let my right hand forget its cunning; if I do not remember thee, let my tongue cleave to the roof of my mouth; if I prefer not thy liberty to life, thy interest above my chief joy! Pray for the peace of Britain, they shall prosper etc. etc. - But I am affraid the margin will not contain it. However, if another edition be cast off, I will correct it.   I was so confoundedly hurried at the time. If you insert the above, score out the preceding clause - being ready to stand forth in the defence of all that is dear to us and - I have also omitted an appropriate text of Scripture just before "These sayings are faithful" etc. in the last head viz. "O the depth of the riches, both of the wisdom and knowledge of God! how unsearchable are his judgements and his ways past finding out!" - I declare I almost long to enjoy the pleasing slumber of the grave! This sermon I fear will gain me enemies. I attack the irreligious example of the generality of the great - and yet I am confident that what I say is undeniable fact. I also speak the words of truth and soberness in my second head; I show that I am no partyman; and consequently what I say in favour of the government will make a deeper impression upon the minds of the people. - Yet I will be condemned for that by your violent politicians. I will even be suspect for what is advanced in the last head. But mens conscia recti etc. That is a comfortable word. If you think you can sell more in Selkirk than the number Clarkson receives, you can send to Armstrong at Hawick for what you want.

I drank tea with Smith. He is well and desired me to send him a dozen and a half. I hope to meet with you at Traquair this day three weeks, and to hear your new proofs of the sleeping opinion. Compts to Clarkson, and to the dear creature. Rob desires his best respects- intends to give them something to chew their cud upon at Traquair. My sermon was well liked here today. Mrs. Ferguson of Raith was in church, and highly pleased. I hope Clarkson will get Paton to preach this day three weeks at Roberton, if Russel refuses, and in case of getting nobody, let Arkle know the sabbath before to intimate no sermon.

> Yours from the heart,

> Will B. Shaw

Courthill 31st 1804

Dear Lorrain,

I was at Jedburgh on Saturday and Sunday last, and had the audience of your friend Mrs. Reid. I did not get my sermon on persecution written out, but luckily the one I gave in the forenoon (which was the only part of the day she was out) was violently heretical. Among other touches was the following - " We must study to divest our religious manners of the indiscreet intollerance of the illiberal bigot" etc. which, if I had known she was in church, and where she sat, I would not have failed to repeat, with a wave of my hand indicating contempt.

Dr. Somerville says he thinks there is every probability that you will get Jedburgh, and even that you will be requested to come. There is only one other candidate who has the least chance, but what his name is I have forgotten. I think he is an assistant in some accademy, but the Dr. thinks he would not do for boarders, and I see that he would very fain have you. The reason of his not writing you was that the meeting was adjourned, but it holds on Thursday next, after which he will write to you. I told him that you had made up your mind to accept of it, provided the wages were such as he mentioned. he thinks they will; only those who learn all the several branches during the same hours are not expected to pay so high for each. He is still not to tell them expressly that you mean to accept, as he wishes them to request you to come; which he thinks will be more respectable. He says there is the clerkship and some other little emoluments which he would endeavour to get increased for you; but does not chuse to hold forth as an inducement anything that is not absolutely certain -

I got notice last week of my brother's ticket having drawn a prize of twenty pounds. With best repsects to Mrs. Lorrain
      I am ever yours sincerely
      Wm B Shaw

            Roberton 11th Sept.1811

My Dear Lorrain,
      You would no doubt be cursing me most bitterly for not being at your examination according to promise. I can assure you it was my sincere intention to have been with you, and accordingly promised to Strachan to come to Hawick from Selkirk the night before, and go down with him next morning. But omnia vincit amor, et nos sedamus amori. In plain English, I was seised with a violent fit of love, and could not forbear going to see my dear angel. - You may laugh, or scold, as you please - but the time was when you would have allowed the force of this argument. Had I not gone that night, I could not have had the pleasure of seeing her for a long time.

I forgot to tell you that I had used the liberty to put down your name for a copy of my acquaintance Charles Gray's poems. This herewith sent, and also a copy for Mr. Brown of Bedrule, which you will be so good as forward to him by the first opportunity. I hope you will pay me a visit during your vacation. With kindest compts to Mrs. Lorrain in which my brother joins

        I remain
          Yours most sincerely
            Will. B. Shaw

Strachan was speaking in the highest terms of the excellent appearance your scholars made.

My Dear Sir,

I have a little ago sent you £14 by Mr. Rutherford, and take the opportunity of writing you this line by Mr. Elliot who tells me he goes to Jedburgh tomorrow. I had the pleasure of seeing your father and brother at L. on the Sunday. They expected to have met you there. Your mother had been complaining a little, but was better. I am highly pleased with Mr. Scott. He will be a great acquisition to me. Brown I have discovered to be a double deceitful rascal. He held forth against me in a company, that I preached dangerous doctrine etc. Mr. Scott had not time to write you, but said, if you get an opportunity, you may send him 6 copies of the Greek collection. The Modn. of my call is on Thursday the eighth of Octr. and I expect the roup will be either the Wednesday before, or the friday following. I shall let you know, as soon as I hear.

Remember me kindly to Mrs. Lorrain, and believe me Yours most truly

Will B. Shaw

The settlement will be the 1st week of Novr.

P.S. As I have not a five guinea note, I will be owing you the 5/-

"The settlement" refers to Shaw's presentation at Langholm by the Duke of Buccleuch. His brother, Robert Shaw, became minister at Ewes, the neighbouring parish, and between them they exerted considerable influence for 36 years. William Berry Shaw and Eliza Scott of Deloraine finally married at Yarrow on 25th March 1813.

My Dear Lorrain,

I was favoured with yours of the 8th in due course, but have been prevented by various avocations from sooner acknowledging the receipt of it. I did not find it convenient to attend the General Assembly, but chose notwithstanding to keep my turn, in order to prevent Brown from going to do mischief. He is making an odd stir at present to get all the parishes to petition Parlt. relative to the propagation of what he calls the Gospel in India. He very slyly tried to get me cajoled into the measure; and though I told him it was contrary to my sentiments, still he did not desist, but with most officious and indiscreet zeal attempted to compass his end in a kind of clandestine way. He made a fool of himself at the Synod. I had a letter, lately, signed by several ministers requesting me to call another meeting about the business, which I peremptorily refused to do; and I have since a letter from Dr. McMorrin signed by a number of the members approving of my conduct. That fellow *Duncan of Ruthwell is a restless animal, and perfect pest. You would perhaps observe, if you get his Paper, that he represented the Assembly as having petitioned Parlt. against the catholic claims - because this suited his own purpose. I was delighted with the spirit of their petition. It does them more honour than any of their proceedings for many years past. And I was particularly delighted at seeing the pompous intollerant Ass, Ritchie, borne down, and obliged to withdraw his nonsensical motion. I was highly gratified with Smith's visit, and intend to repay him in kind in Octr. I had a letter from him a day or two ago, in which he mentions having heard the intention of Duncan &c. to request me to call the meeting above stated, and that they also had thought of petitioning at some time against the Cc claims. They had even the presumption to send me a budget of printed circular letters for the several members, in which I was made to request their attendance, and lobby that they would intimate the same to their ruling elders!!! I returned them by the same conveyance as, being upon fine writing paper, they were of no use to me. I received by Waugh on his return from last meeting of Synod, five guineas from Smith for you, which you will find enclosed - he mentioned them in his letter. That extra meeting which Brown and Duncan procured by the hold of the elders to be appointed for the same foolish purpose, obliged Smith to leave me on the Monday; and not content with the decision of that meeting, which was given against their object by the Modr's vote, they still wish him to raise the business and think to gain the victory. We leave this on Monday for the Forest and Fife. It will not be in my power to be at the Dr's sacrament, but we will see you some time hence. I saw your father and brother yesterday - all well, except your mother who is still complaining. Mine is in the same state, which makes me somewhat anxious about going to Fife. Your suggestion about the Schoolhouse is not unreasonable, and I will keep it in view. We had a meeting there sometime ago and I thought the matter settled, but it seems Sir John wishes to attend himself on the spot, which I am sorry I cannot do for some weeks to come.

You will surely see us here this summer, and if Mrs. L. accompany you, your visit will be the more acceptable.

Eliza joins me in best respects to you both, and I am ever yours most truly -
Will B. Shaw

[*Duncan of Ruthwell was Rev. Henry Duncan who had just initiated the first "System of Savings Banks" to encourage poor people to save small amounts of money in safety. - Ed]

My Dear Lorrain,

  I take the opportunity of writing you by Mr. Turnbull who preaches at Jedburgh on Sunday next. I never saw a young man acquit himself better before a Presby. He officiated for me last Sunday, and gave great satisfaction. Our friend Brown attempted to have him bound very strictly to the Confession, but I opposed the tyranical proposal, and carried my point.

  I was favoured with yours by my namesake, and return you many thanks for introducing to my acquaintance such an excellent young man.

  Your brother had a fever lately, but was getting better last time I preached at Half Morton. I go there on Sunday next, to accommodate our dissenters here, who have their Sacrament this week.

  I have got all my improvements finished now. The expence has been rather more than I calculated upon, this obliges me to borrow ten or fifteen pounds at present. You have been so very obliging in that way, that I have hardly the face to trouble you further; yet, if you could conveniently spare this sum, it would save me the disagreeable necessity of applying to any other person. The fiars have been very low this year, and the Dukes doers are so mean as to pay those of bear, while all the rest of the Heritors pay barley without a scruple. But I shall take care to have the absurdity rectified against Decr. come a year. We are both set on being as economical as possible, and are determined to cut off every needless expence.

  Eliza and little Agnes are doing well. The latter is very stout, and continues amazingly good. My wife and brother join in kind regards to you and Mrs. Lorrain and family, and I remain always, my Dear Sir,

   Yours faithfully,

   Will B. Shaw

If you can favour me with the above, be so good as transmit it by post.

My Dear Lorrain,

  Yours came safe this morning, enclosing ten pounds sterlg. I think five more will do my business but lest I should run short before I draw in any cash, I will gratefully accept of ten. I saw your father on Sunday last. He said your brother is teaching again, but spoke of some others who had the same fever, and intended to write you to prevent your coming at this time. This is a nervous fever and I am affraid there might be some danger of infection. But you can judge for yourself. If you come, I expect of course to have the pleasure of seeing you here, and a longer visit than last time. My sacrament is Sunday three weeks and

I am resolved to have no tent. Which I intimated at the Chapel along with my reasons. I fear your father, honest man, will not like this innovation. But it was a gross nuisance, and I reckon it my duty to reform such a shocking abuse of the ordinance, to whatever reproach and ill will it may expose me.

My wife joins me in best respects to you and yours, and with a grateful sense of your kindness, I remain my Dear friend,

> *Yours faithfully,*
> *Will B. Shaw*

Some of the inhabitants of Langholm had not been married in the "proper" way and Rev. Shaw made it his business to ensure that this omission was recitfied whenever possible. On one occasion he called on a couple who had been co-habiting for years and the woman shouted up to the loft where her man was working: "Jock, here's the minister. Come doon at yince and get Mairit!"

Langholm Manse 23rd July 1814

My Dear Lorrain,

I have been advised to publish my Thanksgiving sermon, which I have agreed the more readily to do, as it was of no further use to me, and if I can make something by it, so much the better. The convenience of a printing office so near, is a great inducement, and perhaps it may be a means of doing some good to our Langholm Malcontents. I send this under cover to Armstrong, and desire him to transmit it to you with two copies, one for yourself, and another for Dr. Somerville which you will have the goodness to inscribe "from his sincere friend the author". I am only to throw off 350 copies, 200 of which I have ordered to be sent here, and the remainder to be kept at Hawick, till we see how it is likely to sell. Mr. Armstrong is so good as to let the type stand a few weeks, in case we should think of throwing off more, which will probably be the case, and then I could advertise it in the Kelso and some other papers, and send a few to Jedburgh, Selkirk, Edinr Dumfries &c.

If there had not happened to be two rainy days before the Thanksgiving day, I daresay it had not been written.

Your friends are all well, when I heard of them, a few days ago.

Eliza joins in kind respects to you and Mrs. Lorrain and I ever am

> *Yours most truly,*
> *Will B. Shaw*

You would hear of Russell's death, which happened on Tuesday night.

[Rev. Russell was minister at Canonbie - Ed]

Langholm Manse 2d March 1815

My Dear Lorrain,

       I was prevented last night from acknowledging the receipt of your kind letter and the ten pound note enclosed. Many thanks for your prompt assistance. I should be sorry to think of subjecting you to any inconvenience, and therefore desire you will not send any more till the second week of April, as I leave this about the middle of next week, and will not return till the beginning of April. My mother has been sadly afflicted with a nervous disorder these two last summers, and I am anxious to pay her a visit at present when she is in a state to enjoy my company. I have got the promise of Mrs. Elliots cart that her father (Mr. Russell) rode in, and intend taking Eliza and the child by short stages to Selkirk, and then riding on old Grey to Fife. We have been sadly plagued with servants. One I turned off, and the next has been away ten days with a sore finger and her neighbour pretended to be ill and also left us, and poor Eliza was obliged to work herself like a slave. The one with the sore finger, however, is returned, but of little use. They are the curse of human existance. I wish we could do without them! - I should suppose after all, you will find yourself more pleasantly situated in Jedburgh, than you would have been at St. Andrews, though indeed the advantage of a university was a mighty consideration for a rising family of sons. My wife and brother join in kind regards to Mrs. L. yourself and family.

    I remain, my dear Sir, in haste,
        Yours sincerely,
          Will B. Shaw

At this time, William Lorrain was contemplating a move. He seems to have considered a post at St. Andrew's before applying to Glasgow High School.

Langholm 8 April 1815

My Dear Sir,

       I found your kind letter awaiting me on my return home last night, and will be much obliged to you to forward the needful as proposed.

    We came to Orchard on Thursday, and got a charming day to come home yesterday. Little Agnes was much the better of the jaunt. I have not seen my mother so well in every respect for many years. The weather was villainously bad during my stay in Fife, I visited my friend Carstairs at Anstruther who regrets you did not take St. Andrews as he would have sent both his sons to you.

I ordain and settle Donaldson next Thursday at Cannobie. I suspect he is rather of the orthodox cast, but seems to be a fine honourable fellow. There was a petition forwarded to Ld. Rothes upon my leaving Fife from the Heritors and Kirk Session of Kinglassie, soliciting his Ldship to appoint my brother assistt and Successor to Mr. Reid, who in testimony of his cordial concurrence adhibitted his name. I have just now received a letter from General Ferguson who forwarded the P. saying he had a very polite answer from his Lordship, in which he expresses his desire to shew every attention to the wishes of the Heritors, but is under a promise, of three years standing, in case of the Living becoming vacant, though he has reason to believe that the person will soon be otherwise provided, in which case my brother will have his support.

Eliza and Robert join me in kind regards to you and Mrs. Lorrain, and I ever am,

> *My Dear Sir,*
>> *Yours most truly,*
>>> *Will B. Shaw*

William Shaw and Eliza had a son George, a brother for Agnes, born in February 1816. Shaw is still in constant touch with Lorrain's father and brother Walter who is having a difficult time with Sir John Maxwell of Springkell *(p.106)* He writes to Lorrain, who has now moved to Glasgow:

Langholm Manse 16 Sept. 1816

My Dear Lorrain,

I was yesterday favoured with yours, and would feign have written you last night, but felt myself so fatigued that I could do nothing. On Wednesday last your father came here bringing a letter to me from Mr. Little, Annan, in which he says, "I am aware that Mr. Wr. Lorrain could recover his arrears of salary from Sir J. M. in the most summary manner, and without any risk of suffering by expenses; but when he applied to me regarding his case, I understood from him, that it was not convenient for him, or indeed in his power, to advance S.J.M.'s rent, without receiving allowance for his salary, and as there is no doubt that his claim against S.J. will serve, by way of exception, equally well as if it were made the ground of direct proceedings, I prosecuted a bill of suspension in his name. A sist and interdict were granted as matters of course; and my opinion is, that there is not the slightest reason to dread the issue, should S.J. attempt to proceed further; but it is necessary, in point of form, in any suspension, whether well or ill founded, that a bond of Caution should be lodged, and it was to warn Mr. Lorrain to come forward with a Cautioner, that my letter to him was written. - He may adopt the mode of proceeding suggested in your letter, if he can raise the rent; but he would, in such case, lose his right of recourse for the expences already incurred by him and might give S.J.M. an argument for treating him rigorously at the settlement of the rent. I wd therefore recommend it to him to pursue the line of proceeding, which has been already adopted, and which must, in my opinion, be successful. I do not think that much time can elapse ere the matter be settled, if the bond of caution were signed; nor do I think the expences could be great; but at the same time, if S.J.M. do appear in the case, it would be very proper to get Mr. Lorrain put on the poor's roll."

Your father had the bond drawn out, and as no time was to be lost, and it was necessary it should be lodged next day, I got your father to sign it conjunctly with me. After it was signed in due form, in Mr. Scot's office "Now," says the good old man, "we are fairly in for it and it will be a bonny business if they come and sweep away all that we have!" I am persuaded there is no danger. S.J. will find himself in the wrong box. It is that scoundrel Sympson, his factor, that is at the bottom of the whole business, and ten to one if S.J. knows properly how the matter stands. I wrote to Sympson by your father, apprising him how the case stood, assuring him that there can be no doubt of the validity of your brother's claims, and adding, that "independent of my private friendship for Mr. L. I could not, in the public station which I hold, stand aloof and keep silence, after being informed of such tyranical proceedings", and I begged to assure him that you would not see your brother wronged, and that he should have all the assistance it was in my power to afford him. - I understand that he does not now pretend to question the legality of the settlement and is even willing to pay for the current year, but refuses to pay all arrears. He sent your brother a list of the farmers' proportion, desiring him to apply to them for it, but your brother very properly returned it. He is a silly, vain, arrogant fool, and is treating several other schoolmasters in the same style. With regard to the poor roll, I conceive there is no meanness at all in getting your brother put upon it. It is a most judicious and benevolent provision made by the law for enabling such as otherwise have not the means to prosecute their just rights before the Court of Session. - Your father had only one note, and I borrowed four in the town to give him to make up the sum required. If the matter were once settled, Sir John will never run in arrears again, but will see the necessity of paying the salary punctually, and in that case, your brother would be much better to have nothing to do with his dear park.   It is probable that, if he has gotten your letter, your father will be over today, so I shall not close this scrawl till night in time for the post.   I am glad to hear that Mr. Easton has got employment under Telford. Sympson finds fault with all his proceedings, but the country in general seems as sensible of the worth and ability of the former, as they are of the arrogance and folly of the latter.   We have had shocking weather for some time past, but this is a charming day.   The children do well, and are beginning to get the turn.   We intend going with them to Deloraine the beginning of next week for a change of air, and will remain there a fortnight.   Next Sunday is Half Morton Day.   I will then see how matters are going on.   But no doubt your father will be at me before then.   Little is well spoken of as a man of business, and a friend to the oppressed.

Remember me to Mr. Byres.   I hope he is making a good use of Emlyn's Tracts among the Students of Divinity.   Mrs. [Dr.] Anderson is with us just now, and two of her children, one of whom has also taken the hooping cough.   We all join in kindest regards to Mrs. L. yourself and family. Your father is a great favourite here.

  I ever am
    My Dear Lorrain
      Yours most faithfully
       Will B. Shaw

Mr. Lorrain of the High School, Glasgow

This completes the correspondence from William Berry Shaw. He and Eliza had six more children and lived in Langholm for the rest of their lives. Neither Shaw nor his brother Robert "came out" at the Disruption of 1843; he died in 1856.

Chapter 14

FINANCIAL MATTERS

*Great care has been taken in accurately transcibing all letters -
errors in spelling and punctuation are as per original*

*Sir,   If convenient for you to pay the Rent of Ashhaugh, I shall either
call, or send for it, before One o' Clock, today - I shall be at Mr. Hendersons
the greater part of the forenoon -   I am*
  Sir,   Your mo Obed. Ser.
                          Fra Brodie
Thursday
11 o'clock

This undated note suggests that William Lorrain rented a house in
Selkirk, since Mr. Henderson was a W.S. (solicitor) there.

From an early date, William Lorrain seems to have had money to spare
and was constantly approached for loans, beginning with his brother
Walter in 1804.   Thomas Robson and Rev. William Berry Shaw both
availed themselves of the facility and on occasion Lorrain received
requests from strangers who heard that he had money to lend. *(p.9)*

Dear Sir,
       *As I am rather straitened to make up my rent, in consequence of
disappointments, might I beg of you to Send me Three Pounds for a
short period which shall be faithfully repaid. I am almost ashamed to ask
it, but my necessity, and the goodness of your heart, will I hope plead
powerfully in my behalf.*
       I am Dear Sir,
              Your most Obe Servt.,
                       Walter Ferguson
Jedburgh 24th May 1814

The British Linen Company opened a branch of their Bank at the north
end of High Street, Jedburgh in 1791

BRITISH LINEN COMPANY'S BANK.

Edinburgh, 27*th* June 1808.

SIR,

INCLOSED, I send to you a Copy of your Account with this Company to the *30th* day of *last month* then balanced by *Twenty four Pounds six shillings & five pence* due *to* you, and carried, of said date, to your *Credit* in a new Account.

In return to this, you will please own receipt of the Account, mention, in words, the balance, and say if you find it right: but if this is not complied with, on or before the first of August next, I am ordered, by the Directors, to inform you that the operations on your Account shall be suspended until it is done, to which be so good as attend. I am,

SIR,

Your most obedient Servant,

Mr Willm Couvrue
Rector of the Grammar School
Jedburgh

Sir,

Inclosed, I send to you a Copy of your Account with this Company to the 30th day of last month then balanced by Twenty four Pounds six shillings and five pence due to you, and carried, of said date, to your Credit in a new Account.

In return to this, you will please own receipt of the Account, mention, in words, the balance, and say if you find it right: but if this is not complied with, on or before the first of August next, I am ordered, by the Directors, to inform you that the operations on your Account shall be suspended until it is done, to which be so good as attend. I am,

SIR,

Your most obedient Servant,
Eb Gelehuit Manager

The tax assessment for 1813 is interesting:

Assessed Taxes.—NOTICE of ASSESSMENT for the Year 1813 ending at Whitsunday 1814.

58 To *Mr. Willm Lorrain Teacher*

TAKE NOTICE, That by virtue of the Acts of Parliament for granting the several Duties under-mentioned, you are charged in my District as under.—Witness my Hand, this *7th* day of *March* 1814.   *Geo: Rodger* } Surveyor.
Residence.

Office included &c

	£		
House and Window Duty, as per Notice formerly given - -	5	2	6
Note.—*The Duty on all the following Articles is charged according to the Number kept, &c, from Whitsunday 1812 to Whitsunday 1813.*			
Duty on Male Servants, viz,			
on Four Wheel Carriages - · - -			
on Two Wheel Carriages - - -			
on Taxed Carts - - - -			
on Horses used for riding or drawing Carriages - - -			
on Work Horses for the purposes of Husbandry - - -			
on ditto for other purposes, 13 Hands high -			
on ditto ——— under 13 Hands high			
on Dogs - - - - - -			
on Armorial Bearings - - - - -			
on Hair Powder - - - - -			
on Horse Dealers - - - -			
on Makers or Sellers of Carriages - - -			
on Carriages made for Sale, or sold by Auction or on Commission			
Deduct Allowance for Children, being 4 per Cent. on the Amount of the Duties (if Total Charge under £45) for every Child above Two maintained by you - - - -	5	2	6
	-	12	3¾
£	4	10	2¼

Which several Duties must be paid to the Collector thereof at his Office on or before the 25th day of *March* next, in terms of the statutes,

If you consider yourself aggrieved by the above Charges, or any of them, you are hereby required to give me Notice in Writing; and to lodge an Appeal, within FIFTEEN DAYS after the date hereof, stating the particular wrong or grievance of which you complain ; without which Notice, within the time aforesaid, no Appeal will be received, The day of hearing Appeals may be learned, by applying to me, or to the Collector *Mr. William Ingram Writer in Jedburgh* - -

Some items were obtained from beyond the Borders:

Leith 8 Feby 1810

Mr. William Lorraine
Bot of Chas. Cowan & Co.
Raw Sugar a Cask

At 3 .2 .0 @ 84/-	£14. 14. 0	
Cask	3. 6	
	———	
	£14. 17. 6	

Sir,

   By order of our mutual friend Mr. John Scott we send you as above *chagd as low as our mkt. will admit* - We annex prices of a few articles we have for sale for which will be glad to receive your order & are
      Your obed. sevt.
         Chas Cowan & Co.

Common Raisins		@ 7d
Figs		7d
Hard Soap	86/-	& 88/-
Lisbon Oranges	85/-	per Chest
Currans	84/-	
Gouda Cheese	72/-	
Common Dutch	33/-	
Congou Tea	6/6-	7/6
Roasted Coffee	2/2	
Red Herrings	42/-	pr Bl

Edinr 4th Oct 1811

Mr. Lorraine
         Bought of James Murray

2 Hair Mattresses @ 52/6 each	£ 5. 5. -	
2 Feather Bolster & 4 Pillows	£ 2. 10. -	
To a Matt for Packing	2. -	
	———	
	£ 7. 17. -	
Discount for Cash	7. -	
	———	
	£ 7. 10. -	

Sir

The above is the lowest I can make them which I will give a receipt to the Carrier next week, should anything else be awanting, I shall be happy to serve you and remain

Sir

Your most obd servt

James Murray

Mr. William Lorrain

1812	Bot. of A Rutherford	
Augt 21	1 Leather Cap	£ - 2. 6

1813		
Jany 29	1 Doz Wine	£2. 18. -
		£3. -. 6

As customary at this season of the year Mr. Rutherford perfixes for Mr. Lorrain his Account amounting to £3. -. 6.

Edinr. 1st Decr 1814

Mr. Willm. Lorrain

Bout of Anderson & Oliphant
2 Cwt fine Raw Sugar   115/ £11. 10

As well as having capital, Lorrain seems to have purchased property which is let out and which attracts tax assessment.

Melrose, 3 September 1808

Sir,

I now annex the particulars of your Property Tax, in Roxburghshire, as assessed for the year ending the 5th day of April 1807. If you are to appeal that Assessment, you must attend the Commissioners in person, at Jedburgh, upon the twenty-eighth day of September Current at 10 o'clock forenoon. And previous to that day you will lodge with me your reasons of appeal, free of postage.

Whatever Correspondence you may find requisite to have regarding your Property-tax for the year above-mentioned, now falls to be with me, and not with Mr. Rodger the Assessor, and you will be sure and pay the postage of all letters.

Mr. W. Rutherford, the Collector, will attend at Jedburgh on the Market days of October next, to receive payment of your Assessment.

> *I am, Sir,*
> > *Yours most obedient Servant,*
> > > *Charles Erskine*

Income from Salary and School Fees	*£70*
Profits from Boarders	*£20*
	£90

Full duty	*£9*
Allowed by the Act	*£3*
Duty payable	*£6*

Dear Sir,

The Heritors have agreed to let us inhabit the Old Manse till the new one one be built: otherwise I would probably have been your tenant.

> *I am,*
> > *Dear Sir,*
> > > *Yours sincerely,*
> > > > *David Brown*

Crailing 22d Decr 1813

> *Jedburgh 23d Decr 1813*

Dr Sir,

I received your Card and fully intended writing you this morning as nothing makes me leave the house but the high Rent, but I perceive you already know believe me you have my best wishes for a good Tenant.

> *I am,*
> > *Sir,*
> > > *Yours sincerely,*
> > > > *Thos. Watmore*

Sir,

In order that you may be assessed to the Property-Tax, from the 5th of April 1813, to the 5th of April 1814, I request that you will have the goodness, as soon after the date upon the back hereof as possible, to lodge at my Office in Jedburgh, free of postage, a return of your Income, mentioning all the different sources from which it arises; and particularly,

1st, In case you occupy any Property belonging to yourself, that you furnish me with a return of the number of acres thereof, classed into different qualities, with the Stock kept upon the Pasture Ground, and what you consider to be the fair annual value of the whole.

2d, In case you entered into any Farm or Farms, Pieces of Land, or Garden Ground, at Whitsunday, 1805, that you furnish me with a return thereof, mentioning what you consider to be the fair surplus rent to be put thereon, and of the number of Acres of which the same consists, classed into different qualities, with the Stock kept upon the pasture ground.

3d, In case you entered to any Property, whether Houses, Farms, small pieces of Land, or Garden Ground, at Whitsunday, 1813, that you furnish me with a return of the rent thereof, and the name of your Landlord or Landlords.

Lastly, That you furnish me with a return of every other piece of information which you may judge necessary for the purpose of assessing you fairly to the Property-Tax for the year foresaid.

I am, Sir,

Your most obedient Servant,

George Rodger, Assessor

TO *Mr. Wm. Torrain Schoolmr.* ———

IN terms of the Statute, 52d Geo. III. cap. 95. I hereby give you notice, that the PROPERTY TAX COMMISSIONERS for the County of Roxburgh, and District of *Jedburgh.* have assessed you as after-mentioned, for the year ending 5th April next. If you have any objections to state against the Assessment, you must, betwixt and the *7th* day of *April next* lodge the same with the Clerk to the Commissioners at Melrose ; and on that day, at ten o'clock, you must in person attend the Commissioners at *Mrs Turnbulls* Inn, at *Jedburgh.* prepared to support such objections. If they relate to the Assessment on Land, you must be able to state the number of acres, or to give such information as to enable the value of it to be judged of. If these Instructions are not particularly attended to, your Assessment becomes final, and no appeal will afterwards be received. The amount is payable to Mr *G. Scott, the* Collector of your District, at *Jedburgh* the *7. 6* day of April next.

	£.	s.	d.
Landlord's Duty, which you retain at paying your Rent.........	1	10	—
Tenant's Duty	—	—	—
Duty on Surplus Rent beyond the Rent you pay..................	—	—	—
Duty on Houses or Land belonging to you, not otherways Assessed..	1	10	—
Ditto for the occupation of such Land as is in your own possession..	—	—	—
Duty on Income arising from Trade, Profession, &c.............	8	—	—
Total..........£	11	-	

Dated this *4th* day of *March,* 1814.

Geo. Hedger Assessor.

Tax Office, Jedburgh,
15 June 1815

Sir,

I request you will immediately order payment of the duty on your property or profession for the year to April last, amounting to £11- -
I am,
Sir,
Your most obedient Servant,
Geo. Scott

211

William Lorrain had always retained an interest in agriculture, having been raised at Oakwoodhill where his father had a farm.   These calculations on the cost of stocking a sheep farm appear to be connected to the letter from George Shaw *(p.91)* son of Lorrain's friend, Rev. William Berry Shaw, and to his proposed purchase of a farm from Mr. Ker:

Cost of stocking Sheep-farm

Cost of sheep farm of 8 @ 10,000 acres	1500	
1000 Ewes @ £2 each	£2000	
20 Rams £3	60	2060
1 Plough	10	
12 Bullocks	45	
1 Waggon	50	
10 do horses	75	
		180
5 Cows	50	
50 Mares	150	
1 Jack Ass	100	
		300
		£4040

Cost of management when an overseer is substituted for a Principal

Wages of overseer per an	£50
8 shepherds labourers @ £1 per mth	96
	146
Interest on Capital invested	200
	346

Income 1st year

1020 sheep will produce on an average 2lbs of wool each	
= 2040lbs @ 2/-	£204.00
The 1000 Ewes should give 750 lambs & each lamb ½lb of wool	37.10
	£241.10

Stock at the end of 1st year

1020 original
 375 lambs - Rams & wedders
 375 Ewe lambs
1770 There would be a loss the 1st year of the £100 difference between the income & expenditure, but the value of the stock would be increased by the young Ewes & Ram lambs - 750 & by 25 to 30 mules

2nd Year

1020 Breeding ewes
 375 young do
 375 do   wedders

1770	@ 2lbs = 3540	@ 2/- -	£354.00
750	lambs @ 1/2lb 375	@ 2/- -	37.10
			391.10

There will be a loss at the end of the 2nd year @ £50 difference between the income & expenditure & the value of the stock would be further increased by the young Ewes & Ram lambs in the sum of £750 & by 25 @ 30 mules

3rd Year

1375 Breeding Ewes
 375 Wedders
 750 Year old lambs
2500 Sheep averaging 2lbs each give 5000lbs wool @ 2/-   £500
1030 lambs 1/2lb each   515   2/-   51
  25 2 year old mules   £15   375
                                                        926
          Less interest & additional capital   400
                      Showing a gain of   £526
between the income & expenditure of the 3rd year & the value of stock will be further increased by the young Ewes & Rams in the sum of £1030

4th Year

1750	Breeding Ewes	
750	Wedders	
1030	year olds	
3530	Sheep = 7060lbs wool @ 2/-	£706
1312	lambs = 600 do 2/-	60
	25 mules	375
		1141
	Less interest & expenses	400
		£741 on the 4th year

& an increase to the value of stock in the sum of £1312

5th Year

2250	Breeding Ewes	
1300	Wedders	
1312	Year olds	
4862	or 9724lbs of wool @ 2/-	£972
1687	lambs 843 do @ 2/-	84
25	mules @ £15	375
250	Ewes £1	250
500	wedders 10/-	250
		1931
	less Interest & expenses	500
		a gain of 1431 on the 5th year

& an increase in the value of stock in the sum of £1687

At the end of 5 years the stock will amount to 6000 Heads & the increased value

1st year	£750
2	750
3	1030
4	1312
5	1687
	5529
Original Stock	4030
	£9559

The stock should now be reduced to & kept at 2000 breeding ewes

2000 wedders

4000

The annual produce of this would be

	1450	Lambs giving 750lbs of wool	£75		
	4000	sheep	8000	800	
sell	725	wedders @ 10/-	362.	10..	
	725	Ewes	£1	725	
	25	mules	£15	375	
		Annual income	2337.	10..	

These calculations are all made on a low valuation & allow a loss of 25 per cent on the sheep for Deaths, Barren Ewes & which from experience is found to be about the true rate, the sales of Ewes & wedders are calculated at only half the present selling price

January 1838

215

Chapter 15

PUBLICATIONS

Great care has been taken in accurately transcibing all letters ·
errors in spelling and punctuation are as per original

William Lorrain took a keen interest in printing and publishing and in due time produced his own well-respected books. His main contact in the printing field was Robert Armstrong who had a business in Silver Street in Hawick. Armstrong was born in 1769 in the parish of Hobkirk near Hawick and would therefore be known to the Scotts of Nether Bonchester, Lorrain's in-laws, as Dorothea was born in the same parish in 1778.

Robert's father, William Armstrong, was the parish schoolmaster and married Margaret, daughter of the Hobkirk minister, Rev. Robert Riccaltoun. Their son Adam, Robert's brother, joined the service of Alexander of Russia and became a major-general.

Armstrong and Lorrain's first recorded contact was shortly after the latter's arrival in Selkirk. William Berry Shaw had given Armstrong an order to print his sermons *(p.192)*

Sir,

Mr. Shaw informs me that you are so obliging as to take the trouble of sending the copies of Taylor to the Subscribers in and about Selkirk. I feel myself highly obliged to you; and if I can be of any service to you in this quarter, I shall esteem it a happiness to receive your commands.

I am, Sir,

Most respectfully yours,
Robert Armstrong

Hawick Novr 14, 1801

LIST OF SUBSCRIBERS.

Mr. Wm. Lorraine	2 copies
Mr. John Lang	2 "
Mr. Andw Henderson	2 "
Mr. John Anderson	1 "
Mr. George Dobson	1 "
Mr. Ebenr Clarkson	2 "
Mr. Wm. Nichol	1 "
Mr. Alexr Bell, Preacher	1 "
Mr. John Riddell, Schoolmaster	1 "
Miss W. Henderson	1 "
Mr. Alexr Park, Writer	1 "
Mr. Archibd Park Hartwoodmyres	1 "
Mr. Geo. Anderson, Bridgehaugh	1 "
Mr. Geo. Roger, Selkirk	1 "
Mr. Ballantyne, Whitup	2 "

P.S. Any of the above that it is not convenient to send to the Subscribers, you may return. R.A.

Edinburgh 8th February 1803

Received from Mr. William Lorrain, Selkirk, through the hands of Walter Clarke, the Sum of One pound Nineteen Shillings Sterlg being payment of Account to the above date

£1.19 - for J. Guthrie
James Tait

Edinr 9th February 1803

Mr. Lorrain to J. Guthrie

To Chopin Bottle and Ink	1/2		£-.	-.	10
" 2 Arroll's Cordery	1/-	9d		1.	6
" Almanack	2/6			2.	3
			£-.	4.	7

Dear Sir,

I send as above and am sorry that I can get no secondhand Dictionaries to send you. Ainsworth new sells at 13/- and Young at 10/6
I am Sir yours for J. Guthrie
James Tait

In 1807 Lorrain commissioned Armstrong to print his publication "Bookkeeping by Double Entry":

Hawick 27 Nov. 1807

Dear Sir,

You will think me extremely negligent in not furnishing you with your multiplication tables ere this time. - The truth is that however simple a piece of work the Table may appear, it requires so many figures of one sort (for instance 1 & 0) that my stock of large figures was not equal to the work. I borrowed all Mr. Ballantyne's of Kelso*, & I find I shall have to get a few more still from Edinr. - I could easily have done it on small figures, but thought that it would not suit you so well.

I am now quite at liberty to go on with the B. keeping, and shall be able to finish it in a very short time. Hardie's Extracts will be out of the press soon, and then I shall have nothing of any moment to interrupt me in the printing of your work -

You may command what number you please of Hardie on the same terms as formerly, viz. paper & print. By the bye, can you suggest any improvement on Elliot's Lessons. - He is preparing a new edition, & will be thankful for a hint from you. You will see by the volume that accompanies this, that your friend Christophe has commenced author.

> *I am, Dear Sir,*
> *Truly yours,*
> *R, Armstrong.*

[*"Ballantyne of Kelso" was James Ballantyne, editor of the Kelso Mail as well as printer. He had recently produced the first edition of Scott's "Minstrelsy of the Scottish Border". - Ed]

"Hardie's Extracts" refers to sermons by Thomas Hardie, D.D. who was minister at Ashkirk. Lorrain's friend Smith, teacher at George Watson's in Edinburgh, had just received 20 copies:

Geo. W. Hospital Decr. 10 1807

My Dear Sir,

I received both yours by Messrs. Usher and Aikin, the latter of whom I saw about 8 days since. Your Extraordinary which I have expected some time has not yet arrived, altho' it may this day as I hear your carrier is expected - By it I expect all your news and much information - What from the South? Do you ever hear now of Russell or from Canobie?

This day I received from Kelso 20 copies of Hardy's Collection; but no Acct. which I request you to send by the Carrier next week regularly discharged. If you can include the 40 copies that are to be sent of Next Edition, as we wish always to settle for the whole quantity ordered at once. I wish those to be sent bound likewise - your binding is cheaper than here. I am just informed by Miss King that her brother proposes practising as physician & Surgeon in Jedburgh - I hear him spoken of as sober and well qualified for his business - I am desired to mention the circumstance to you and request your countenance and good wishes, wh I have no doubt you will be ready to do as far as you prudently can. It will be towards Whitsunday before he can remove to Jedburgh. I suppose you will now be satiated with Classic Lore - I hope the present Cargo wil give equal satisfaction as the former. If the carrier comes next week neglect not to send the accompt and receipt. With best wishes to Mrs. Lorrain and Willy &c.   I remain

My Dear Sir

Yours &c.

A long letter & many good news   D. Smith

Books sent Mr. Lorrain

Livii Historia 6 vol.	£1.	5.	0
Podarem Scot. Missa Sacro 2 vol		4.	6
Nelsons Gr. Exercises & Key		6.	6
Willymote on Use of certain Words		3.	0
Dante's Phaedrus		1.	0
	£2.	0.	0
Discount on Livy		1.	0
	£1.	19.	0

Decr. 10th on paying Livy this day received 1 shilling discount - the text were bought at Auction.   D. Smith

Mr. Lorrain   To R. Armstrong

Printing 600 Multiplication Table - Post 4to - Paper included   £1. 10.   0

Dear Sir,

I intended seeing you on Tuesday, but was under the necessity of going to Yarrow with my son on that day. - I shall see you on Monday or Tuesday next.

> *I am Dear Sir,*
> *Yours truly,*

Decr. 11   *R. Armstrong*

Hawick   18 Dec. 1807

Dear Sir,

After trying all the various length of lines and form of pages, I find that no form will answer so well as the old one. At the same time that it makes the Book look better, it will insure correctness - Upon consideration, I find that the single Entry when done up by itself will cost you little more than the price of stitching, on account of its forming part of the other work.

After next week, there will be nothing to interrupt your work till it be completely printed off.

> *I am Dr Sir,*
> *Yours truly,*
> *R. Armstrong*

THE ACADEMIC READER & RECITER
or Miscellaneous Pieces in Prose & Verse

Selected from the Best English Writers and arranged under Proper Heads designed for the Improvement of Youth in Reading, Speaking and Reciting the English Language with Propriety and Ease and to inculcate Some of the Most Important Principles of Piety and Virtue By William Lorrain, AM Rector of the Grammar School of Jedburgh and author of Book-keeping etc.
Doctrina sed vim Promovet Insitam, Rectique Cultus Pectora
Roborant Horatius   Hawick 1810
Printed by Robert Armstrong for A. Thomson & W. Renwick, Jedburgh
Sold also by them & by A. Rutherfurd, Kelso.

"Education is a subject of such general importance, that every production which has a tendency to lessen the drudgery of the Teacher and to heighten the pleasure and promote the improvement of the Scholar merits the attention of the Public. Our School-books had long and loudly called for reprehension. The many excellent Selections, however, which have appeared within these few years, have in some measure remedied the evils of which Parents and Teachers complained. To these Selections, the Academic Reader & Reciter forms a valuable addition & must be an acceptable present to the friends and instructors of youth. The Extracts of which this work is composed, and the arrangement of the various pieces do credit to the taste and judgement of Mr. Lorrain; they are calculated to combine amusement with instruction; to engage the attention of the Scholar, and at the same time to inculcate the most important principles of Religion and Virtue. - The third part of the Academic Reader & Reciter contains select pieces for Recitation arranged under proper heads. This necessary appendage to a schoolbook, renders the work now before us, perhaps the most useful of its kind. We can with confidence recommend it to the attention of Teachers, & have no doubt but its merits & cheapness will procure it a ready admittance into our Schools."

In September 1811, mention is made of Lorrain's publication on bookkeeping for Ladies *(p.232)*

Newcastle, Sept. 28th 1812

Dear Sir,

Some time ago I sent you a parcel of copy-slips accompanied with an order for a few of your readers, which I suppose you received, - I have expected them for some time, as by your last letter, you expected the new edition would be ready in July.

I should like to have 3 Doz. of the new edition - but if it will be more than a month in being ready, be so good as send me one Doz. of the old immediately.

I am sorry that my hopes of seeing you in Newcastle this summer have not been realized. - but it gives me great pleasure, to see in our papers, so good accounts of the examination of your school. - You have I dare say raised Jedburgh to a degree of celebrity for learning which before it never knew.

I am

Yours very truly
Geo. Gowinlock
No. 6 Saville-row

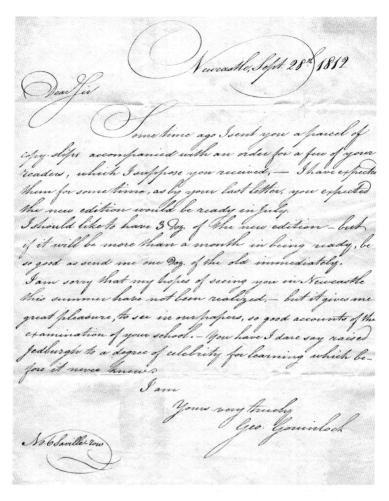

Newcastle, Sept. 2d 1814

Dear Sir,

Being again entirely out of Academic Readers I embrace the opportunity by the bearer of enquiring if you have got the new edition printed. If it will not be ready for two or three weeks could you let me have a Dozen of the first edition as soon as possible.

Being rather hurried

I remain

Yours Sincerely,

Geo. Gowinlock

Hawick 26 Oct. 1812

Dear Sir,

It will be quite impossible for me to finish your Essay sooner than tomorrow fortnight. Perhaps you could put off your west country journey till after that time. Were you at hand to correct the proof sheets, you might have it done in half the time.

I cannot help thinking that some passages of the Essay require your attention in looking over the proof - I have marked them thus X .

For instance at page 4, would not the word view or picture be better than group? - In the same sentence there is a confusion of tenses and I think it would run better thus- "A corporal who has fought in the German wars, who had nearly forgot or never understood his own language, and who had just acquired", &c. &c. "An old soldier who had" &c. Is "summed the legitimate characteristics" a proper expression?

Again at page 6 "Happily for us that these times," &c. - the word that should either be expunged, or the adjective adopted in place of the adverb - "Happy for us that these times" &c. or "it is happy for us" &c.

I beg your pardon for taking the freedom of making these remarks, which are probably wrong - you will, however, place my officiousness to its proper account.

Mention the exact number you wish thrown off - and return the proof by tomorrows post.

If you see Renwick, tell him that I expected to have heard from him ere this time.

I am, Dear Sir,
> *Most sincerely yours,*
>> *R. Armstrong*

In 1822, while he was teaching at Glasgow High School, Lorrain produced "Nomina Virgiliana Propria".

Robert Armstrong outlived William Lorrain, dying on 7th July 1852 in the 83rd year of his age. In the kirkyard at Hobkirk, the inscription on his gravestone describes him as " a man of uncommon talents and of great independent spirit - a pattern of rectitude and fidelity. He lived in the upright discharge of the offices of life until his closing sickness which he bore with exemplary patience, sustained by firm faith in the Redeemer and died in the blessed hope of a glorious immortality".

Chapter 16

THE PROFESSION OF SCHOOLMASTER

*Great care has been taken in accurately transcibing all letters -
errors in spelling and punctuation are as per original*

"I do not know a more useful or more honourable one than a
schoolmaster; at the same time I do not see any more generally despised,
or whose talents are so ill-tempered"
- Oliver Goldsmith

Despite the passing of a bill for "the betterment of Schoolmasters" in
April 1803, it took many years for the recommendations to be brought
into effect. Lorrain's friend James Smith reports on his experiences:

St. Andrews 24th of June 1807

My Dear Sir,
*Yours of date 26th of March I received in Course of Post and a
few days thereafter one dozen of Your Book keeping - I have sold only
two Copies of it, but I trust I shall dispose of them all in a Year or two -
Wiseman at Cupar has volunteered his services I therefore hope that
with his assistance I shall soon need a Supply - You may depend upon
every exertion in my Power - Agreeable to my promise I shall send per
next Carrier a dozen Copies of Wisemans Arithmetic and Mensuration;
price to Teachers 2/6d they sell it at 3/-d per Copy - When we meet in
Sept (as meet I hope we shall) I will settle with you for the whole - I
wrote Dr. Adam lately and recd his answer in Course of Post - from his
Statement, I hope that our Bill will receive the Royal Assent this Summer
- it is rather unlucky for us that neither Henry Erskine, the late Lord
Advocate, nor Horner have been returned to Parliament - Adam has
already advanced £100 - Walker I see is still in the pay of the Schoolmasters
notwithstanding his Stupid Bill & the unhandsome manner in which he
was introduced amongst us - Moores ungenerous Conduct to me has
enraged all the Brethren in Fife against him - At the Annual Meeting of
our Society on the 20th instant, I was elected Preses, Mr. Melvill, Kirkaldy,
Secretary and Moore holds now no Office not even that of a Trustee, -
The Brethren previously had resolved upon this, to convince Mr. Moore
that they were dissatisfied with him - as soon as our Bill shall receive the
Royal Assent, I am to summon a Meeting of our Society to adopt such
Measures as may appear most eligible for dissolving our Society, in order*

that we may have it in our power to enter into the National Fund at its first establishment - Our Capital Stock is now several hundred pounds. I should not be much disappointed although the Parliament should not take up our Bill in the Summer Session - The multiplicity of national and most important Business that must be attended to immediately may occupy all their attention and I suspect that the present Rulers of Scotland will not be so sanguine in our Cause as the former - However a few weeks will determine this - When you have anything to communicate, Write me. Let us stand firm together and let us muster all the Strength that we can to go along with us - Adam must be our Cashier and Irvine our Secretary - and if they will employ Walker or any other Scribe under them, let them do it - but both must be responsible for their Depute and must pay him - Irvine will and ought of course be Adam's Successor.   I am,   My Dear Sir,

Yours sincerely,
James Smith

Compts to Mrs. Lorrain & the Misses Shaw when you see them.

Locally, efforts had already been made by Mr. Dymock *(p.34)* to stimulate joint action by schoolmasters and after his departure to Glasgow William Lorrain himself followed his example by calling a meeting in Jedburgh.

Extract of a Minute of Meeting of Schoolmasters
Jedburgh Presbytery 30 July 1808

Which day met here the following Schoolmrs. of this Presbytery viz. William Lorrain Schoolmaster of Jedburgh, James Kirk, Schoolmr. of Hawick and James Turnbull, Schoolmr. of Cavers, having chosen Mr. Kirk Preses they proceeded to elect a Collector and Clerk in Terms of the Act for Raising a fund for the relief of Widows and Families of Burgh and Parochial Schoolmasters in Scotland and accordingly made choice of Mr. Lorrain to fill these Offices, who immediately found Security to the Satisfaction of the Contributors present....

William Lorrain often received letters from younger schoolmasters asking for advice or guidance, and from those looking for recommended teachers to fill vacant posts. Rev. James Wood, minister of Falstone, Northumberland, falls into the latter category:

Dear Sir,

I was favoured, just about a fortnight ago, with two Copies of your Academic Reader & Reciter, the one addressed to James, & the other to William, for which, I beg you will accept my very sincere & hearty thanks.   The Selection of the Pieces has been performed with real judgement & taste, & the Book is, I think, one of the best of the kind, I have ever seen. May your useful labours be rewarded by a rapid Sale, as well as by the Consciousness of having devoted your time & talents, to promote the true interest & happiness of Mankind. My Dear little Boys are accustomed to consider useful knowledge & virtue, as the most precious things they can possibly acquire in this World, & consequently they are in the habit of esteeming Books, which are calculated to aid & to direct their pursuits, as the most valuable of all kinds of presents. The perusal of Your Book is a mental feast to them, & they tell me that they feel a lively sense of gratitude to you, for your kind & respectful attention to them.

I am happy Sir, that I can now assure you that our Schoolmaster, Mr. Laidlaw, seems, in every respect, to deserve the ample recommendation with which you were pleased to favour him. I feel much inclined to procure him all the encouragement in the compass of my power, & for that purpose, I have applied to Some of the most respectable & wealthy people of this place, to make up for him, by way of Voluntary Subscription, a yearly Salary, over & above quarter wages, & other little perquisites.

In this attempt, I shall, I hope, prove Successful. The first public proposal I made of a Salary for our Schoolmaster, was in the Company of ten Neighbouring Gentlemen, with whom I was one day dining, not one of them refused me, & their Subscriptions amounted to Six pounds yearly. When the Subscription paper has been circulated throughout the bounds of the Congregation, the annual Salary, will, I hope, be tolerably decent. Mr. Laidlaw, however, has not, I understand, Studied English under you, & consequently his taste in that particular branch, is not so correct as I could wish it to be. He has, at my request, lately introduced into his School, the method of teaching the English Language Grammatically. This will at once improve himself, & be very agreeable to the people.

My family join me in kindest Compts & best wishes, to you, Mrs. Lorrain, & your Young family, And I am,

Dear Sir,

Yours, very respectfully, & Sincerely,
Jas. Wood

And from a former assistant of Lorrain's who has started on the professional ladder:

Edinburgh 15th February 1811

My Dear Sir,

The spirit of procrastination is with me such a prevailing principle, that it often makes me transgress against the clearest light; and with all propriety I may call it the sin which most easily besets me. Often have I heard a voice within telling me of my negligence, but as often has that baneful propensity to defer, found a pretext to silence its remonstrances. It is needless to attempt to make apologies. I confess I have done wrong, or rather I have not done right. (for you will observe my fault lay in omission, and it is proper to make logical distinctions.) But I think I am conscious of a resolution (for I must speak in the metaphisical strain) to be more attentive to my duty for the future. Let this suffice then. One good resolution is worth a torrent of penetential tears. That I may not, however, appear altogether unworthy of your attention and friendly regard, suffer me to tell you, in a few words, the circumstances in which I am placed; and I have no doubt but you will look upon me with a more favourable eye. You must know then I have four classes to attend to, and two hours private teaching which occupy me in all six hours a day. Some preparation at least is necessary to attend these classes with advantage; and as one of my pupils is a student at College, I find that I cannot do him justice without a good deal of study. He is a very smart young man and would soon detect ignorance or inattention. From these circumstances you will perceive that my hands are pretty full, and that I have not much time left for triffling. But I have filled my letter with apologies: however, I have given you by the way a sketch of my proceedings.

I have taken out a day for my exhibition in the Hall, and I am really in bodily fear as to the consequences. For you must know, that a man's fate here depends very much upon the state of the atmosphere, or other little incidental circumstances no less precarious. O! on that eventful morning may the sun rise with unclouded splendour, may the Dr's servant delight him with her melody, when they join together in their morning devotions - Ye powers! protect the china - Last of all may no disagreeable sight, may no nauseous smell assail him in his way to the class. Let these be granted and I am safe, I am highly pleased with Mr. Aitkens productions. They are just such as I expected from him.

I have not leisure to give you a particular account of all your old pupils, that are attending the classes here. I shall only say that, in general, they are all as far as I hear diligent sober, and make a respectable figure in their several pursuits. James Pott is still the pedant, and disgusting to all his acquaintances; and withal, I do not think that either his abilities or his information at all justify his high pretensions. But I should not write scandal; speaking it is bad enough. I met with your friend Mr. Fogo of Leith lately, when he desired to be kindly remembered to you and Mrs. Lorrain. He desired me to mention to you a new plan of teaching writing; (p170) of which he seems highly to approve. But this I have not time to describe. Mr. Aitken will describe it to you. Will you be so kind as write me. Your advice will always be received with gratiutude. I know you have much to do, but you might try to find a spare moment. With best respects to Mrs. Lorrain,

I am,

My Dear Sir,

Yours etc. in very deed while

A. Rutherford

Favd by Mr. Aitken

Edinburgh 12th April 1811

Dear Sir,

I received your kind letter of the 21st ult for which I return you my hearty thanks. I am much obliged to you for the proposals it contains, which I ought certainly to have replied to long ere now. I have remained however so long silent, only that I might be able to give you a decisive answer; and the truth is that I am still as unable to do so as when I first received your letter.   You must know that I have a situation in view, which I think would answer me exactly, and I do not yet know whether I shall be so fortunate as to succeed.   Should this fail (which is very likely to be the case) then I shall return to Jedbr and I should be extremely glad to accompany you in your labours. I should not wish this to be spoken of as I have not yet mentioned it even to my friends, but I thought it but fair to mention it to you that you might not be drawn into any inconvenience on my account. If I am in Jedbr in summer you may depend upon me but as this is uncertain and as you must have an assistant you had better provide against any disappointment.

I delivered in the Hall on Wednesday and got off as well as I could wish. There is nothing stirring here worth mentioning. Robert joins me in best respects to Mrs. L. and yourself.

I am always

Dear Sir,

Yours &c. &c. in very deed

Andw Rutherford

A well-known bookseller makes a recommendation:

Kelso 4 March 1811

Dear Sir,

Mr. Lowrie the bearer of this, has for some months past profesed teaching vocal Music in our town, and now means to follow the same line in Jedburgh, if you will be kind enough to give him your countinance. I believe it will be bestowed on a good Character - for his abilities I know nothing, as I hardly know one Psalm tune from another myselfe, but he has given satisfaction here, and his conduct has been unreproachable.

I am Dr Sir,

Your Most Obed Servt

favoured by Mr Lowrie

Archd Rutherfurd

Mr.Lorrain   *Sunderland 18th March*

Sir/   Could you recommend any young man as able to teach English Arithmetic and Latin? I am requested by two Gentlemen in this neighbour hood to make inquiry for such a person - and warranted to say that he will, for teaching the Children of these said Gentlemen, meet with very good encouragement.

If you can recommend any, be so good as write me immediately - and the conditions will then be agreed to - By delivering the letter to my Father it will reach me - and confer an obligation on Sir yours etc

Moses N. Williamson

Sunderland 10th May 1811

My Dear Sir/

I return you a thousand thanks for your kind attention to my request. It is answered to the utmost desire of all concerned. For my own part I shall have in Mr Hills a companion with whom I have been formerly acquainted and who is certainly highly qualified for the office he has undertaken.

With gratitude I am Sir

Your obedient servt

Moses N. Williamson.

Perhaps prompted by these many experiences and need for high standards in the teaching profession, on 29th June 1811 William Lorrain proposed the formation of the "Roxburghshire Friendly Society of Parochial and Burgh Schoolmasters". In response to an advertisement in the "Kelso Mail", fourteen teachers met in Kelso in October to "take into consideration the utility of forming themselves into a Society with a view to promote more effectually the interests of education and to establish a fund for the benefit of indigent and infirm brethren". Laws and regulations conforming to the spirit and sense of the Act of Parliament 33 George III cap 24 were drawn up and submitted for inspection and sanction to H.M. Justices of the Peace.

Membership of the Society was open to all parochial and burgh schoolmasters in the county of Roxburghshire; in addition tutors in families or private tutors were eligible, as were "respectable" teachers in other counties until such time as they formed their own society. One of the main objects of the Society was to provide a fund for members who were no longer able to support themselves or their families due to infirmity. Not less than 5% of their contributions was to be invested in a Widows Fund, but those who did not contribute were to pay a sum not less than 3/- per annum. One half of the total collected was to be paid in grants; the other was to be allowed to increase until the capital amounted to £100 sterling, then lent on heritable security. When £1,000 had accrued, $2/3$ of the amount of annual contributions and the interest of the capital was to be expended. Once £2,000 was reached, the full amount of the contributions and capital - with agreement of $2/3$ of members present - could be spent in making grants to indigent brethren. The committee was empowered to receive legacies or donations from well-wishers.

Mr. Lorrain laid great stress on the educative aspect of the Society - rule VII - "That the different modes or plans of teaching shall be liberally and freely discussed, in order that members of this Society may adopt that which has been found most successful. It is expected that every member will be candid and sincere in answering any queries that may be put to him respecting his plan of teaching any branch of education which he professes and that he will annually report to the general meeting the result of his experience upon such a plan, either personally or by a written report under his hand."

Mr. Lorrain   Jedburgh

Bot of James Smith

1811

March 5th	*50 copies 1st Spell. in Sheets at 2 d*			*£*	*11.*	*5½*
	50 Ditto 2 Spell.	*do*	*4½d*		*18.*	*9*
	50 do Reader	*do*	*at 1/-*	*2.*	*10.*	*0*
				£ 4.	*0.*	*2½*

My Dear Sir,

    It will not be in my power to attend our Genl Meeting this year, - Mrs. Smith is in so feeble a State I dare not leave home for one day - This will be delivered to you by my Nephew Mr. James Brown who is here at present and who intends to look in upon the Meeting - After you return home you will send me 24 Copies of your Ladies Book keeping - If convenient for you, after deducting the price of the 24 copies, you may pay the Bal of the above account ot Mr. Brown who will forward the Cash to me - I hear that Dr. Monro is to be Preses -

    With best Compts to all the Brethren I am

        My Dear Sir,

           Your sincere friend

St. Andrews   *James Smith*

16th Sept. 1811

Christopher Armstrong, son of printer Robert, writes from Hawick:

Hawick   26th Nov 1811

Dear Sir,

    Will you be so kind as send me on Thursday per Postboy a list of your proclamation fees and if possible the date of my Certificate respecting John Gordon's proclamation - if not that - you will can inform me when and how many days he was proclaimed in your Church and what he paid - I was from home when the Shabby-wretch was married and he now refuses to pay the fees allowed by the Session - I therefore mean to have the honourable Serjeant before the justice court - Inform me respecting Thompson & Wood Writers as I have a piece of business in the law to do and they are recommended as good lawyers &c. - I hope Mrs. Lorrain has got quite stout and is doing well with all the little ones - Has there anything been said, done or wrote, respecting the rules for the association of the Schoolmasters of Roxburgh What are your thoughts of the matter - I have not hitherto got time or rather I have not been able to think about the business -

    Yours truly   Christopher Armstrong

William Lorrain had an assistant, James Anderson, who later went on to become schoolmaster at Makerstoun, near Kelso.

Jan 1th 1812

Sir I hereby acknowledge the receipt of thirteen pounds sterling which together with other items makes thirty five pounds sterling being payment in full of my last years salary terminating upon the 22d Nov last for which I returned you my sincere thanks and am,

> *Sir,*
> > *Your Obt huble Servt,*
> > *James Anderson*

Mr. Lorrain, Jedburgh
1812   *A.C. James Smith*
Feby. 22nd

For			
100 Copies of Reader in Sheets		*£5.*	*0 . 0*
200 Ditto Spelling in Ditto 1st part		*£2.*	*2 . 0*
		£7.	*2 . 0*

Dear Sir,

I am favoured with yours of the 17th inst. and in the meantime send you as above.   After receiving your former Letter, I wrote Mr. Wiseman and had for answer that the Statement was correct & that he would settle with me - but that he had a small Charge against you, and that as soon as he had time to inspect his Book he would inform me.   I have not heard from him since.   When he settles with me I shall write you.   I have very few of the 2nd Part in hand at present.   The Printer is just finishing a New edition of it.   I have made a little Addition to the reading Sessions, (Extracts from the Bible) as most Teachers thought that it would be an improvement.   The Selling Price of this edition will be 10d instead of 8d.   Bound to Teachers, the Selling Price 1/-.   I cannot exactly say what it may cost in Sheets till the whole edition is thrown off but you may depend that it will be as low to you as possible.   The paper is better than the former.   As soon as it is finished, I shall send you 200 Copies in Sheets.   I am sure that you will be pleased with the Addition - agreeable to the Conversation that we had upon the Subject.   They consist of Jobs Description of the Reverse of his fortune - the Deitys address to him out of the Whirlwind, Hannah's Song &c.

I rejoice to hear of your Meeting & the object of it, I did not hear of it before.   It is singular that Davidson & I have been corresponding about a Meeting of the Brethren of this County upon the same subject - and on Wednesday last I summoned a Meeting of this Presbytery on Wednesday last to take the subject under Consideration previous to the County Meeting which is proposed to be held in May next. Our Object is to establish a fund for superannuated Brethren & for those that are incapacitated by distress to superintend the Management of their Schools, and also to consider what improvement may be made in the plan of conducting the education of Our Schools. We vainly flattered ourselves that we were again taking the lead in this, but I find that you can claim the Palm, no matter may you succeed. I hope that the other Brethren in Scotland stimulated by our example will join us from John o groats to the Tweed -

If the Schoolmasters of Scotland would unite their Wisdom & experience, I am convinced that they might form a better plan for the Management of Schools than these that have been brought forward by Bell & Lancaster. - Come forward to next General Meeting with some specific Motion upon the Subject, if in health and there I shall support you heartily - and although a General National Plan may be found incompatible, yet it will do much good to communicate our Ideas upon the Subject. It will rouse the indolent, stimulate the languid and encourage the industrious to persevere. When you have anything to communicate write me. With Compts to Mrs. Lorrain, family and all the Brethren of your quarter. I am,

Dear Sir,

St. Andrews		*Yours*
Feby 23rd 1812	*with 2 parcels*	*James Smith*

Selkirk 6th May 1812

My Dear Sir,

I duly received your favor of the 5th inst. with the other documents enclosed, by Mrs. Lorrain - and immediately called on Mr. Oliver, to whom I communicated the instructions contained in your letter, and made a demand for the amount of the claim against him. - He stated to me, that altho hitherto he has declined entering into the Society, yet it was his intention to do so immediately, and was partly prevented by an ill natured letter he received from you. - This statement however being foreign to my instructions, I told him there was no other alternative, but to raise an action and arrest his Salary. - Upon this threat he begged to let the matter lye over until the last Saturday of May as he would have an opportunity of seeing you at Hawick, when he had no doubt a settlement would be effected; and in the meantime hoped that I would take no steps against him - my answer was that I would inform you of what passed, in order that you may say, whether any indulgence is to be given. - I therefore wait your further orders - and in the meantime have suspended any proceedings against him. -

I doubt not Mr. Oliver would wish to avoid this yearly contribution of £2-2-0 which goes to a fund for the relief of the Widows of Parochial Schoolmasters; he honest man, will more than likely never enter into the matrimonial state - as I have been told he is unfit for generation - and before doing so it will be necessary that he undergoes a regeneration.

We really had a merry party at Jedburgh on the 1st, altho we, boys of Ettrick Forest, gave the Jed Forest Lads, a licking in the way of pushing round the Glasses - and left a number of slain in the field of Glory. I doubt not if we all live to see the 1st of May 1813 - the meeting to be then held will be equally pleasant, and more numerous. - In the meantime I remain

> *My Dear Sir,*
> *Yours very respectfully*
> *Robt. Henderson*

A receipt signed for a scholar by William Lorrain on 26th May 1812 gives an indication of the poor rates of pay:

Received from T..... R..... five pence sterling, amt. of Schoolmaster's salary from Whitsunday 1807 to Whitsunday 1812 at the rate of 1d stg. per annum.   *William Lorrain*

Scholars were expected to give extra at Candlemas and of course parents paid fees for boys who were boarders. The sum paid by Burgh proprietors towards the schoolmaster's salary was £21/16/4 and this amount was raised by voluntary assessment. They and the Heritors, who also contributed, had an equal say in electing a master. In addition, the Kirk session gave a quota, the schoolmaster acting as session clerk and Scripture-reader.

On 30th May 1812, the second annual meeting of the Society was held in Hawick and Lorrain read a paper entitled "Practical Education". [A printed copy of this paper is supposed to be held at the Mitchell Library in Glasgow.] He then joined a group including Mr. Armstrong and Mr. Kirk of Hawick and Mr. Gillies of Kelso to hear a case raised by Mr.

Little, schoolmaster at Kirkton. The minister of his parish, Mr. Elliot, had been denying him access to his house on the pretext that it had been built on the glebe. It was agreed to support Mr. Little in asserting his right and in taking his grievance to a proper court and before the heritors.

Shittleheugh - mill - 19th Octr 1812

Sir,

 You will receive from the bearer hereof, My Brother, for the two parcels of Books which I owe you with thanks for the long credit you have given me - I have yet a few of them which I hope I shall not be long in vending, this done I shall again apply to you for more if I find any demand. I am at present with my friends at the mill as I have had a vacation which is now near terminated when I will have to return to my Course of care - My situation as yet has proved satisfactory. If you have any of Gowenlocks line you will be so good as send two slips with my Brother, of the Text which he will pay for.

 I am, Sir, Yours
   With the greatest respect
    Matthew Anderson
     Redwater

At the Society meeting in Jedburgh on 29th May 1813, Mr. Oliver of Selkirk read an essay on "Practical Education" and Mr. Anderson, Lorrain's assistant, made remarks on "the power of figures in a new and general application of them". Lorrain himself was appointed Cashier and Clerk and it was decided that subscriptions be altered to a flat rate of 3/- per member per annum.

Lorrain writes to John Weir ("AMICUS") at Kelso:

Jedburgh 4th March 1814

Dear Sir,

 Your favour of the 2d Currt with Mr. Buchanans Introductory Lessons I received this morning per Posty and was sorry that I had not as much time as to answer you by the same.

 I have never heard anything about your new appointment untill the receipt of yours. I rejoice in your prosperity, long may you live to enjoy the respect due to your Merits - the Regulations of our Society have not been neglected by me. They are now nearly reduced to such a form as I flatter myself will give satisfaction to every individual of the Society & I expect that they will be ready to appear before the next Meeting of the Justices of the County which takes place about three weeks hence - From a conversation which I lately had with the Sheriff I find that we can make any alterations that we may think proper at any time posterior to the approbation of the Justices in which case they can again come under the review of the Next General Meeting. I am sorry indeed that our Society is to lose so valuable a member in you. It may however expect your good wishes and all its members hope that you will by your exertions establish a Society of a similar nature in the County of Stirling. Such measure will give the amplest testimony of the regard which you bear to this Society at the head of which you now stand. To me it is a matter of regret that I am not again to see you in your official Capacity as a Meeting just now of the Committee at Kelso would strike at the root of the Regulations I shall be happy to meet with you and such of the members of the Society as you may think proper to ask on any Saturday previously to your departure to Dine & talk over matters which I think would be of importance to us all. I use all Dymocks Classics but as I formerly told you keep no books myself on sale. Do you know who is to be your successor? I put the question because I know of a young man of considerable experience who may in all probability offer himself a Candidate if so be that the matter is not already determined.

Let me hear from you soon fixing the day of our meeting at Kelso to say (God Bless You)

> *My Dear Sir,*
>
> > *Yours truly*
> >
> > > *Wm. Lorrain*

To Mr. John Weir
  Schoolmaster
  Kelso

Before his departure for Stirling, Weir writes:

Kelso 29th Augt 1814

Dear Sir,

> *I beg to apologize for having delayed so long to send the fishing rod. I would have forwarded it the day after I saw you, but observed that a top belonging to it was wanting, which I supposed might have dropped out of the bag Kersmains where I dined I therefore wrote to Mr. Jafferey to learn if it was there - His answer has not yet come to hand. Should it not be found, I have given directions to Mr. Archbd. Rutherfurd to pay the value*

Nothing would give me greater pleasure than to see you at Stirling during the holidays. Pray try to make it out.

> *I am*
>> *Dear Sir*
>>> *Yours Truly*

with a fishing rod   *J. Weir*

By May 1814, James Anderson had become schoolmaster at Makerstoun and was succeded as assistant in Jedburgh by Mr. Scott. The latter read an essay on "Education" that year at the Society Meeting, while Anderson read one on "the science of figures and practical mathematics". A short time later Anderson wrote from his new post:

> *Makerstown 11th Aug 1814*

Dear Sir,

I received yours & was happy to hear of your success. I certainly will do myself the pleasure to attend the Examination of your School (should nothing of very considerable importance take place previous to that period) As the harvest is fast approaching here It is most likely my Vacation will take place much about the same time. My School is not quite so throng as in winter, as you know it is not commonly the case in Country Schools. Our Annual Meeting for the Widows Fund took place on Saturday the 30th of July. I was much surprised to see so few of our Brethren there, the following is a list of their names.

> *Present:*

Mr. Gilles, Kelso; Mr. Turnbull, do; Mr. Riddle, Ednam; Mr. Fairbairn, Stitchel; Mr. Davidson, Nenthorn; Mr. Robertson, Sproustown; Mr. Calbrath, Eckels & Mr. Knox from Morbattle. Mr. Gilles Preses.

The Meeting held in the Grammar Room. After Business was transacted, we went in Co. to Mr. Lauder's Inn and dined there. For my part I must confess I never felt so disagreeable in my life. During our stay there, nothing but quarrels and animosities took place amongst us. A very particular dispute took place betwixt Mr. Robertson & the rest of the Brethren whether Mr. Weir could be considered as a Parochial Teacher (while he remained in Kelso) or not. Mr. Robertson denied that he was. I shall be happy Sir to have your opinion upon that subject & what constitutes a Parochial Teacher.

My leisure hours are at present mostly occupied in the study of the Diaphantine Problems, a branch the most curious & perhaps the most abstruse of all the Analytic art. As no general Rule can be given that will suit all cases, every particular question puts us upon a new way of thinking,

*and furnishes a fresh vein of analytical treasure, which cannot but be
very instructive to the mind in conducting it through almost all difficulties
of this kind whenever they occur.*

With Compts. to Mrs. Lorrain, Mr. Scott & Mr. Laidlaw
    I am,

        Dear Sir,

            Yours most truly,

                James Anderson.

Enthusiasm for the Society was on the wane, for only £3/3/- was collected in 1814, with eleven non-payers. It was suggested that every member who failed to attend the General Meeting should pay an extra shilling with his subscription, which would be applied to the interest of the fund. It was also decided to produce a magazine for schoolmasters to facilitate the objects of the Society, profits going to the Fund. Robert Armstrong, printer in Hawick, was ready to undertake the printing and other expenses himself and donate any profit to the Society.

James Oliver, had been at Selkirk High School since 1808. Education was so close to his heart that he later made a bequest of 25/- per annum which was eventually administered by the School Board of the Burgh of Selkirk. A silver medal - the Oliver medal - was awarded to the best scholar.

                    Selkirk 13 Feby 1815

Dear Sir,
    *I have since I saw you a thousand times thought of writing to
you but have never found anything to say that might indemnify the
postage. As I must send this to the bearer immediately I have only time
to say that I long to hear from you. I intend seriously to push for an
advance of Fees, would you if yours be advanced since you wrote to me
state what you receive per qr for Latin, English and Writing inclusive. Is
the Schoolmasters Magazine set on foot? May I not expect you will spend
a night with me in the course of spring? in doing so you would greatly
oblige me. I intend to visit Edinr about the end of this month. If there be
any commission I could perform for you I shall be happy to serve you.*
    Excuse haste write me soon and informe me of all our affairs.
        Remember me to Mrs. Lorrain
            I am

                Dear Sir

                    yours truly

                    J. Oliver

Selkirk 29th March 1815

Dear Sir,

  To what cause shall I impute your long continued silence? If I have offended you tell me my fault and I shall endeavour to atone for it. You are almost the only person of our own class with whom I ever correspond. I wrote to you some time ago and as I presume you got my letter I shall not repeat its contents. I would be glad to hear if the Magazine be set on foot. I have been informed that you have been offered the Grammar School of Dundee and have rejected it - Pray what is become of Mr. Scott?

 Can you mention to me a young who is well acquainted with the Greek Latin and French languages and with Mathematics and qualified in every respect to undertake the instruction of a gentleman's children? As the Gentleman has written to me to air the subject and mentions you in the most respectful terms I would be happy you could assist me. He is a Member of parliament and his family I understand is remarkably agreeable. He would wish one who would devote himself to the instruct. of his children and would therefore chuse one who has been assistant in a Gramr School than one who intends to become a preacher.

 The situation is very desirable for a proper person - If you Know of any write me - Remember me to Mrs. Lorrain I haste as the post sets out Adieu

J. Oliver

Selkirk 6 Apr 1815

Dear Sir,

  Wm E. Lockhart* Esqr Borthwicks Brex is the gentleman for whose family a tutor is wanted. He resides during the greater part of the year at Old Melrose. He will give any reasonable salary to a proper person, who is qualified to teach Latin Greek French, Mathematics etc. and who will devote himself to his business on which acct he would avoide a preacher, or student who must attend a university. he would rather have one who has been an assistant in some Gramr. School and who intends to be a teacher. I have had several applications from young men who I believe perfectly qualified and fit for the situation, but the above terms render it difficult to find a proper person. To such, however, as it suits it will, I am persuaded, prove a desirable situation. Mr. E. L. is an excellent man and has, I am told, a very pleasant family.

240

Most of those who have applied to me (in consequence of mentioning it to some persons in Edin.) wish if possible to attend the University a few months annually - one such I wished Mr. E.L. to accept, as I had a young man of excellent parts in view, - he would however prefer one of our own order - please write me if you know any proper person The term of entry will be about midsummer.

"The Misses Buchan return compts to Mr & Mrs Lorrain and are happy to inform them that they are well".

Say that Mr & Mrs Lorrain will take a dinner, supper, or Breakfast with a brother on their visit to Selkirk and you will oblige

> Dear Sir
>> Yours truly,
>>> J. Oliver

[*William Elliot of Borthwickbrae married Marianne Lockhart of Cleghorn and, on the death of his father-in-law, he assumed the name of Lockhart. He was M.P. for the county of Selkirk 1806-30. - Ed]

Sir,

Having called at your house this night and spoke to Mrs. Loarene concerning a School for teaching Church Music, but she told me that she had little hops of me succeeding upon the account of the dancing -

I am truly sorry I had not the pleasure of seeing yow and hearing your opinion of whether or not I might Make a triel -

If you think there is any prospect of a school take the trouble of writing in the course of next week with the following adress

A. Wood Teacher of Music, Morebattle
your so doing will oblige yours etc.

> A. Wood

Jedburgh
8 Aprile 1815

> Falstone Manse, March 16th 1815

Dear Sir,

Some respectable persons belonging to my Congregation, having now resolved, steadily to encourage an able Teacher at this place, I request the favour of you, as a Gentleman in Whose Judgement we can fully confide, to recommend One, fit to answer our views & expectations. The Schoolmaster we wish to employ, & to encourage, must be well qualified to pronounce the English Language with propriety, & to teach it, Grammatically. He must also be fully qualified to teach all the following particulars of Education, in the most approved manner: Viz. Writing, (for a good hand of write is much, & generally esteemed on the English side) Arithmetic, Vulgar and Decimal, Book-keeping, Mensuration, Land Surveying, Gaugeing, Geography, Latin, & the first Principles of the Greek. The Salary will be about £30 per Annum to be paid half yearly, & the quarterly payments of the Scholars are as follows: English Readers, 4 Shillings each. Readers & Writers, 5 Shillings each. Writers, Arithmeticians, & Latin Scholars, 6 Shillings each: To be paid punctually, at the end of every quarter. The Schoolmaster's income cannot be less, I think, than between 60 & 70 pounds per Annum, & if he can undertake to be Precentor, & Session Clerk, he may make about £5 yearly by these Offices. We have a very good School-house; but I regret that we have not, at present, any convenient house for the accommodation of the Master. It is probable however, that a married man, (& one of that description would suit us best) might, in a short time, be accommodated with a house, & a branch of business connected with it, which would prove a very considerable augmentation to his income, & would be attended with no inconvenience to himself. If you can find a Schoolmaster, whom you can fully & freely recommend, & who would be Willing to Accept of this place, about the 12th of May next, you will confer a very obliging favour upon the public here, in general, & upon me in particular, which we will certainly be disposed to remember with the most lively & lasting sense of gratitude. I have lately heard of a Mr. Tait at Camptown, in your parish, but it was not by a person on Whose Skill I could depend, & consquently I could pay no attention to that recommendation. If you should happen to find out a Master fit for us, be pleased to take the trouble of addressing a few lines to me, by Hexham, & Bellingham. I am really happy Sir, to hear of your eminent usefulness, prosperity, & success. May you long enjoy all your domestic Comforts & continue to derserve & to receive your Well earned public Applause.

   With Kindest Compts & best Wishes to Mrs. Lorrain, to your young family, & to yourself, in which I am Joined by Mrs. Wood, I remain, Dear Sir,

Yours very respectfully, and Sincerely,

Jas. Wood

P.S. If Mr Wm Laidlaw be still with you,
please, Offer him my kind Compliments. J.W.

After the annual meeting of the Schoolmasters Society in May 1815, William Lorrain prepared to leave Jedburgh for Glasgow. He handed his successor as Cashier the sum of £7.8.10$^1/_2$ - an amount far short of the goal of £1,000 capital! The meeting of 1816 was deferred until June to allow Mr. Lorrain to attend in person. He not only brought his own subscription but also paid in those of his brother Walter and of Dr. Chrystal of Glasgow. Nevertheless, subscriptions were down again and the committee were only granted 3/- each to defray expenses.

Chapter 17

EPILOGUE

*Great care has been taken in accurately transcibing all letters -
errors in spelling and punctuation are as per original*

William Buckham Lorrain entered the medical profession and, on 6th
June 1842, in Barony parish, married Jessie Grieve who was 12 years his
junior. They had two daughters, both named Jessie, who died in infancy.
In December 1847 a son was born and named William after his
grandfather.

Shortly afterwards, Dr. William was being recommended for a post at
Glasgow University:

> *8th Feby 1848*
> *41 Wilton Crescent*
>
> *My Dear Douglas,*
> *In reply to your letter of the 6th Inst. I have to report that I
> have this day a written to Lord John Russell to bring to his notice Dr.
> Lorrain as a candidate for the Professorship of Anatomy in the University
> of Glasgow & should I receive any reply you shall hear from me again.*
> *I trust to your making known the contents of this note to Mr. Grieve.*
> *Yours very truly*
> *J.E. Elliot*
> *Arch. D. Douglas, Esq.,*
> *I have been more or less unwell ever since I came to town but am I hope
> getting right again.*

The following year, in May 1849, a daughter, Dorothy Scott, known as
Dora, was born to William and Jessie.

Meanwhile Walter Scott Lorrain, William's younger brother, had
become a prosperous Glasgow merchant and bought a house at 12, Royal
Crescent. In March 1848 he married Grace Paterson Gillespie and they
had a daughter, Helen, born in January 1849. Their second daughter,
confusingly also known as Dora, was born in February 1851. At this
time, both families were living in the Blythswood area of Glasgow.

At the beginning of 1852, William and Jessie were preparing to leave Glasgow for the foreign missions at Point de Gaulle in S.W. Ceylon (now Sri Lanka) Brother Walter was appointed guardian of their two children, William and Dora, and custodian of their affairs.

W.S. Lorrain & Adam,
12 St. Vincent Place
Glasgow   *Thursday Jany 29th (1852)*

My dear William,
    In case I should forget I will here jot some memoranda.

1st   *Pray pop a note to Mr. Ritchie anent your likeness in terms of ourlate conversation.*

2nd   *Think of making out an inventory of your Books and all articles you wish to leave under my care (in duplicate - one copy for you & one for me) & I will give you a receipt for same.*

3d   *Give me an idea of date of our Mother's birth. I must have a suitable monument erected at Rothsay.*

4th   *Date of your marriage. Names & date of death of your two children.*

5th   *Leave me written instructions as to your wishes in regard to your bairns Wm. & Dora.*

6th   *I rather think it will be necessary for you to leave me a Power of Atty in order to enable me to deal with Mother's bank Shares (20 in No., value about £350.) according to your wishes, for I am now getting them transferred into your name. Frank & I wish the above to be yours: irrespective of which, I make you a present of your passage and outfit.*

7th   *Don't forget to write a line on your way out from Gibraltar, Malta, Alexandria, Suez, Aden & Point de Galle. You & Buttery can make up one dispatch.*

8th   *Pay all outstanding Bills ere you leave, & leave receipts behind in case of disputes. Let me know what Coin is wanted.*

                  Yr. ever Affect
                    W.S. Lorrain

To Dr. Lorrain

William and Jessie had a second son, James Grieve Lorrain, born in February 1852 and they took the infant with them to Ceylon. Jessie had a cousin, Nellie Aitchison, daughter of Canonbie farmer Andrew Aitchison and Janet Grieve, sister of Jessie's father. Nellie, one of a large family, is looking after the older Lorrain children.

Howden
15 of July 1853

My dear Mrs. Lorrain,

I am very glad to inform you that your Father is very well, much better than he has been for a long time and upon the hole his Spirits are pretty good again and realy he is better than what he could expect at his time of life. William & Dora are both very well excepting a slight cold coffing a little they are both very happy and very noisy William likes the Scool very well and to day has come on very best and we have sent the boy down for him he is not coming home to night it is to night he says he stops at Marjory Richardson's and takes his dinner there this is the first night he has stoped all night I supose he is very bright and when the boy went in he said he was not going home and he was lectering away to Marjory he is a very happy child he is always either whistling or singing soon and late but he is a very rompish fellow like all Boys Dora is not at the School Mr Scott said she was too young and I give her a lesson every day at home and she says she thinks that she will be as good a reader as William Dora is very much improved both in her looks and temper tell Mary that Dora is far bonier than William most of people think and she is very good and behaves very well at church both William and hir Dora speaks far more about Papa and Mama.....than William Dora has always to kiss your letters two or three times when they come she sees what pleases grandpapa William has none of that He cannot make a fuss cany Boy We are to have the Langs and all the Rodgers some Saturday William & Dora have been asked twice to Mrs. Langs but were always prevented Mrs. Langs Baby took hooping cough so they have never got yet you mention in your letter about *Mr Sorley your Father says it is not true but I mind of hearing something about some of them wanting their Church the same as the established Church we were to have Miss Sorley Mr Sorleys Brother and his wife and daughter this afternoon to tea but they have not come with the heat and you wished to know the date of your Mothers Funeral day it was on the 11 of the Month Thursday at 2 o'clock and the Funeral would just be at Bull haugh at half past the o'clock no doubt your Mother's death would be a shock to you but we must expect nothing else but to be taken from one another

*your Mother was very patient in hir dark hour and just resined she had
no wish to live and spoke of her death with great composure and told
what was to be done with hir cloths She often expressed a wish to hear if
you were safe landed but that was not to be. The children spoke much
about grand Mama for a good while but they don't often speak of her
now. My Mother has been very poorly for some time. She is much better
and your Father wished her to come and stope a while I have wrot to hir
but I have not received a letter from hir yet Miss Isabela Buckam wished
to be remembered to you Miss Smithson's married Mr. Roberts Miss
Clarkson has had another Message Dora is standing next to me and she
says tell Mama that I have got a new Black polka and that I go to the
Church every good Sabbath day Next that she would like to see Jimmy
and the Black Boys and the flowers are very bonie and she is sending
some of them to papa ask Mama if she has a nice garden and if she has
any daisies in it read ones for I have non and plenty of weeds. Tell Mary
that there is nothing new about Selkirk Miss Grieve has left and gone to
Hawick and the Muirs have taken their shop Hatty who Mary used to
speak of and a Brother and Agnis Richerdson has a Daughter which she
is very proud of*

Give my respects to Doctor Lorrain and Mary
I remain your Affectionat
Cousin Nelie Aitchison

*P.S. Mr & Mrs Sorley's complements to Dr. Lorrain your Self your
Father will write*
N. Aitchison

*Rev. William Sorley had been minister at Dunbar. At the Disruption
of 1843 he transferred to the Free Kirk at Selkirk.

This is the last letter of the collection and unfortunately there is little
information about the fate of the family beyond this date.

From other family letters it would appear that William and Jessie visited
relatives in Ohio and Canada. William's uncle Frank had emigrated in
1805 and Jessie's uncle Elliot Grieve also took his family to Canada.
Another of Jessie's uncles, Archibald Grieve, had settled in Ohio.

Walter Lorrain continued his successful business career but he and
his wife Grace both died before 1871. They were outlived by uncle
Walter Lorrain, schoolmaster at Half Morton, who died in 1872.

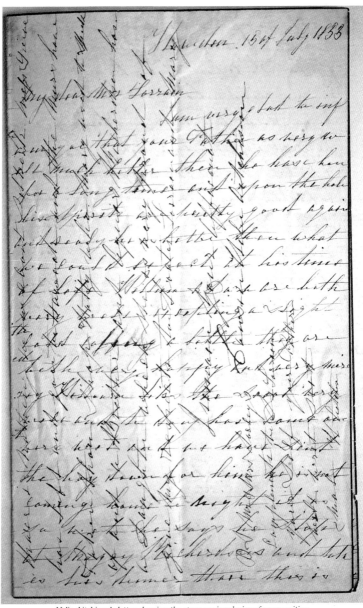

Nelie Aitchison's letter showing the space-saving device of cross-writing

INDEX

SOURCES

Archives Departementales de la Seine -   Paris
"The High School of Glasgow" -   Harry A. Ashmall
Border Almanac Advertiser 1893
"High School of Glasgow" -   James Cleland Burns
"History of Selkirkshire" -   Craig Brown
Census Records
"The Rutherfords in Britain" -   A. R. Davis
"Army Life under Napoleon" -   Doisy
Dumfries Weekly Journal 1841
Selkirk 1714 -   Walter Elliot
Fasti Ecclesiae Scoticanae
"Home Life of Sir David Brewster" -   Mrs. Gordon
First Statistical Account
"French Prisoners of War" -   Hawick Archeological Society 1912

Glasgow Herald 1841
"Yesterdays in a Royal Burgh" -   J. Lindsay Hilson
"Langholm as it Was" -   Hyslop
"History & Antiquities" -   Jeffrey
Old Parish Records
Service des Affaires Culturelles -   Le Havre
"Border Highways"   John James Mackay
Memoirs of Susan Sibbald
"Jedburgh Worthies" -   Thomas Smail
"Somerville's Life & Times" -   Thomas Somerville
"Personal Reflections on Mary Somerville" -   M. Somerville
"Two Centuries of Border Church Life"-   Tait
"Annals of a Border Club" -   Tancred
"Rulewater & its People" -   Tancred
"History of Jedburgh Grammar School" -   G.Watson
"A History of the Scottish Borders Militia" -   Rev. Robt. Weir
Imperial Gazeteer of Scotland -   edited Rev. Wilson